D0594360

#23

NOAH'S
OTHER
SON

NOAH'S
OTHER
SON

Bridging the Gap Between the
Bible and the Qur'an

BRIAN ARTHUR BROWN

continuum

NEW YORK • LONDON

2007

The Continuum International Publishing Group Inc
80 Maiden Lane, New York, NY 10038

The Continuum International Publishing Group Ltd
The Tower Building, 11 York Road, London SE1 7NX

T&T Clark International is an imprint of the Continuum International Publishing
Group Inc

www.continuumbooks.com

Printed in the United States of America

Library of Congress Cataloging-in-Publication Data

Brown, Brian A., 1942–
   Noahs o ther son : bridging the gap between the Bible and the Qur'an /
Brian Arthur Brown.
      p.   cm.
   Includes bibliographical references.
   ISBN-13: 978-0-8264-2797-7 (hardcover : alk. paper)
   ISBN-10: 0-8264-2797-9 (hardcover : alk. paper)
   1. Koran—Relation to the Bible.   I. Title.
BP134.B4B76   2007
261.2'7—dc22
                                        2007001809

CONTENTS

FOREWORD

Noah had another son who drowned in the flood? The Qur'an says Jesus was the Messiah, that he was born of the Virgin Mary, rose on high and will return prior to Judgment Day? Biblical women had names that are preserved in the Qur'an? The coming of Muhammad was prophesied by both Moses and Jesus? Who knew any of these things?

Noah's Other Son is structured around twenty-five familiar biblical figures whose teachings also appear in the Qur'an. As an invitation for Christians and Jews to understand the place of the Qur'an in Muslim and world culture, this book is an easy entry point for people still struggling to get a handle on the modern Muslim phenomenon. As such, it is also intended as a tool to help equip moderate religious people to deal with extremism wherever it is found, whether in Christian fundamentalism, the Jewish Defense League, or Islamic extremism.

Noah's Other Son is equally an invitation for Muslim believers and Islamic scholars to appreciate the techniques of scriptural "criticism" or analysis, as developed and refined by Christian and Jewish scholars in the last century. This aspect of the book is a direct result of a challenge to "community leaders inside the Muslim world as well as outside it" by Salman Rushdie, published first in the *Washington Post* on August 7, 2005, and carried in the *London Times Newspaper* on August 11, 2005.

Following the terrorist bomb attacks on the British transportation system in July of 2005, Rushdie called on the Muslim community to address a closed-mindedness of its younger generation that he attributes to a self-defeating isolationism in the older generation, even among Muslims in the West. He goes directly to the heart of the matter: the continuing reticence of many traditionalist Muslims to read and interpret the Islamic Scriptures in a manner adequate to serve as a foundation for faith in the twenty-first century. Then he issues his challenge.

What is needed is a move beyond tradition—nothing less than a reform movement to bring the core concepts of Islam into the modern age, a Mus-

lim *Reformation to combat not only the jihadi ideologues but also the dusty,
stifling seminaries of the traditionalists, throwing open the windows of the
closed communities to let in much-needed fresh air.*

*It would be good to see governments and community leaders inside the
Muslim world as well as outside it throwing their weight behind this idea,
because creating and sustaining such a reform movement will require, above
all, a new educational impetus whose results may take a generation to be
felt, a new scholarship to replace the literalist diktats and narrow dogma-
tisms that plague present-day Muslim thinking.*

*It is high time, for starters, that Muslims were able to study the revelation
of their religion as an event inside history, not supernaturally above it. It
should be a matter of intense interest to all Muslims that Islam is the only
religion whose birth was recorded historically, its origins uniquely grounded
not in legend but in fact.*

*The Koran was revealed at a time of great change in the Arab world,
the seventh-century shift from a matriarchal nomadic culture to an urban
patriarchal system. Muhammad, as an orphan, personally suffered the difficulties of this transformation, and it is possible to read the Koran as a plea
for the old matriarchal values in the new patriarchal world, a conservative
plea that became revolutionary because of its appeal to all those whom the
new system disenfranchised, the poor, the powerless, and, yes, the orphans.*

*Muhammad was also a successful merchant and heard, on his travels, the
Nestorian Christians' desert versions of Bible stories, which the Koran mir-
rors closely (Christ, in the Koran, is born in an oasis, under a palm tree). It
ought to be fascinating to Muslims everywhere to see how deeply their
beloved book is a product of its place and time, and in how many ways it
reflects the Prophet's own experiences.*

*However, few Muslims have been permitted to study their religious book
in this way. The insistence within Islam that the Koranic text is the infalli-
ble, uncreated word of God renders analytical scholarly discourse all but
impossible. Why would God be influenced by socioeconomics of seventh-
century Arabia, after all? Why would the Messenger's personal circumstances have anything to do with the Message?*

*The traditionalists' refusal of history plays right into the hands of the lit-
eralist Islamofascists, allowing them to imprison Islam in their iron certaint-
ies and unchanging absolutes. If, however, the Koran were seen as a
historical document, then it would be legitimate to reinterpret it to suit the
new conditions of successive new ages. Laws made in the seventh century
could finally give way to the needs of the twenty-first.*

The Islamic Reformation has to begin here, with an acceptance that all ideas, even sacred ones, must adapt to altered realities.

—Salman Rushdie, August 7, 2005

I contacted Mr. Rushdie immediately, through his agents, after his opinion piece appeared in the *Post* and the *Times*, and I decided to address significant elements of this book to his challenge. I am one of those "outside" the Muslim world, with a contribution that may serve a role complementary to much of the best that is going on within that religious culture. We will refer to the many reformist trends inside Islam, but, as Mr. Rushdie indicates, we all have a role in this dialogue.

I hope to illustrate how much the West and the world as a whole can learn from the Qur'an, and to boldly offer the fruits of more than a hundred years of biblical criticism among Christians and Jews. I do so in the belief that Muslim lay people will be inspired by these techniques of scriptural analysis, and that Islamic scholars may use them increasingly to unlock the treasures of the Qur'an for the benefit of themselves and their followers, as well as for Jews, Christians, and humanity as a whole.

Salman Rushdie's challenge demands an answer to the outstanding questions we all have about the Qur'an, as increasingly does the Muslim world itself. I am grateful to Mr. Rushdie for articulating the issue so precisely, and for his personal permission to quote his words in this foreword, in order to set up this dialectic with the Muslim community.

Many people have assisted in answering Salman Rushdie's challenge, but none is more eloquent than the eminent American Reform scholar Rabbi Reuven Firestone, who addresses certain Jewish concerns. Professor Firestone is Director of ISEMJI, the Institute for the Study and Enhancement of Muslim–Jewish Interrelations, a program of the Center of Religion & Civic Culture at the University of Southern California.

Reuven Firestone guided me through certain complexities of messianic theology as it relates to traditions other than my own. He has also added a gem of his own to the text. The scriptural grounds for Christian–Muslim relations and for Jewish–Christian relations are substantiated by two appendix documents from the United Church of Canada, but nothing exists as a specifically scriptural basis of support for Jewish–Muslim relations. Professor Firestone is one of the world's leading authorities in this field and kindly consented to pen an original contribution to fill that gap for this publication. It appears as Appendix III, which I expect may be widely quoted.

I therefore hold the agendas of one of the world's leading critics of Islamic extremism and one of the world's leading Jewish reformers in creative tension as we attempt to understand Torah, Gospel, and Qur'an in reference to the parable of *Noah's Other Son* in our time.

A question remains about what is often called the Christian or Protestant "mainstream." Mainstream denominations are increasingly joined in their positions on social issues by liberal Roman Catholics and Emerging Evangelicals. When this broader mainstream of Christians becomes comfortable with the interfaith agenda, Progressive Muslims and Reformist Jews will be part of a world-changing alliance in the shared-faith arena, which is the subject of this book: equipping the world's people to heed the warnings ignored by Noah's other son, Canaan, and by multitudes today.

—Brian Arthur Brown

INTRODUCTION

People of the Book

WHERE WERE YOU ON September 11th? I was at church working on a sermon, two-thirds of the way through a "mega-series" called *The Year of the Bible* at Lansing United Church in Toronto. We had reached the Minor Prophets by September. On 9/11 I was writing a sermon on Amos, the passionate Prophet of Social Justice, a popular theme in my church.

Very soon all this biblical material looked different to me. Our television screens were filled daily with people who looked and dressed much like the people about whom I was preaching, except that, in many cases, they were presented on TV as the enemy.

Had there been some kind of time warp? Had these folks gone astray and lost their bearings, or were we the ones who had moved so far from our roots that we could no longer understand them? Through the rest of the year 2001, my Sunday sermons changed. I was gripped by something that needed exploration from a spiritual perspective.

By late September, after the Minor Prophets in the Hebrew Scriptures, I was into the Christian Scriptures, in which the first parts to be written down were the epistles of Saint Paul. In this new context, these letters required us to worshipfully enquire about the movement of the Christian community away from Judaism. Part of this was obviously occasioned by the inclusive message of the gospel, which was addressed to a universal constituency. However, after September 11th, the split between the church and the synagogue in the second generation of Christians took on new significance. Could the bitter divisions between the ancient citizens of Jerusalem be related to the modern global context of questions about Islam and its relations with Christianity and Judaism?

The stories of the birth of Jesus were among the last parts of the Christian Scriptures to be written down, which puts them near the end in a Year of the Bible series. So by Christmas, I was blending the gospel accounts of the birth of Jesus with additional material about Mary and Jesus from the Qur'an. The congregation was moved when a new friend, Mehboob Kamadia, recited the nativity stories from the Qur'an in haunting, resonant tones, in the presence of several dozen Afghans who also joined us on Christmas Sunday in the year American and Coalition Forces began the bombing of Afghanistan.

The Year of the Bible ended on New Year's Eve with the now truly apocryphal tones of readings from the Book of Revelation. With our new sensitivity and awareness, it was impossible not to notice the striking similarity in style between the last book of the Bible, as we knew it, and the Qur'an, as the next Scripture from that region.

By this time, in that Toronto neighborhood, we had several Iranian Muslims worshipping with us on a semiregular basis, not "converting" but exploring. They joined increasing numbers of Jewish Russian émigrés, who had been attracted to our choir by several Russian members, in their own quest for a value system to replace the recently collapsed communism with which they had grown up. Has there ever been a time of such spiritual questing, opportunity, and even a demand for new understanding?

This amazing multicultural congregation, at that point, realized with me that we had missed something important in the first run through the earlier chapters in the Year of the Bible. My colleagues in ministry there—a Russian, a Jamaican, and a native Canadian—took the pulpit through Epiphany to allow this preacher to regroup. Then we redid the stories of Adam and Eve, Cain and Abel, David and Goliath, and others, except that we included perspectives from the Qur'an, where the same characters were re-called to the stand as Aadam and Hawaa, Habeel and Qabeel, and Dawoud and Galoot.

This took us through a new kind of Lent and Easter season. This time through, we were more cognizant of the Jewishness of Sarah and Isaac, especially since they were now seen in juxtaposition with Hagar and Ishmael, who we now saw in a new light in a Lenten sermon series we called *Under the Shadow of War*, in the runup to the second Iraq campaign. One of the great thrills for us was the realization that appreciating the stories of what the modern world might call "Abraham's dysfunctional family" in no way diminished our Christian faith. Rather, it deepened our understanding of the role of the Messiah and the purpose of His reign, as we understood it, even as we began to recognize and appreciate the different understandings that others have for the messianic concept.

It was members of the congregation who urged me to consider a third draft of some of this material in book form. I got this encouragement first from older "White Anglo Saxon Protestant" Canadians and then from younger new Canadians of the rich mosaic that now makes up our country. Two dynamic churches in the Niagara Falls area invited me to come to them on the understanding that I would continue working on *Noah's Other Son*, and they would provide the opportunity and the support needed to complete this undertaking.

In adult study programs, my new churches assisted me in working through a review of the material in publication format. Here I am within driving distance of the publishing offices of T&T Clark in Harrisburg, Pennsylvania, and their marketing team on Maiden Lane in New York, and also near the Niagara Islamic Center, where friends pored over my work to prevent egregious errors.

In the past year, I have also had the benefit of collaboration with Jewish scholars in Buffalo, New York, as well as input from Christian clergy and their spouses. With all this, plus assistance from my wife, Jenny, and intense discussions with my children, Arthur and Indira, this work is a collaborative effort. Acknowledgments at the end recognize many debts, especially to Salman Rushdie, Rabbi Reuven Firestone, and Rabbi Harold Kushner, whose personal contributions are priceless.

The book format of this material still has traces of its origins in the two series of sermons, the Year of the Bible and *Under the Shadow of War*. I have eliminated first-person singular pronouns from that more intimate style, and refrained from attempting to inspire as we lean toward critique and study. However, this book comes with a Warning Label: THIS MATERIAL MAY CONTAIN TRACE PARTICLES OF EXHORTATION AND RHETORICAL FLOURISHES. While publication of sermons was once common, the "trace particles" of exhortation and rhetorical devices contained in this book may be the closest we will get to that genre of publication in our time. The Muslim world is an exception to this rule; published collections of sermons are in vogue now more than ever, so perhaps some faint echoes of that genre are acceptable in this work.

The history of relations among Jews, Christians, and Muslims in Europe is well known. There might be value in at least acknowledging the origins of the three Abrahamic traditions in North America. Christians have had a presence there since the arrival of the first Europeans. The first recorded instance of Christian worship by lay people was in the year 1000, in the Nordic settlement established briefly by Leif Ericsson in Canada's Newfoundland. The first Catholic mass in North America was with Jacques Cartier in Quebec in 1535, followed by Huguenot Protestant communion services in Champlain's 1604 Nova Scotia settlement, and Anglican communion celebrated in the far north by Henry Hudson's crew in 1610, all three with the benefit of clergy chaplains.

Jewish history in the Americas goes back to the Jews in the crews aboard the ships of Christopher Columbus. They were fleeing the Spanish Inquisition and a small Jewish community was soon established in Trinidad, West Indies. The first American Jewish congregation was established in New Amsterdam twenty-five years after that colony was established by the Dutch, but the Mill Street Synagogue—America's first—was not built until 1730.

There were no Jews in Canada until a party arrived in Montreal with General Jeffery Amherst in 1760. Since then, Jews have played a role in every part of the country, with a section of Saskatchewan even being settled by a party of Zionists in 1887. Those settlers of Moosomin, near the present city of Yorkton, were sponsored by Leo Tolstoy of Russia and the Rothschild family of France.

This was the first attempt to establish the kind of "Jewish Homeland" that later succeeded in Israel. One has to wonder if a million Jewish refugees arriving in Saskatchewan after World War II, forcibly displacing established Canadian farmers, would have been any more welcome than Jewish settlements in Palestine. As it is, the Jewish community is as secure and as much appreciated in the Canadian mosaic as any other element, much as it is today in the United States of America.

The theory that Muslim sailors from Africa reached the West Indies at about the same time Nordic sailors reached Canada is the subject of ongoing research. More certain is the presence of Muslims with Christopher Columbus. Dr. Youssef Mroueh describes the situation in *Islam in America*, found at www.everymuslim.com, the website of Al-Islaah Publications.

Columbus and early Spanish and Portuguese explorers were able to voyage across the Atlantic (a distance of 24,000 kilometers) thanks to Muslim geographical and navigational information, in particular maps made by Muslim traders, including Al-Masudi (871–957 CE), in his book *Akhbar Az-Zaman (History of the World)*, which is based on material gathered in Africa and Asia. As a matter of fact, Columbus had two captains of Muslim origin during his first transatlantic voyage: Martin Alonso Pinzon was the captain of the Pinta, and his brother Vicente Yanex Pinzon was the captain of the Nina. They were wealthy, expert ship outfitters who helped organize the Columbus expedition and repaired the flagship Santa Maria. They did this at their own expense for both commercial and political reasons. The Pinzon family was related to Abuzayan Muhammad III (1362–66 CE), the sultan of the Marinid dynasty (1196–1465 CE).

The romantic notion that Muslims, Jews, and Christians together "discovered" America discounts the fact that Native Americans had not lost it, and requires a docile attitude on the part of the few Jews and Muslims in the face of the robust, even chauvinistic Christianity of Christopher Columbus and his crew. However, given the skills of Muslim sailors in particular, and the eagerness of non-Christians to get out of Spain to escape the horrors of the Spanish Inquisition, the evidence would appear to be valid.

It is beyond question that most of the slaves brought to America were Muslim in origin. The story is well known from *Roots* by Alex Haley, where the 1767 capture and enslavement of Kunta Kinte is documented. Kunta Kinte was a Muslim born in 1750, in the village of Juffuee in Gambia. He was shipped to Annapolis, Maryland, and put on the slave market. His story has become emblematic of the twelve million slaves forcibly removed to the Americas. They were mostly Muslim, the largest number of whom were settled in the United States, where they lost their identity and adopted Christianity. This was partly at their own volition, in the circumstances, a related scriptural tradition embraced with a passion and understanding of the essence of the Christian faith that has engendered renewal at its core in American life.

The first mosque in America was possibly the Albanian Mosque built in Maine in 1915, but records are sketchy. Muslims began arriving in Canada from Turkey in the 1880s, and the scattered community built its first Mosque in Edmonton, Alberta. The land was provided by Christian politicians at City Hall, who personally contributed cash and encouraged the Muslim women who approached them. The funds for the building itself were raised by mainly Jewish business leaders on Jasper Avenue, who were approached by the same group of Muslim women. The Muslim men did much of the work under the guidance of a Ukrainian–Canadian builder who produced a dome with more Orthodox "swoop" than traditional Muslim expanse. Jews and Christians (including the Christian Arab mayor of nearby Hanna, Alberta) assisted the renowned Indian translator of the Qur'an, Abdullah Yusuf Ali, in opening the historic Al Rashid Mosque in 1938. It is the highly regarded Yusuf Ali translation, with its Canadian connection, that we use in this study as a *continuo* of shorter verses supporting a hybrid compendium of Qur'an translations.

There are early indications of Jewish and Muslim interest in this book, and I am grateful for the input and reviews of many from those communities, who will also to be acknowledged later elsewhere. The United Church of Canada, of which I am a minister, has recently completed a nationwide consultation called *That We May Know Each Other: United Church–Muslim Relations Today*, pointing "toward a United Church of Canada understanding of the relationship between Christianity and Islam in the Canadian context." This consultation resulted in a statement for study by congregations. That statement is included in Appendix II following another highly regarded appendix document, *Bearing Faithful Witness*, which is a similar interfaith study of Christian–Jewish relations. These resources are much in demand among Christian denominations around the world as the moderate majority seeks to develop a positive response to the challenges of extremism. This book is offered as a further contribution to that process.

I was surprised to realize how much we, as reasonably well-informed people, did not know about Islam. We knew Muslims believed in Jesus as some kind of prophet, but did we know that they believe he is the Messiah, born of a virgin, and that they are awaiting his second coming? I don't think so. We knew a little about Muhammad, but did we know that Muslims believe Jesus was speaking about Muhammad when he promised to send an advocate or comforter? Who knew that women who are nameless in the Bible have their names recorded in the Qur'an? And who would have imagined that Noah had a rebellious son who refused to get on board the ark and drowned (such a preachable story), or other details from the biblical cast of characters who populate the Qur'an?

This is all amazing news to religious people, in North America at least. What else is there that could help bridge the gulf between Jews, Christians, and Muslims in our time? Of course, knowledge is not everything, or Jews and Christians would not have such a troubled history. Nor would the Crusades have taken place, based on such ignorance as they were. Along with new information, there must be a spirit of understanding, and even accommodation, without compromise. Is this even possible?

If it is, it would be helpful to remind ourselves that this is no longer a secular age. The twentieth century was a secular age, when even the best-selling books on the future, such as *Future Shock* and *The Third Wave* by Alvin Toffler, had no need to discuss religion. Not so in the latest book by Alvin and Heidi Toffler, *War and Anti-War*, "a preview of the twenty-first century" that deals with the role of religion as perhaps the key difference between these two centuries.

Population figures for Jews, Christians, and Muslims given here are statistically inclusive, despite the practice of church leaders who count only those who go to church as "Christian." Jews do not differentiate between those who attend synagogue and others whose moral and spiritual ethos was formed by Jewish upbringing, and Muslims have a similar approach.

On the fifth anniversary of the events of September 11th, for example, I did an unscientific "snapshot poll" of 200 visitors at Ground Zero and discovered that, on that day, the visitors self-identified their "religious background" as follows: Jewish 17 percent, Christian 67 percent, Muslim 7 percent, other religions 9 percent, none of the above 0 percent. The exercise was a deliberate take-off on a poll done in Red Square on New Year's Day 2000, which interviewed 201 Russians before finding a nonbeliever in a place where twenty years earlier one would have questioned at least that many before finding a believer.

I almost found one person who was "none of the above," but after her husband identified himself as Jewish, she said she was a "nonbeliever." I deadpanned the next question as if it was in my questionnaire: "Would that be Christian nonbeliever, Jewish nonbeliever, or Muslim nonbeliever?" To this she replied in a very definite tone, "I am a Christian nonbeliever." We chatted and she acknowledged that "there is probably a God somewhere" and she knew that she got her moral ideals from the same "organized religion" that had deeply offended her otherwise.

There may be still a few elderly atheists in New York, but even they could probably identify themselves as having elected to absent themselves from church, synagogue, or mosque. Nor are we suggesting that all those whose moral framework and social ethos has been formed by these religions necessarily grasp the profound mysteries of the faith that formed them. In a 2005 article on Christianity, *Harpers* reported that 12 percent of Americans think that Joan of Arc was Noah's wife, though that also indicates that 88 percent know better. Interestingly, while 12 percent of the population is unsure of the identity of Joan of Arc, none of the respondents were unfamiliar with the story of Noah. It is possible that all or most of them could give an outline of that story and some rational explanation of its meaning.

Pollsters may continue to ask the twentieth-century question of how many people attend church every Sunday, receiving lower and lower figures, but times have changed. Weekly attendance is not the pattern, but belief patterns remain strong, as do identity patterns. Recent research is based more on connections than on the old Gallop Poll question showing the declining number of people who attend worship every week. Canada may be a useful example, a country less overtly religious than the United States and less secular in appearance than Europe. A collage of recent polls of religious connections would show respondents' actual participation in religious life as: 30 percent regular (though not necessarily every week), 30 occasional ("Christmas and Easter"), 30 percent rarely ("Weddings and Funerals"), 10 percent never ("at this time"). Adjusting the festival names, this picture might not be very different among Muslims and Jews in Egypt or Israel.

Social systems and action programs without God (atheistic communism on the left, secular humanism at the center, and pagan Nazism on the right) were all given hearings and opportunities, for better or worse, in the twentieth century. They reached their apex, proclaimed their ideals, and now appear to be in the same dustbin of history to which they once consigned religion.

There is clear evidence that religion is in a worldwide resurgence in the twenty-first century. At the very beginning it seemed that this trend was limited to a fundamentalist revival, but a rising tide lifts all boats. This is the time for religious moderates to get serious about the opportunity that lies before them instead of perpetually lamenting the decline of their influence. With the failure of religious extremism in America, for example, and the rejection of the religious right at the polls, the temptation for those with a twentieth-century mentality might be to give up on religion altogether. But the evidence is that religion is here to stay, and it is loaded with power. Our task is to practice religion properly, moderating into spiritual maturity, not sinking beneath the waves of the flood with Noah's other son, Canaan, whose story we will consider in detail.

Yet there remains a dangerous delusion, a cop-out in media, political, and academic circles when it comes to religious and spiritual matters. Old habits of mind die hard, and the older dogs have not yet learned the new tricks. A 1960s mentality persists, particularly in liberal church circles: many liberal Christians continue to speak of this as a "post-religious" age, in spite of the religious content in the daily news.

Religious reporting is not limited to extremism and wars, but is extended to everything from arts and science to cultural wars and politics. This religious phenomenon is not limited to the "deep south" or "the Bible belt," but is found in the Middle East, the Old West, the southern hemisphere, the far north, and the far east, especially in China where this phenomenon is becoming the main counterbalance to the government. Moreover, the moderate majority is dominant everywhere except in the deep south or the Bible belt, where shrill voices grabbed headlines at the beginning of the new century, while moderate Muslims, Jews, and Christians were still finding their voices.

The delusion that this is a "post-religious" age is dangerous because some of our creative thinkers and committed activists are therefore blind to one of the most important realities of our post-9/11 world. This is a more religious era than we could have anticipated, as witnessed by the popular influence of leaders from Pope John Paul II to Billy Graham, each of whom attracted millions of teenagers to the largest stadiums in the world in the

early years of the new century. Indeed, it is the moderate influence of Ayatollah Sistani with the youth of the Shi'ite militias that has initially prevented civil war in Iraq. None of them may live to see it, but they have
helped set the tone for a new religious era, one almost ignored by liberal
media and liberal religious leaders.

The material presented here is intended to be as spiritually inclusive as
possible, while respecting the resurgent neo-orthodox base of the three religious traditions under consideration. The methods of scriptural interpretation fall within the generally accepted limits of orthodox Christian, Jewish,
and Muslim norms, while also "pushing the envelope" to investigate the
limits of more radical positions in all three traditions.

No model is entirely adequate, but I have become personally comfortable
with the view that Judaism provides a *Foundation* for the three traditions,
for "western civilization," and for an emerging world civilization. Christianity has become a *Spiritual Temple* for many people, no longer a white
western religion, but now a truly multinational, multicultural, and multira-
cial phenomenon. Islam has saved some valuable antiques in the attic and,
with its focus on the final judgment, or ultimate principles, is pressing its
claim to be seen as the *Dome* roof over this family shrine, and others need
to understand that.

None of this diminishes the fact that all members of Abraham's household have much to learn from the other religions and faith communities of
the world—their mission may be to bring us all home to God in the fullest
sense. But it is the concept of Islam as the dome of our family shrine that
will be the most difficult for Jews and Christians to accept, believing, as
many still do, that embracing Islam may be a step backward.

In truth, Islam is beautiful; the problem is in the eyes of the beholders.
We hear about the beauty of Islam but the media tend to look critically at
Islam as a religious organization. This is like judging Christianity by the
worst actions of the church. Some inappropriately regard Muhammad as a
warlord with too many wives, which is like judging Judaism by only the
reputed sins of King David, without reference to his great faith. The solution
is to focus not on the leaders and not on the followers, but on the Scriptures
of each tradition. This is more a book about Torah, Gospel, and Qur'an
than about Judaism, Christianity, and Islam, or even about David, Jesus, and
Muhammad, even though the well-known characters of the Bible and the
Qur'an provide most people with a comfortable entrée to the Scriptures.

There are problems for new readers when we first come to the less familiar material of the Qur'an: the revelations of God to Muhammad. The
Qur'an is as hard to read as the books of Daniel or Revelation, and it is

presented in a similar style. It is buttressed by sacred literature called the Hadith, which is comprised of the stories and sayings of Muhammad as related by his companions, including information about the lives of the biblical prophets, but not enjoying the same status as revealed Scripture. The Hadith contains yet another cast of supporting characters from the Bible, including Samuel, Isaiah, Jeremiah, and dozens of others who did not make it into the Qur'an, but who are as well-known among Muslims as they are among Jews and Christians. The Qur'an, standing alone, could be compared to the Book of Revelation if the latter were taken alone as the only Christian Scripture, with the Gospels, Epistles, and Hebrew Scriptures as appendices about which outsiders know little.

It is tempting to open the Hadith with its wealth of information and spiritual insight. However, this book is based on scriptural characters, and the Qur'an alone is the Muslim Scripture. There is enough there for us to see what Islam should be, without the distortions of history or individual failings. Moreover, we do not need to examine the Hadith as a sequel to the Qur'an because we have two "prequels." Those would be the Jewish and Christian Scriptures, which the Hadith summarizes and interprets in its own way. Muslims would want us to take their Scripture itself at face value, and Jews and Christians will be afforded the same respect.

This brings us to an important point. I have always considered the assertion that the religions of the world all have some version of the Golden Rule to be a shallow attempt at syncretizing the differences. When it comes to the study of traditions and experiences of other faith communities, all of us need to think about the Golden Rule in a new way.

To understand others as *they* would want us to understand them, we must put forth the most favorable interpretation of any cherished belief, as long as it does no real damage to our own. We would hope that others might look at our tradition through *our* fond eyes, rather than looking for every inconsistency and hypocrisy they can find. This is not the same as saying we should look at them as we would want them to look at us. Rather, it is a step further. We are to look at them as *they* would want us to look at them, and vice versa.

This will be helpful as we seek to understand each other and to grow in our own appreciation of ultimate truth. I am a Christian, orthodox in both faith and practice, but I shall attempt to follow this "new and improved" Golden Rule throughout this investigation. As we share our treasures with each other, someone may get "converted" but that is between them and God. In this post-9/11 era, the world desperately needs members of Abraham's family to start talking to each other with greater respect.

This is the true role of religion in an era teetering on the brink of an apocalyptic "clash of civilizations." The dangers of racism, anti-Semitism, and Islamophobia are all around us. Their roots are partly religious, and so the solutions must be at least partly religious. If the religions themselves are to surmount traditional animosities and contribute positively to the resolution of the conflicts threatening to engulf the world, they need to begin afresh with their essential bases in their Scriptures, as opposed to politics, traditions, or cultures. The moderate majorities in Christianity, Judaism, and Islam have the capacity to do this, and are perhaps longing to do so, if a solid basis for such an approach can be provided.

A secondary purpose of writing this book is to make a modest contribution to peace from a generous Christian perspective, in response to the highest motives on the part of our cousins in the Abrahamic family. Along with the main focus on biblical characters as they appear in the Qur'an, we will attempt to apply their encounters with God to our situation under the shadow of war in the opening years of the twenty-first century. To do so, it will be necessary to begin well before Abraham, with Noah and his son, among others. Canaan, the "other son," is not mentioned in the Bible, but is a twentieth-century type of skeptic. He does not survive, and we must move beyond his mentality.

For that reason I present a prologue which was "preached" by Muslim, Christian, and Jew together at a multifaith service hosted by Lansing United Church at the Toronto Centre for the Arts on October 6, 2002. It was a year after September 11th, and we gathered with our congregations, as well as Hindus, Sikhs, Buddhists, and other Christians, to worship God and to raise funds for a project to rebuild a mosque in Afghanistan that had been bombed accidentally by Coalition Forces in an operation that included Canadians.

The sermon was preached jointly by Javed Akbar, a Muslim businessman who is a frequent contributor to the *Toronto Star* as Outreach Director of the Pickering Masjid, a mosque in suburban Toronto, by me as host minister, and by Margarita Vinnikov, a Jewish university student active in the synagogue at a North York Jewish Centre and a translator at the Lansing Food Bank. Others provided prayers and music from various cultures and faith traditions, but it was left to the main protagonists to address the fundamental concern about Jews, Christians, and Muslims entering a period of mistrust and war.

PROLOGUE

Exploring Common Ground, From Ground Zero to Holy Ground

Javed Akbar

ONE OF THE BIGGEST challenges for believers in the world today is that of interfaith relations. We know people have experienced God in so many ways and have experienced the spiritual dimension of human existence within many different cultural and symbolic systems. In promoting the fullness of life, believers benefit enormously from dialoguing with one another.

Those of us who follow the Abrahamic religions strongly believe that it is our moral and spiritual responsibility to overcome obstacles by building bridges of understanding among each other. Never before has there been such a need for faith groups to explore and discuss the mechanisms of peace, particularly in the climate of militarism, brinkmanship, and media war hysteria.

The challenges and opportunities facing Jews, Christians, and Muslims today provide epoch-making prospects to open the doors of understanding. From a Muslim perspective, there is a compelling human bond that binds all of us together, wherein the Qur'an calls God's creation a family. And, as a family, we can better serve God's purposes in the world by reaching out beyond our own community for the common good of all. This approach does not diminish our faith, but rather enhances it.

Christians, for example, can see in dialogue an obvious but demanding example of Christ's commandment to love our neighbor as ourselves, an injunction he quoted from the Hebrew Scriptures, with which he grew up as a Jew.

Love requires understanding. Through dialogue, we may, therefore, come closer to the attitude of Saint Francis, who is famously said to have prayed "not so much to be understood as to understand"—a prayer that those involved in dialogue might do well to inscribe deep in their hearts.

Muslims can also find that the experience of dialogue prompts fresh reflections on their relationship with the "Other." A much-quoted Qur'anic text states that religious uniformity is not God's will ("Had God willed, He would have made you one community") and that the relationship between different faith groups is to be characterized by striving toward mutual dignity and respect.

"The dignity of difference" is a challenging but exciting reality that we all must address in the conviction that we will be enriching humankind when we understand our differences. We can discover much that is good and true in those who are different from ourselves and, at the same time, come to a deeper understanding of our own traditions.

The relentless quest for justice and the act of carrying out virtuous deeds are two fundamental principles of Islam that have also been hallmarks of the universal paradigm of intellectual development. These guideposts can help renew our civilization at a time of worldwide moral decline.

An important priority is the potential for Judaism, Christianity, and Islam to work together and with others for peace and justice. Such a dialogue should involve not just reaching out to members of a different faith, but also a willingness to turn our attention to common challenges like globalization, the environment, and poverty.

What lies at the heart of our relations is how we travel together into the future for the benefit of all. The journey involves building new bridges of friendship and respect. It is those bridges we will have to be working to build today, tomorrow, and in years to come.

Brian Arthur Brown

I thank my very good friend, Javed Akbar, for introducing this topic as Outreach Director of the Pickering Masjid and lately one of my several tutors in the quest to retool a professional understanding of Islam. The new commonality that humanity now requires depends not on new technology or new facts, but on a new spirit among us, or rather a new openness to the Spirit of God. This "turning" is called *t'shuva* by Jews, *conversion* by Christians, *submission* by Muslims, and other words by the other great religions represented here today. It is only as we turn toward and submit to God that our issues are resolved. The closer we are to God, the closer we are to each other.

Hindus, Buddhists, Sikhs, and others here may have to excuse us for just a few minutes, since it is the dysfunctional family of Abraham that has been causing most of the trouble in the world lately. Many people now realize that Jews, Christians, and Muslims all have religious roots in Abraham. Secular magazines like *Time* and religious journals like *Christian Century* have cover stories on Abraham this very week, as an attempt to understand his descendants. But as a matter of fact, Abraham is just one of some twenty-five personalities and prophets who are featured in both the Bible and the Qur'an. These are "The People of the Book." So are the three of us in this pulpit today, as are many others.

If I may say so, the hot issues of the twentieth century have been moved to the back burner. Civil rights between blacks and whites no longer cause riots in the United States. Language rights no longer divide Canadians in such a threatening manner. The Iron Curtain of communism in Europe came down with the Berlin Wall. There is still work to be done on these and other issues left over from the last century, including caste concerns in India and human rights in China, but something else preoccupies us at this time.

The hot issue in the world of the new century is the ongoing family feud involving Jews, Christians, and Muslims, whether in Afghanistan, Indonesia, Chechnya, Iraq, Jerusalem, New York, Paris, London, or Madrid. Abraham's dysfunctional family has displaced the Cold War, the nuclear arms race, civil rights, and human rights as the issue of the new century, though the others remain of concern, along with poverty, disease, and climate change.

As with Irish Catholics and Protestants, this fight is not about religion. The Irish fight about power, land, and money and this fight is about water, oil, and blood, but a spiritual answer is needed, since communal battle lines are often identified by religious affiliation.

We have a good deal more going for us than a common ancestor. For example, the Abrahamic texts give rise to a "covenant theology," which these three religions hold in common. God says, "Behold, I make my covenant with you and your descendants." Out of our sacred texts and traditions, Jews, Christians, and Muslims also have well-developed messianic theologies, which represent an ongoing quest for Jews ("The Messiah is coming"), a present reality for Christians ("Jesus is the Messiah"), and a higher priority among Muslims than others have realized ("Yes, Jesus was Al Masih, and He is coming again at Judgment"). "Judgment" and the expectation of heaven is a third theological construct held in common by these three. Scholars call this eschatological theology, or the study of the last days. Fourthly, it is monotheism, belief in the oneness of God, that sets the Abrahamic religions apart from other religions. After hints from "Adam,"

monotheism began with Abraham and was developed by God through
Moses, all equally revered in the three traditions.

Perhaps it is time for Christians and Muslims to more generously recognize Jews as People of the Book, as those who laid a *Foundation* for western
civilization and contributed much to the whole world. Perhaps it is time for
Jews and Muslims to more generously recognize the role of Christianity as
a *Spiritual Temple* of faith, for at least a third of the people of the world.
Perhaps it is time for Jews and Christians to more generously recognize that
Islam is vitally concerned about the last days, a magnificent *Dome* that shelters our family shrine. The image of foundation, temple, and dome is an
example of a more generous spirit Jews, Christians, and Muslims might
extend to each other. Rita Vinnikov is a young, articulate new Canadian of
Russian origin, a Jewish female university student with some radical
thoughts in this direction.

Margarita Vinnikov

I greet you in the name of God, by whichever name you know God best
in your own hearts.

This summer, the *Religious News Service* reported a breakthrough
between Roman Catholics and Jews that should be of interest to us here
today. A joint task force of Roman Catholic bishops and Jewish rabbis concluded that targeting Jews for conversion is "no longer acceptable in the
Catholic Church" because Jews "already dwell in a saving covenant with
God." These are phrases from a twelve-page statement released jointly on
August 12, 2002, by the U.S. Conference of Bishops and the National
Council of Synagogues. The Catholic part of the joint statement refers to "a
deepening Catholic appreciation of the eternal covenant between God and
the Jewish people, together with a recognition of a divinely given mission
for Jews to witness to God's faithful love."

Commenting on the report, the executive director of the National Council of Synagogues Rabbi Gilbert Rosenthal said, "Neither faith group
believes that we should missionize among the other in order to save souls
via conversion. Quite the contrary, we believe both faith groups are beloved
of God and assured of God's grace."

As a Jew who is personally comfortable with this, and happy to hear it,
and as a young person in this wonderful city where we do make every effort
to include everybody in community life, would it seem out of place for me
to recommend to all my Protestant and Muslim friends here today that they
might issue a similar statement to each other? Who knows where such
things might lead?

Of course, there should be nothing to prevent anyone from joining another religion. What should change are organized campaigns by religions to coerce whole groups to switch religions, as a few Christian groups still do, or to prevent individuals from switching, as a nervous Jewish community tries—and a practice absolutely forbidden in Islamic countries that have Sharia Law. Such coersion belongs to the spiritual mentality of previous centuries. Religious respect and religious freedom are recommended by the bishops and rabbis to Catholics and Jews. I recommend both to Protestants and Muslims, and, of course, to all others. This is what I and my generation expect in this new century, and we will not accept less.

Thank you all, and may God truly bless you.

CAST OF CHARACTERS

The English and Arabic Names of
Scriptural Personages

English	*Arabic*
Aaron	Haroon
Abel	Habeel
Abraham	Ibrahim
Adam	Aadam
Children of Israel	Bani Israel
Cain	Qabeel
David	Dawoud
Enoch	Idris
Eve	Hawaa
Ezekiel	Zul-Kifl
Goliath	Galoot
Isaac	Ishaq
Jacob	Yaqub
Jesus Christ	'Isa Masih
Job	Ayyub
John	Yahya
Jonah	Yunus
Joseph	Yusuf
Lot	Lut
Mary	Miriam
Moses	Musa
Muhammad's wife	Khadija
Muhammad's daughter	Fatima

Noah	Nooh
Pharaoh's wife	Asiya
Queen of Sheba	Bilqis
Satan	Shaitan
Saul	Talut
Solomon	Sulaiman
Zechariah	Zakariyah
Potiphar's wife	Zulaika

PREFACE

Translations, Versions, Sources, Context, and Spellings

THOUGH I PERSONALLY PREFER THE New Revised Standard Version of the Bible for personal study and devotion, as well as public worship, I will use the King James "Authorized" Version, or paraphrases thereof, throughout this study, with rare exceptions, when quoting Hebrew or Christian Scriptures. There are two reasons for this, one relating to Jewish usage and the other to the Qur'an.

For 350 of the last 400 years, the King James Version of 1611 was the translation known best to English-speaking Jews. Despite his well-documented anti-Semitism, Jewish scholarship clearly influenced Martin Luther's watershed German translation, which was a guide for the English translation by William Tyndale, which in turn became the single most important model for the King James Version. The English-speaking Jewish community returned the compliment by adopting variations on that English Bible as its own for many generations, completing a circle of European scholarship.

The Introduction to the modern Tanakh version of Hebrew Scriptures, produced jointly between 1955–1985 by orthodox, conservative, and reform scholars for the Jewish Publication Society, comments on the relationship between the King James Version and previous Jewish translations: "The more modern English versions (of Hebrew Scripture), such as *The Holy Scriptures* by the American rabbi Isaac Leeser (1855), the (British) *Revised Version* (1881–1885), the *American Standard Version* (1901), the Jewish publication Society's *The Holy Scripture* (1917), and the (American) *Revised Standard Version* (1952), all made extensive use of the King James."

The King James idiom is what Jewish children learned. Its translators also had an acknowledged influence on traditional Roman Catholic versions, but the KJV fell into disuse among most Protestants in the second half of the twentieth century. This period of biblical scholarship saw more original translations in fifty years than in all the years of Jewish and Christian history combined. The newer translations are more accurate textually, and some of the words in the King James Version have dramatically changed meaning in 400 years. However, in the twenty-first century, the wish to replace King James English has begun to seem less important than the spiritual authenticity it somehow conveyed. There has been a revival of interest in the KJV, or what was often called the "Authorized Version" in previous times.

The 2003 publication of *God's Secretaries: The Making of the King James Bible* by Adam Nicolson was a best-seller on both sides of the Atlantic. It signaled a new appreciation of the intrinsic mystique of the King James Version in both scholarly and popular circles. The KJV is one of the bedrock sources of the English language in its highest literary form. The political intrigues, theological balancing acts, and personal peccadilloes of the fifty-four brilliant KJV translators, working in four teams, far from compromising the translation, actually contributes to its hybrid character. It would seem that the Holy Spirit used this spectrum of dynamics to ratchet up the spiritual tone to its finest pitch. It was as if the voice of the redeeming God was actually heard in English.

Other individual translations may be poetic, scholarly, or more accessible, but only the King James Version captures anything like the sacred intimacy with God characterized by the Qur'an in its very text. For that reason, the King James Version is more suited to our purpose of comparison than any other. Accordingly, I will use the King James for most quotations of Hebrew and Christian Scriptures, although paraphrased sections will be enhanced by phrases from the *New Revised Standard Version*, the *New International Bible* (New Century Version), and the *Good News Bible* (Today's English Version).

The best-known English translation of the Qur'an, that by Yusuf Ali of 1934, is a classic that deliberately emulates the King James style. For purposes of reviewing the Qur'an, I will use brief verses from the Yusuf Ali Version as a *continuo* throughout this book. I personally benefit from the recent Thomas Cleary translation, but it has yet to receive general acceptance in the Muslim community. To introduce a richer variety of texts, I will include one significant quote from each of the other three most highly regarded twentieth-century English translations, appropriately identified, to distinguish from the verses quoted from the Yusuf Ali Version.

Farooq-i-Azam Malik, who is one of the most respected American Muslims today, presents a very modern translation in the Malik Version. Equally well regarded internationally are the Pickthall and Asad Versions, the former by Mohammad Marmaduke Pickthall, the English son of an Anglican clergyman who converted to Islam, and the latter by Muhammad Asad, born Leopold von Weiss, a Jewish journalist working in Austria, Saudi Arabia, Pakistan, and America who also converted to Islam. Both of these scholars have won high praise inside and outside the Muslim community for their academic standards and spiritual integrity.

Typically, Pickthall insists that his is not a translation, but a transmission of the meaning of the Qur'an, for it is often said that the Qur'an is untranslatable. It is in the hearing of it recited, usually in Arabic, that one experiences the Qur'an. With a nod to the verbal patina of the King James style employed by Yusuf Ali, we will review samples of all the above, the last two of whom also use the noble KJV English because they recognize that the sound of that noble expression of English language comes closest to the Qur'an.

We have now hinted at one of the main differences between the Muslim Scriptures and those of the Judeo-Christian tradition. For the latter, translations are not only acceptable—they may even be part of the work of the Holy Spirit in God's great communication of His Word, as contained in the words of Scripture. For Muslims, the Qur'an is not only the *Word* of God but also the *words* of God. This is a view of Scripture held now by only a few literalist minorities among Christians and Jews. The vocation of literalists is to prevent Catholics and Orthodox and mainline Protestants from straying too far from the essential connection between the words and the Word. To literalists, the Bible contains the inerrant *words* of God, a position virtually identical to the Muslim view of the Qur'an.

One of the most significant movements among Christians in the early years of the twenty-first century involves a more mature relationship to the Word that cuts across denominational lines. Many churches formerly identified as Fundamentalist or Evangelical now identify themselves as Emerging or Missional Churches. Joining the Protestant mainstream, or even becoming the mainstream in parts of America, Brazil, Europe, and Africa, the Emerging Missional Churches tend to embrace cultural norms, often reviving traditions of ritual maintained by orthodox and Catholic Christians, but in an open, eclectic style of worship. The movement includes some Catholics, many Evangelicals, and increasing numbers of Protestant (old mainstream) Christians. They believe that in Jesus, God has given his Word, and that every word of Scripture points the believer toward that living Word.

The Emerging Missional Church movement has several hallmarks. Black EM churches revel in liturgical embellishment and vestments, for example. An emphasis on inclusive community and social justice is another feature of this movement. Instead of piously asking, "What would Jesus do?" in making moral decisions, white Evangelicals now raise environmental concerns, asking, "What would Jesus drive?" However, it is a third hallmark of EM Churches that is of interest here. Both the eclectic use of liturgical traditions and the new commitments to social justice have emerged from an understanding of the Word of God, which is compatible with the advanced scholarship we will investigate in this study.

This twenty-first-century spiritual approach to Scripture distinguishes between the "words" of the precious text and the "Word" of God to which they witness. Gone is the old liberal–conservative dichotomy in a fresh appreciation of the depth of meaning that comes from God's Word to humanity, presented uniquely through the words of Scripture.

Through the twentieth century, conservative Christians displayed an essential warmth of emotion and spirit within their fellowship, but seemed to expend much of their passion and energy opposing everything from Sunday shopping to abortion instead of providing positive alternatives. Liberals appeared to have more politically correct views, which is a way of caring for your neighbor, and a prophetic dedication to social justice, but starved the soul and wondered why their children agreed with their politics but lost the faith it was all built upon.

For Christians, the resolution to this debilitating situation has come through a new consensus on the depth and value of the Word of God. Conservatives used to insist on a literal understanding of the Book of Jonah and an allegorical interpretation of the Song of Solomon, while liberals did just the reverse. In this post-conservative and post-liberal era, both are simply looking for the meaning of the Word within the words. For many, the change is not one of essence but of style, symbolized by less emphasis on being "born again" (John 3:16) and more focus on the equally valid expression of being "transformed" (Romans 12:2), a phrase that has equal power but less negative baggage.

As a new century began to unfold, the agendas of the Emerging Missional movement quickly became so all pervasive across the church spectrum, even among clergy and others unfamiliar with the term, that it began to sweep all other agendas into its embrace. Its principal features now almost describe the whole church, especially in relation to the Word of God. As the Emerging Missional movement begins to disappear, almost as quickly as it appeared, its invisibility is precisely because it was merely an articulation of trends ripening across the spectrum, and increasingly adopted in thousands of postmodern contexts, each different and all valid.

In contrast to all this, for Muslims, the Word comes not only through the meaning of the words but through their sound, the emotive impact of divine poetry, and the experience of reciting the words. This aspect of the Qur'an can be partially understood by Jews and Christians in reference to their own understanding of ecstasy in the Prophets and rapture in the Book of Revelation, but we will need to return to this topic if we are to appreciate fully the Muslim reverence for the characters in the Qur'an that also appear in the other Scriptures.

For many, the Bible is divided into Hebrew Scriptures and Christian Scriptures, the description that has respectfully replaced the phrases "Old Testament" and "New Testament" employed by Christians for many years. This "politically correct" observance is challenged by the views of Rabbi Reuven Firestone, one of America's leading scholars on such matters, in his work at the Hebrew Union College in Los Angeles. Firestone contends that "Old Testament" is actually an acceptable description for that text since it actually gave rise to three new religions: Christianity, Islam, and Rabbinical Judaism. The flowering of Rabbinical Judaism as a separate religion is a multitextured enrichment of the religious fabric of the world, especially through its intimate connection with biblical Judaism, which is so foundational to the faith of Christians, Muslims, and Jews. However, I shall often use the designations Hebrew Scriptures and Christian Scriptures and, for purposes of this study, I will refer to the Qur'an simply as the Muslim Scriptures to extend this connection to all who read "The Book." At other points, I will refer to Torah, Gospel, and Qur'an.

Meanwhile, there is a final aspect of the different appreciations of the characters in the Scripture that needs to be addressed before we begin. Some of the most helpful Muslim scholars (thanked in the acknowledgments at the end of this work) were aghast at my first reminders that Jewish and Christian Scriptures present many of the great figures of the Bible "warts and all" (as Oliver Cromwell required of the artist painting his portrait).

They urged me to acknowledge that the Qur'an presents Noah, Abraham, Lot, and others as messengers from God who were models and examples of the morality that pleases God. They are held in reverence and with a respect that does not countenance tales of foul misdemeanors from Hebrew and Christian textual sources that may have been corrupted over the centuries. The Christian Scriptures resemble the Qur'an in this respect, because no one questions the "saintliness" of the saints, and to question the purity of Jesus is a blasphemy that always creates public controversy. It is in the

Hebrew Scriptures, which Christians also regard as sacred, that this issue comes to the fore.

That Abraham could have passed off Sarah as his sister, so she could have an intimate relationship with Pharaoh, is an offensive slander in the eyes of Muslims and, to them, an illustration of how the Judeo-Christian Scriptures have been corrupted. Likewise, Noah would not have gotten drunk after the flood, an intoxicated Lot would not have been seduced by his daughters, and David would not have stolen another man's wife and had him killed. Muslims wonder what kind of Scripture would report such things of those chosen by God and entrusted with His message. As we shall see, even riots over offensive cartoon depictions of the holy Prophet Muhammad, "peace be upon him," can only be understood in the context of this Muslim interpretation.

It is important that Jewish and Christian readers recognize that difference as we begin. It is equally important that Muslim readers understand that the Jewish appreciation of God's response to the human quest and the Christian doctrine of God's grace both depend on the fact that God redeems these great prophetic characters *in spite* of their sins, not *because* of their virtues. The point is that this redemption is available to all.

The Christian understandings that "all have sinned and come short of the glory of God" and that "while we were yet sinners, Christ died for us" necessarily includes the prophets among the great examples of this truth. It includes the saints too, except for those mentioned in the Christian Scriptures, who are given the same respect the Qur'an accords to the prophets. Of course, the notion of God's Masih, or the Messiah, being crucified like a common criminal is also abhorrent to Muslims.

Early in my ministry a grateful bride and groom presented me with a Bible in thanks for my part in their wedding. I already possessed several, but accepted the gift graciously, only to realize later that I had received an original copy of the Bishops' Bible of 1568. Published at the dawn of the Protestant Reformation, two generations before the King James Version, among its prominent features are the leather straps and metal hasps used to padlock the Bible in an era when the church was still struggling with the idea of a Bible open to all.

The fear was that if everyone interpreted its meaning for themselves, any trustworthy understanding would be lost in the confusion. The church decided to trust the Holy Spirit to guide the readers, and now anyone can benefit from its meaning on their own terms. The role of the church in teaching and the benefits of scholarship have increased, not diminished, as "blind faith" is replaced by faith with "eyes wide open," which is ever so much more fulfilling for the believer. Today Islam and its authorities, scholars, critics, and believers, may be preparing to unlock to Qur'an, and to proceed from the uncertainties of "blind faith" to a new era of faith with "eyes wide open."

It is my hope and prayer that in these pages Jewish and Christian readers may find a new appreciation for Muslim reverence for the Scriptures, and that Muslim readers may find inspiration from Christian and Jewish experiences with the techniques of critical analysis that will open their sacred treasure more widely, to the benefit of the whole world.

It is an honor to be published by T&T Clark, the world's most prestigious publisher of theology from Mahatma Gandhi through Karl Barth to Rowan Williams. As part of the international Continuum Publishing Group, this publisher requires adherence to the *Chicago Manual of Style*, but I have dared breach the rules to capitalize the word Scripture and the divine pronouns in deference to a preference of certain intended readers. Footnotes have been avoided by including references within the text and other information is placed in the acknowledgments and the bibliography in hopes that both scholars and general readers will be satisfied with the flow of material.

Finally, a brief note about the spelling and usage of Arabic names of biblical characters in this study. In the preface to a later edition of *Seven Pillars of Wisdom* by T. E. Lawrence (Lawrence of Arabia), his brother attempted to answer the critics. One critic had questioned Lawrence's inconsistencies in the spelling of proper names. In reply, A. W. Lawrence quoted his famous brother, "Arabic names won't go into English, exactly, for their consonants are not the same as ours, and their vowels, like ours, vary from district to district." The critic had given an example of inconsistent spellings where "Sherif Abd el Mayein" on one page becomes el Main, el Mayein, el Muein, el Mayin, and el Muyein elsewhere in the text. To this, in shrugging off the criticism, Lawrence had replied, "Good egg. I call this really ingenious."

There really is no standard translation of these names that come to us from the Arabic alphabet. The various English translations of the Qur'an reflect the communities from which they come, in South Asia, Egypt, Iran, America, or elsewhere. I have attempted to employ the most widely recognized North American usage of names that are increasingly common in the fast-growing Muslim community where I live, but surely I shall be subject to questions on this matter. For example, notable commentators, including literati such as Salman Rushdie, continue the English spelling of the word,

Koran, whereas I have adopted the increasingly accepted Arabic spelling, Qur'an, though one also sees Quran and Alcoran, as well as the Turkish Kur'an.

It might be simpler to use English translations of names: "David" and "Jesus" instead of choosing between Dawoud, Dawood, and Daud (David) and between 'Isa and Esa (Jesus), for example. Several variants are found in the Muslim world. I chose Dawoud and 'Isa from among the translations of David and Jesus simply because that is what Canadian and American children now hear most often in the schoolyard. Part of the purpose of this study is to familiarize ourselves with our new neighbors by recognizing these scriptural/cultural connections. I depart from Yusuf Ali's usage of English names at this point, as on some others, and it is the Asian appellations rather than Arab that are more common in North America, at least.

The lines of communication are open now, with the likes of "a self-described Muslim feminist cowgirl," Asma Gull Hasan (author of *American Muslims* and *Why I Am Muslim*), reaching out to Jews and Christians with love. This book is an attempt to reach Muslims with love, but also to help Jews and Christians to become more confident in loving Muslims, in spite of the daily horrors reported on both sides in other media.

1

Higher Than Angels

Adam/Aadam

BARASHEET BARA ELOHIM et ha shemyim va et ha eretz. Va ha eretz ha yeta tohu vavohu. Ve hoscheech al penay tehom. "In the beginning God created the heavens and the earth, and the earth was without form and void. Darkness covered the face of the deep." Thus begins the original Hebrew Scripture, followed by the majesty of the Old English rendering in the traditional Protestant Christian version. This story also sets the context for the creation of Adam and Eve in the Qur'an.

Fourteen and a half billion years ago, as scientists now estimate, there was nothing—no creature to observe what happened next and no material out of which to make something. There was nothing—no sound, no light, no movement, not even a smell. What caused something to emerge from nothing science cannot explain. Theologians have simply said, "God created *ex nihilo.*" Today, most scientists whisper about God as the Prime Mover, and science is nearly unanimous about what happened next, except for the question of how life emerged out of the rubble that followed.

Energy somehow "spontaneously" transformed into matter, and all the atoms of the universe came into being with a "big bang," which is still reverberating through the galaxies over fourteen billion years later. Not until Albert Einstein's theory of relativity was expressed in the famous formula $E = mc^2$ were mortals able to compute the relationship between energy and matter, and to measure their convertibility. If one could imagine the sound of a nuclear explosion from the splitting of the atom, as at Hiroshima, consider the sound and the flash of light in the conversion of enough energy to create all the atoms of the universe. The universe was so hot for billions of years that nothing could live in the rubble and, frankly, except for this little

29

planet, we do not yet have evidence that much of anything lives anywhere else, even now.

Among the first people who did much thinking about the meaning of all this were the ancient Jews, at the time of their second enslavement, not in Egypt, but in Babylon (Iraq). We may acknowledge that the ancient scientists of Babylon, Egypt, China, and later Greece all did a reasonable job of analyzing what happened in creation. But the Hebrews asked the further question, "Why did this happen?" Is there any purpose in creation and, if so, how does that affect the lives of humans? Can we attune our activities to a purpose reflected in the creation of the universe? Is this the way to happiness and fulfillment of a destiny that includes everyone in the human family? This question was a puzzle to Jews.

By this time, around 600 BCE, the Jews had campfire stories about Abraham, Isaac, and Jacob that were more than a thousand years old, stories of Moses only 600 years old, and even more recent stories of King David, most of which had been written down in the recently invented Hebrew alphabet. As they retold their campfire stories, the children, perhaps attending Babylonian schools, offered the then current stories of creation. These tales from primitive science were repeated in remnants of the Babylonian texts that we can find today in the recently rebuilt museums of Iraq. Scholars compare them to biblical texts, and we discover that biblical science does, indeed, come from Iraq. The Jewish tribal elders and priests did not leave it there. "Whom do you think was behind the Big Bang, my child? And why do you think God would do all that, my child?"

The day after 9/11, Dr. Lawrence H. Summers, the new President of Harvard University, came to the Divinity School. He calls himself an "agnostic," one who does not know about something, usually God. But he came to the Divinity School on September 12, 2006, to acknowledge that the Harvard Schools of Law, Business, Government, Arts, Science, and Medicine had no idea what to say about what happened. He said, "If ever there was a week when the importance of what you study and what you think about was manifest, it was this one. You at the Divinity School are the carrier of Harvard's oldest traditions, of what was Harvard's original mission, but you are charged with what is, in some ways, most new: finding eternal truth in a world that appears to be in complete flux."

One of the less recognized facts about the aftermath of the terrorist strike against America on September 11, 2001, has been a Muslim push toward a reformation or "renaissance" of the Islamic faith based on a fresh understanding of the Qur'an. Of course, Muslims have always been attached to the Qur'an, and most can recite more from it than Christians or Jews can recite from the Bible. The Muslim religion has evolved from revelations to the Prophet Muhammad, "the peace and blessings of God be upon him," and from the testimony of his "companions" as well as later historical traditions. The current renaissance is based on a rebirth of the deepest understandings of the Qur'an, in which there may be treasures unrecognized in recent times in the Muslim community, as well as for Jewish and Christian children of Abraham, and for descendants of Adam worldwide.

For many, the surprise about this is that the material in the Qur'an appears to be so biblical. Christians and Jews are in nearly total ignorance of the close relationship among the Hebrew, Christian, and Muslim scriptures. Muslims believe that Jewish and Christian texts have become jumbled and garbled but, whether the rest of us accept that or not, even a cursory reading of the Qur'an makes it clear that it is like the third book in a series, ostensibly from the same source. One cannot read the Christian Scriptures without knowledge of the Hebrew Scriptures, and no one can read the Qur'an without knowledge of the Bible stories, known by many Muslims through material in the Hadith. The Qur'anic understanding of figures like Adam and Eve, or Abraham and Sarah, or Hagar, is incomprehensible on its own, and the Muslim community has always acknowledged that.

The Qur'an reads or recites as if the reader or hearer already knows the stories of Noah and Moses. David and Goliath are not introduced when their story "comes up," because everyone who reads the Qur'an is expected to know that story already. They know the story of Jonah, which is brought up in the Qur'an in the same offhand manner as the references to Jonah by Jesus in the Christian Scriptures, where familiarity is presupposed in exactly the same way.

This new understanding of the relationship and the common roots of Judaism, Christianity, and Islam, based on their Scriptures, is an inconvenient fact for Muslim extremists who want no part of any such renaissance. It is no less inconvenient for Christians, Jews, and any others whose psychological make-up requires an enemy, a focus, or projection of all that is wrong in their own society. This role as enemy of the rest of the world is a role that an Islam based on the Qur'an cannot fulfill, in spite of seeming evidence to the contrary in various historical situations.

To judge all Muslims by standards set by Osama bin Laden or Saddam Hussein is as mistaken as to judge Christians by the Crusades or the Ku Klux Klan, or to judge Judaism only on the basis of violence in Hebrew scriptural accounts of the invasion of Canaan, or Israeli incursions into Palestinian refugee camps in Lebanon, authorized by Ariel Sharon in one of the more violent eras of his varied career. People who say they can bring peace by violent means are perverting the Scriptures, which present such endeavors as exceptions to God's greater purpose.

More to the point, in terms of this investigation, instead of reviling and vilifying each other, it is becoming apparent that one of the most dynamic and mutually helpful theological exchanges of the nascent twenty-first century could be an interchange among Jews, Christians, and Muslims, which would contain both benefits and surprises for all. To begin with, given the xenophobia current in extremist Islamic circles, and the Islamic image portrayed in the popular media, perhaps one of the greatest surprises to many is the universalism taught to Muslims in the Qur'an, a universalism prefigured in the person of Aadam.

Far from being "Chosen People" like Jews or having the "only truth" like Christians, in the Qur'an, Muslims are not asked to convert Jews, Christians, or anyone else. According to the Qur'an, Muslims are to recognize God's graciousness to all the peoples of the world and to respect their responses to God. That may not be everyone's experience of Islam, the religion, just as there may be differences between the ideals of the gospel or the message of the prophets as compared to the record of Christians or Jews.

In this investigation we are not comparing the religions. We are comparing their Scriptures. The Qur'an calls all who submit to God "muslims," and the religion of Islam originated as just one more group joining the universal family of those who give their total allegiance to God. The Qur'an goes so far as to recognize this in the religions of India, Africa, and elsewhere, but especially among faithful Jews and Christians. This aspect of the Qur'an is a surprise for most Jews and Christians, and for many Muslims.

Modern science believes that life emerged out of "the primordial soup" or silt of the ocean bed. In Genesis 2:7, the Bible says that God made Adam from dust or "clay." The Qur'an (Surah 18, ayah 37) refers to human origins as coming from dust mixed with a drop of divine sperm. All three views are in close accord, scientifically, poetically, and theologically. Like the Bible, the Qur'an blends reality with symbolic expression so dynamically that there is scope for those who believe in an intelligent design in the creation of humans, those who believe in evolution, and those who see evolution as the most intelligent design imaginable.

The Qur'an presumes that we know the story of Adam, because it launches into deep theological questions without any of the detailed background we might require. His name is spelled Aadam and Eve's name appears as Hawaa, just a slightly different rendering in related languages. The Qur'an says that after creating Aadam from clay (dust and sperm) and breathing His spirit into him, God called all the angels together and announced that Aadam would be His vice-regal representative upon the earth.

The angels protested that such a person could create havoc, even resulting in bloodshed, as compared to themselves, who were programmed simply to praise and honor God. God replied that they were unable to understand His purpose, and He explained no further. God discussed the names of all creatures with Aadam, just as in the Bible. Naming implies giving or recognizing meaning and purpose. When the angels again confessed their confusion, God appointed Aadam as their teacher.

The angels are beautiful for their purpose: producing music and poetry that reflect God's glory. In making human creatures who could choose freely between God's will and their own, God brought in a whole new order of creation, above even the angels. The Bible says in Psalm 8 that mankind is "a little lower than the angels," and this is one of the differences between the Bible and the Qur'an. The Qur'an places humans a little higher than the angels, because they were given choice. God required the angels to bow down to Aadam, and they did, except for one known as Iblis, or "Lucifer" in English literature. He also has the name Shaitan (or Satan) in the Qur'an.

Iblis was one of another class of forces in the universe with a level of freedom lower than humans, but Iblis had so pleased God by good behavior that he had been elevated to the status of angel. These "Jinns," or Forces, were created from fire, whereas angels were created from God's own light, or "Noor." That is why angels are incapable of sin: they see things so clearly that they never make a mistake. Though Iblis now had the rank of angel, the honors bestowed by God on Aadam were still too much for Iblis to bear. God asked him why he refused to bow before Aadam and he said, "I am superior to him. You made me of fire and him from clay, which needs to be fired. I will not bow down to him."

With that, God ordered Iblis away from His presence, but not into eternal hell because Iblis had asked to be permitted to contend with Aadam and his descendants until final judgment. God agreed, believing humanity would choose to love Him and fulfill His purpose. The Qur'anic images are familiar to us from their use in *Paradise Lost* by the English poet John Milton, in which the story leads to an episode familiar to us from the Bible.

God invited Aadam and Hawaa to enjoy all the pleasures of Paradise except for a certain tree and its fruit, which God kept for Himself. Now Satan whispered to them, "God only forbade this tree because its fruit has juice that can make you wise as angels. With the authority God has given you, this would make you too powerful. Trust me on this!" When Aadam and Hawaa tasted the fruit, they became aware that they were actually naked in every way. In an effort to cover things up, they clothed themselves with leaves from the garden. They pleaded with God for forgiveness and, though He now restricted their movements, God forgave them and taught them how to pray. This paraphrase summarizes the story as it appears in the Qur'an.

Chapter 1 of Genesis has a short version of the creation story of the first humans, in which God made male and female mortals at the same time. It refers to them in the plural, acknowledging that there were many Adams and Eves from the beginning. The insight of the human story in Chapter 1 is the part about mortals being made in God's image, not physically, but spiritually. God has freedom of choice—so do humans. God is responsible, as well as free, and God is creative, merciful, graceful, and moral—and this is how God intends mortals to be. This is why Muslims continue to believe that Aadam was made higher than angels, not a "little lower than the angels" as the Judeo-Christian Scriptures suggest. The rest of creation is amazing, but humans have a potential and a capacity for a truly divine lifestyle.

Chapter 2 of Genesis has a more colorful presentation. A single man is created first and then one woman, though again their names are plural. He is Man, as in mankind or "men," in much the same way that tourists realize the meaning of the word *Adam* when they see it on the door of a washroom of a kibbutz in Israel. The name does mean "men," but even that comes originally from *adama* meaning the wet soil or clay in the silt from which he came. The great, God-inspired author of this biblical story put a capital A on Adam and he became Mr. Man, so that we would all get the point that his is the story of every man. The roots of the Hebrew words "Eve," Mother, and "Eden," Contentment, give us an immediate hint that this is a story rich in symbolic imagery.

In this most insightful story of humanity, opportunity, and iniquity, the snake is made up of just one muscle, just like a particular feature of the male anatomy, which is why this story has always had a certain sexual overtone. A snake tempts the woman, "You can do this. It won't kill you; it will make you fully alive. Trust me!" She did, and she became more alive than ever she had been, receptive to both pleasure and pain. Then she convinced Adam that this was a good thing and they shared it. Insightful as it is, if we focus only on the sexual dimensions of this story, we may become as fixated as our own sex-crazed society. The Bible uses this image wisely as a profound illustration of an important universal point.

In their new awareness, humans realized that they could face each other in the sexual embrace. No other creatures can do this but, at the Genesis moment when conscience developed, it suddenly mattered with whom one shared the embrace. Sex symbolized a growing awareness of the importance of relationships. Such new knowledge was a major challenge to manage, but they could face each other, and that really mattered. It was a big step in the development of human responsibility. They sometimes had difficulty in facing God, so they hid, as we still do. When God confronted them, as God confronts us, they blamed each other, and even the snake, as we still do.

Then they were forced to leave the Garden of Eden (the state of contentment) to work for their daily bread, to labor to beget children and to feed them. Note what just happened here. Just as God had elevated humans above angels, at least in the Qur'an, they now distinguished themselves from animals. They were no longer content with instinct as the basis of activity, whether eating, sexual activity, relationships, migration, jobs, or anything else. For better or worse, humans have emerged into the realm of choice and responsibility—exactly what we hope our children will do when they are ready, and just what God intended men and women, Adam and Eve, to do when he set up this scenario.

The eminent psychiatrist Carl Jung was sure that God intended us to bite the apple, to face the consequences maturely, to work things out, to work for a living, to know both pain and pleasure, and to have a conscience. Unless we learn from our mistakes and accept God's redemption of our situation, we remain immature, interesting animals, but incomplete as companions for a moral God. However, when given freedom of choice, wrong choices could lead to death, as one of Noah's sons learned. Adam experienced this risk, as do we all.

The great Christian St. Augustine had a handle on "what went wrong" when he recalled how he and some teenage friends had stolen ripe pears from a neighbor's tree but did not even bother to eat them. It was the stealing that was the thrill, an instinctual "original sin" they had yet to overcome. In the same way, a child's favorite toy is usually one belonging to a brother or sister. This original sin, the quest to touch and possess everything, especially any fruit or any toy that is off-limits, is a step between animal life and mature humanity. Arsonists lighting forest fires and hackers spreading computer viruses have not moved beyond this stage. Nor have terrorists. But the quest for the rest of us is to choose rightly, living up to our Qur'anic destiny, higher than the angels.

Darwin was the first to notice that humans are the only creatures who have the ability to blush. Nowhere in literature or science has our transformation been better described than in Genesis. The defining moment when human beings became distinct from animals was not when we stood up on hind legs, or when we used thumbs, or made tools, or communicated. Bears can stand up, monkeys use their thumbs, apes even make tools, and dolphins appear to communicate. It was when we developed a conscience that we became fully human, just as God designed and created us to be.

But the importance of the human trait of "freedom of choice" is left to the Qur'an, which thereby accords humans a place higher than angels. This may seem strange to Jews and Christians alike, who have always decried Islam as mere fatalism. This could be an important area of discussion.

In his book, *How Good Do We Have to Be?*, Rabbi Harold Kushner develops an idea introduced to many of us by Carl Jung, who was not only a psychiatrist, but also the progeny of a Protestant preacher. The idea was that eating the fruit from the Tree of Knowledge of Good and Evil, or the Tree of Conscience, was not entirely a bad thing. We advance by pushing the limits, though we must discover the proper limits. Kushner suggests that biting the apple was one of the bravest and most liberating events in the history of the human race, and in the personal development of each person, and that God planned it that way. Its consequences are painful in the same way that growing up and leaving one's home can be painful. In the same way, marriage and parenthood can be painful and cause us to wonder, "Why did I give up my less complicated life for all these problems?" For the mature person who has experienced the complex, hard-earned satisfaction of seeing these things through, there is no doubt it is worth the pain.

The woman is not necessarily the villain of the story, enslaved by her appetites and bringing sin and death into the world. She can be seen as the heroine of the story, leading her husband into the brave new world of moral demands and moral decisions—the only kind of world in which love can be found. In his chapter on "What Happened in the Garden," Rabbi Kushner devises an alternative ending to the story of Adam and Eve. It seems like a happy ending at first, but who would want to live it?

So the woman saw that the fruit was good to eat and a delight to the eye, and the serpent said to her, "Eat of it, for when you do, you will be as wise as God." But the woman said, "No, God has commanded us not to eat of it, and I will not disobey God." And God called the man and the woman and said to them: "Because you have harkened to my word and not disobeyed my command, I shall reward you greatly." To the man he said, "You will never work a day in your life. Spend your days in idle contentment with food growing all around you." To the woman he said, "You will bear children without pain and raise them without any trouble. They will not need anything from you and never depend on you." God told them, "Children will not cry, nor even grieve if their parents die. Parents will not cry if their children die; they can have as many more as they wish. No one will ever laugh or cry, and nobody will ever receive something they have always longed for, because they will have everything." And the man and the woman grew very old in the garden, and very fat, eating daily from the tree of life and having more and more children. And the grass grew high around the Tree of Conscience until it disappeared from view, for there was no one to tend it.

2

Raising Cain

Cain and Abel/Qabeel and Habeel

IN THE BEGINNINGS of civilization (as presented in the Scriptures) we find the basis of our complete humanity, which climaxes in the crowning achievement of human life: both personal and communal relationships with God. However, in almost every other way, civilization as we know it has not advanced much since the story of civilization as found in Chapter 4 of Genesis.

Religion has not advanced much either, except that the direction established by our ancestor Seth has continued in the Jewish vision of a Messiah, fulfilled for Christians in Jesus Christ and celebrated by Muslims as 'Isa Masih. The topic of Messiah, Christ, and Masih deserves a chapter of its own. But who on earth is Seth? He is the younger brother of Cain and Abel and his name means Appointed or Anointed, a hint of the beginning of the Messiah theme as the core of the whole story.

His name is Shiith in Muslim tradition but Shiith is hardly mentioned in the Qur'an. To learn more, we would turn to the Hadith (the sayings of Muhammad, his companions, and later apostles), the collection that has near scriptural authority. The relationship of the Qur'an to the Hadith is similar to the relationship between the Torah (the basic Hebrew Scripture) and the rest of the text (the Nevi'im or Prophets, and the Kethuvim or Writings), all of which are accorded scriptural status by both Jews and Christians.

Examination of biblical characters in the Hadith is not on our agenda, though that would open up additional material on Samuel, Isaiah, Jeremiah, and many others. Suffice it to give one small passing example in the case of Seth. In the Hadith, Muhammad Ibn Ishaq related how when Aadam's death drew near, he appointed his son Shiith (Seth) to be his successor, and taught him the hours of the day and night along with their appropriate acts of worship. He also foretold to him the flood that would come. Others attributed the invention of writing to Shiith, and Abu Dhar narrated how the Prophet Muhammad had once said: "Allah sent down one hundred and four psalms, of which fifty were sent down to Seth."

Seth is the younger brother of Cain and Abel in the Bible and, of course, Jews, Christians, and Muslims all know who they are. These three brothers are the only ones of the many children of Adam and Eve that we know by name in that generation, and what interesting names they have.

The names *Adam* and *Eve* are plural words meaning "Men" and "Mothers," implying that there were many people in that time and that modern people, too, may be included in the story. But the names of these brothers are every bit as interesting as the names of their parents. We have already noted the Messianic implications of Seth's name, and perhaps he deserves more attention, since Abel was murdered and Cain was banished.

Seth became the ancestor of Jews, Christians, Muslims and others, as Christians are reminded in the last verse of Chapter 3 in the Gospel According to St. Luke, the conclusion of Jesus' genealogy. It is somewhat ironic that Christians and Jews are only now beginning to appreciate how the Muslims have maintained ancient Middle Eastern lore of great interest to them. It is uncertain whether this material is now to be understood mythically, spiritually, culturally, or historically—probably a combination of all the above, in the same rich appreciation that modern Jews and Christians have for the depth of their own Scriptures.

Abel is an ancient word for "shepherd," though it can also mean "breath." The name is spelled Hebhel in Hebrew and Habeel in the Qur'an. Abel represents the era in human history when humanity developed beyond hunting and gathering food. The era of animal husbandry is the first era of civilization. His is the first occupation to be mentioned, followed closely by that of his brother Cain who was a tiller of the soil, the first farmer who actually used manufactured tools or implements.

While shepherds breathing deeply on the open range were well regarded in ancient times, farmers were not always seen as the salt of the earth, as we sometimes think of them now. *Cain* is actually the word meaning "smith," as in blacksmith. As a tiller of the soil, he had made tools that would actually interfere with nature. He put up fences to keep Abel's animals out of the garden and he used technology to domesticate the crops. People must have thought it was unnatural to force plants to grow in rows, to use animal waste as fertilizer, and to harvest so much more than a family could eat. They may have speculated, "Next he'll want to be selling food to his neighbors."

Compared to the more natural life of Abel, the shepherd breathing freely out under the stars, Cain was seen as positively decadent in lifestyle and activity, much the way we feel about farmers using herbicides and pesticides, or the possible curse of genetically modified foods. The names of the agrichemical giants like *Monsanto* and gene harvesters like *Biocyte* have almost the same frightening ring to some modern people that the name Cain had to the ancients. This explains why primitive religious folk believed that Abel's offering was acceptable to God and Cain's was not. Genetically modified food may be here to stay, but we do not yet know the price. There are warnings to be heeded.

Before we begin to look at the biblical and Qur'anic texts in reference to the brothers known to us all, let us recognize that all the stories, so far, and several to follow, are stories about humanity as a whole. They have no particular reference to the Jewish people or the Hebrew stories, which dominate much of the Hebrew Scripture as it unfolds in the story of the Jewish people. These are proto-Hebraic and pre-Christian stories, and only Muslim to the extent that, prior to Muhammad, all who submitted to God were considered "muslims," though not part of the Islamic religion. These are stories with universal application as the Qur'an more explicitly acknowledges.

———— ⊱≋⊰ ————

With those words of explanation to set the context, let us examine Chapter 4 of Genesis and take the story of Abel and Cain, or Habeel and Qabeel, not quite verse by verse, but concept by concept. It is interesting that the opening of this drama comes out of the worship experiences of Cain and Abel. They present their offerings to God, though presumably not in public worship, which does not appear until the end of this chapter, in connection with Seth. Both worthy persons like Abel and putative sinners like Cain had a consciousness of God, at least in personal and private devotion, which was one of the finest human instincts from the beginning.

We pick up the story at verse 8, remembering that, just as Adam stands for men and Eve stands for mothers, Abel stands for nature in the life of a shepherd, and Cain, the blacksmith, is associated with implements, or perhaps technology. This is a brilliant story, unmatched in figurative literature. Technology goes out into the field with nature and guess which one gets killed? It is the story of Chernobyl, Three Mile Island, Love Canal, and Global Warming. The warnings continue.

When Qabeel kills his brother Habeel in the Qur'an, a raven appears to urge him to hide the body, as if nature is offended by the crime, but at this point Qabeel's pumping adrenaline has him in such a state of agitated excitement that he is not paying attention. It is a scriptural image of what happens to troops in conflict and even the mass psychosis of the mob in the time of war.

Then comes the biblical "cover up" in verse 9 of the Genesis text. "Cain, where is your brother, Abel?" What follows, if seen as the corporate story of humanity, is akin to the Holocaust denial motif and the denial of knowledge by those who were complicit. Cain gives God the famous line that answers itself, "Am I my brother's keeper?" Those are the familiar words of the King James Version of the Bible, but it is just as poignant in modern English, "Am I supposed to take care of my brother?" This is the question raised every day on the latest newscast. The warning and the consequences are implicit.

God's reply in verses 10 through 12 is also a reproach for every war, especially the religious wars that pit brother against brother, as in Afghanistan or Iraq, or equally poignantly, cousin against cousin in Israel or Ireland. "Your brother's blood is crying out to me from the ground."

Then the story shifts as Cain no longer defends himself but casts himself on God's mercy. His concern about anyone killing him for the murder of his brother is an interesting allusion to what English Common Law calls "misprision of treason." The best example of this may be the traditional Chinese custom of police destroying neighbors' houses in cases of domestic murder when no one stepped in. We are all our sisters' keepers.

But, taking the story on the personal level for a moment, how could Cain know that, if he beat his brother, his brother might die, if, as according to the story, there had never yet been a death in the human family? He must have been stunned at the result of his actions, as we are at ours sometimes. But Jesus actually equates an angry attitude with murder, because that is where it can lead—so, we are all implicated, at some level or other. As Oscar Wilde put it in his *Ballad of Reading Gaol*:

Yes, each man kills the thing he loves,
By each let this be heard.
Some do it with a bitter look,
Some with a flattering word.
The coward does it with a kiss,
The brave man with a sword.

Consequences can result from a deed done (or left undone), or a careless word (spoken or written). We are all implicated, but God is merciful. The consequence of the risks involved in civilization cannot be ignored, so God offers protection to Cain. Technology then proceeds to spread out around the earth and develop. As civilization expands, we examine descendants of Cain by name—Adam's grandchildren and great-grandchildren.

As we consider the meaning of the names of civilization's children and grandchildren, the mythic and plural aspects of all their names is hinted at in what comes next in the marriage of Cain. Sunday School children have sometimes mischievously challenged their teachers with the question, "If the only humans were Cain and his parents, then who did Cain marry?" Literalists read further in Chapter 5 that Adam and Eve had many other children and are stuck with believing that Cain married one of his sisters. This assumption rationalizes incest as a nasty requirement of the circumstances and misses the deeper levels of these texts.

As we see in verse 16, Cain went to a land called *Nod*, or Wandering, and married there. There really were other people, and this fits perfectly with the obvious plural meanings of the names of our biblical ancestors. This land was east of Eden, which was in the Tigris–Euphrates valley (Iraq and Iran), which would put Cain in Afghanistan, his land of exile, a coincidence of at least passing interest to us in the twenty-first century.

In verse 16, Cain and his wife beget enough descendents to establish the city of Enoch, named after their son, whose name is Chanoch in Hebrew and Idris in the Qur'an. The name means Initiated, as if to suggest that Cain's descendants are not finally "beyond the Pale" of civilization. The Bible says Enoch walked with God, while the Muslim tradition gives him the name Idris, meaning Instructor. Enoch is mysterious, as one of those few who were assumed bodily into heaven in all three traditions, but the point stands that children of industry and technology too were able to experience redemption.

In verse 20, Jabal (whose name means watering hole) re-establishes animal husbandry in an organized fashion. In verse 21, we meet Jubal (ram's horn) who began the production of music by harp and flute. Verse 22 introduces the bronze age and the iron age through Tubal-Cain, the "metalsmith" of bronze and iron. In a more civilized society, these various elements of community now coexisted in harmony.

Meanwhile, back at the ranch, Adam and Eve gave birth to the other son whose name we have also remembered. The name Seth, too, is significant. Eve believes that God has given her this son to replace Abel, not just as the man of nature in the sense of shepherding and herding as his occupation, but as the one whose offering is acceptable to God. At the conclusion of the fourth chapter of Genesis, Seth introduces "organized religion" as an element in the progress of civilization.

This points to the responsibility of religion in civilization today. Industry does severely challenge nature, as we have known since the industrial revolution at least, but, with care, we can survive and prosper. Only a few of those protesting pollution actually ride bicycles regularly, and few objectors to the research of Monsanto want to turn the clock back to a time when every person needed to hunt and gather for themselves. So why do religious people so often seem to oppose progress at every turn? Somewhere between the risks and the warnings, humanity finds and fulfills its destiny.

The key to advancement for Muslims in the twenty-first century may be renewal of confidence in their own theology regarding the freedom of choice given to humans, placing them higher than angels. Warnings are important, but freedom cannot be stifled. To find this same balance, Jews and Christians, at least those in Western cultures, may have to become more conscious of the warnings they are so prone to ignore in matters such as global warming, materialism, and militarism, to name some of the most obvious issues.

We all seem to have a natural conservative instinct that Abel's offering is more acceptable than Cain's. That is the notion that the old ways—the country ways—are best. However, while many modern people admire the simple ways of the Amish Mennonites, few join them. We know that reversion to organically grown foods alone would cause mass starvation around the world within a year.

It would seem that the role of religion, in addition to offering warnings in the name of God, is to provide the protection that God offered Cain in a world where risks must be taken, technological or otherwise. Preachers are not to encourage turning back the clock at every juncture, but rather to offer encouragement and wise reflection on the trends, guiding progress rather than preventing it. This is the meaning of the story of Habeel and Qabeel in the Qur'an, and Abel and Cain in the Bible. The People of the Book, as Jews, Christians, and Muslims are called in Islamic tradition, have preserved these stories of universal significance for themselves and for the world. Will these stories be conveyed in the twenty-first century by religious fanatics or through a mature spiritual culture?

Among Christians, renewal of moderate mature religion may mean fewer shrill fundamentalists, but also fewer trendy agnostic pastors. For the Jews it means that the ultra-orthodox must be faced down, but that secular Judaism is equally passé. In the Muslim community, Sunnis and Shia traditionalists must stand up to the Islamofascists, but Salman Rushdie's putative atheism is not the way of the future either. It is out of step with the community, and he knows it. In the twenty-first century, in these three related religions, there may be fewer liberals explaining what we don't have to believe, and fewer conservatives telling us what we must believe.

Many old mainstream Christian congregations may never be as robust again as they once were, nor as robust as many Evangelical churches are now in what may be the new mainstream. This is because, on a point of principle, old mainstream churches do not even try to encourage their large nominal memberships to make the congregation the main focus of daily life. Serving God in the community and in the world is the new agenda. This does not mean that occasional worshipers are not deeply rooted in the Christian ethos, even some who have not been to church for years.

The seeming decline of the old mainstream may be just a shift to cultural religion, and that may be just what civilization needs on some level. Some historic churches are perhaps called to become "shrines," as centers of cultural religion. Such sacred precincts will offer the undoubted privilege of greater involvement to a small core of dedicated members, but two levels of involvement may be appropriate. However, each person must finally decide whether they are getting onboard the ark or not, regardless of how their commitments and devotions are expressed.

While the political extremes of the American Christian "right wing" appeared dominant until recently, the ax had been put to the root of that tree by the trends in theology among the more mature of the Evangelical churches at the turn of the century. They now bring the warmth and verve of Christian spirit and orthodox belief to a "new mainstream" that is able to sustain the essence of the Christian faith with confidence, even while opening the hearts of Christian people to see and hear what else God is doing, and where else God is active in relation to the divine agenda of human destiny. At the same time, Evangelicals in America need to prepare for the twenty-first century when their megachurches may not have ten thousand worshipers every Sunday. But as the religious ethos changes toward "cultural religion," all is not lost. Indeed, a new maturity may be replacing the almost fanatical devotion of the late twentieth century. Such a development may be the only way to avert the disasters associated with religious extremism, whether in America, the Middle East, or elsewhere.

3

Noah's Other Son

Noah/Nooh

THESE ARE DAYS in which Noah's ark could be an almost universal symbol for times when people should again be prepared for worldwide calamity on almost any front. Sunday School children, kids in *synagogue schule*, and those in the nursery at the mosque have all made models and colored pictures of the story of Noah with the animals marching into the ark, two by two. The Bible says some of them entered by sevens, an odd number, to allow for food and sacrificial slaughter, a detail skipped over in the Qur'an in its haste to get to the meat of the matter, the meaning of the story, and the "warnings" given by Nooh.

Again, Christian and Jewish readers will be struck by the realization that the Qur'an presumes the reader knows the story. Unlike the biblical account, the Qur'an does not give us Nooh's family tree, nor set a context for the story, except to acknowledge that Nooh was living in an age of immorality, the likes of which modern people know equally well. Three Surahs contain significant portions devoted to Nooh: 11, 26, and 71, namely: Hud, Shuara, and Nooh, or Noah, as Jews and Christians call him in English translation.

The Qur'an is structured differently than the Bible. It opens with its shortest chapter or "Surah," a little "psalm" that actually has a biblical ring, so much so that it is a favorite at interfaith gatherings and mixed marriages. The other 113 Surahs are all arranged merely according to length, beginning with the longest (the size of Mark's gospel), down to the shortest (the length of Psalm 23, "The Lord Is My Shepherd"), without any sense of chronology or unfolding meaning.

While this may be disconcerting to the Jewish or Christian reader, this seeming mishmash of powerful themes is very similar to the lack of formal "arrangement" of the Psalms. Yet, those who recite the Psalms in worship take no notice of this "disorder," from a human perspective, since they have become accustomed to this in familiar material.

Without putting too fine a point on it, Noah's Hebrew name means Rest, not as when one is tired, but as in coming to rest like an arrow that has completed its flight. Just as Neil Armstrong is remembered as the one who landed on the moon, and could have been nicknamed Lander, it is believed that Noah came to rest on Mount Ararat, and he is remembered as the survivor of the flood.

So the name or nickname must have come late in life unless, again, we simply have a Hebrew retelling of a universal story picked up in Babylon and massaged by old rabbis to illustrate its meaning. The Scriptures are not the record of science or of history or even, in this case, geography or climatology. The Scriptures are God's response to the world's quest and need for meaning.

Immanuel Velokovsky, in his 1956 watershed investigation, *Worlds in Collision*, was the first modern author to systematically document and compare the remarkable similarity between legends of deluge and flood from ancient cultures, though Plutarch noticed the coincidence in an essay written in the year 110 CE. The flood stories that we know best are *The Gilgamesh Epic* from Babylon and the ancient Greek flood story of *Deucalion*, to which Plato refers in *The Timaeus* (in which he also compares it to an older Egyptian flood legend). There are also such tsunami stories in India's Vedic Scriptures and in the records of the ancient Aztecs of the Americas.

Some stories may have borrowed material from others, as did the Hebrew version, almost certainly, but others are too widely separated for that. The common thread is water both falling down and rising up; the destruction of society and information about a few survivors who had built a boat—a family and their animals. There are a few hints of awareness about the wrath of the gods toward corrupt civilizations, but only the Hebrew account is focused on the cleansing and redemptive purpose of it all, the rainbow of God's love, the grace involved in second chances, and the quest for meaning.

That is precisely why we continue to read this account, and not the others, to our children at bedtime. We also read it ourselves in synagogue, church, and mosque, because this account is laden with adult meanings that are not improved upon by philosophical comments on the text provided by literary giants, from William Shakespeare in the King James era to Sigmund Freud a hundred years ago or the preeminent modern-day literary critic the late Northrup Frye, who pointed to the postmodern meanings in all biblical material.

The Qur'an is an exception to this observation about the impact of later comments on the biblical original. The Qur'an, as we have noted, is presented from Allah as an update, an extension, correction, or commentary on the Hebrew Torah and the Christian Scriptures.

After the flood, humans eat meat for the first time. This is taken symbolically as the end of the age of harmony in nature, when humans coexisted with beasts. It may also indicate a more "civilized" ability to cook meats properly, for better or worse, rather than to eat raw flesh. Likewise, the family and generation of Noah were the last to measure time by cycles of the moon rather than the sun, so that they lived to be 600 or even 900, rather than 50 or even 100, as time spans were calculated thereafter. This flood was truly a "tsunami" experience that engulfed whole cultures, rather than just the coastline fringes of countries.

Jungian and other schools of psychology believe that, at the deepest level, the story is about differentiation between the conscious self and the unconscious human psyche, both individual and communal. Water is widely used in art, poetry, and analysis as a universal symbol of the subconscious, whether in books like *Moby Dick*, the art of aboriginals, and other painters, or the probing of the meaning of one's troubled dreams on the analyst's couch. The Noah saga may be a brilliant portrait of the emergence of human self-awareness, though to suggest it is only that is to diminish the scope and the spectrum of meanings addressed in the scriptural texts.

Modern science has come to a consensus that such a prehistoric flood, deluge, or tsunami was responsible for raising the level of the Mediterranean Sea just enough to crumble the land barrier separating a populated valley to the north of modern Turkey. The Black Sea was then formed in a populated area about the size of California when the wall of water suddenly pushed through the Bosphorus Channel about ten thousand years ago in a flood no one forgot. Was this part of a universal catastrophe with few survivors? Did other cultures have similar experiences, or did they simply hear about this one? Or is the universality of the story related to floods and catastrophes we all experience? It may not matter, as long as we discern what it takes to survive—the very point of these Scriptures for those who heed the warnings.

Genesis 6:9–11 in the Hebrew text summarizes the description of the ark, rich enough in symbolism to satisfy the needs of both Christianity and Islam as well as Jewish analysis. In the Christian Scriptures, for example, the apostle Peter refers to the ark as the vessel of salvation for the eight survivors, and suggests that the church has such a role for those who have come through the waters of baptism. Through the ages, the church has used this image. When people go to church, they sit in what is called the nave—they are the navy of God and the crew of the ark. The Qur'an is no less graphic, as we will see.

Genesis 7:11–24 tells the story of the flood, plain and simple. The possible historical parallels, far from diminishing the biblical account, actually buttress it so that the meanings ascribed to the experience have universal application. In a typically biblical literary pattern, the Jews call the experience of coming through the waters of the deluge with Noah a midrash. Coming through the waters of the Red Sea with Moses, through the waters of baptism with Peter, and through the flood of each modern person's catastrophes, are all demonstrations of God's faithfulness and grace. In the Qur'an, Allah simplifies the story into a graphic presentation of the consequences of our unwillingness to heed the warnings, assuming we know the story.

Genesis 8:13–22 says the ark landed on the "mountains" of Ararat, not Mount Ararat, as we sometimes say. Ararat is a range of mountains between Turkey, Syria, and Russia, roughly where modern Armenia is situated. The Muslims believe the ark settled on Mount Judi, a mountain with two peaks in a range of mountains in the Kurdistan region of Iraq, while Orthodox Christians have traditionally pointed to Mount Massis in Turkey. Gullible North American "Bible tourists" believe it was wherever they find unexplained lumber, which is identified by the tabloids as the ark.

Ararat is the mountaintop that changes everything, like Mount Moriah to Abraham and his son, Mount Zion to David, the Mount of Transfiguration to the disciples, and Mount Calvary to the dying thief. Each believer is invited to come to rest on a mountaintop. If we heed the warnings, we can survive the flood, though many are still swimming for dear life. Here again, we have a Jewish midrash, a pattern for understanding the ways of God, picked up by Christians and Muslims. Before turning to the Qur'anic account, we need to review just a few more Jewish verses, known equally well by Christians and Muslims.

Genesis 9:8–17 is the rainbow episode, sometimes illustrated by Sunday School children blowing bubbles in church to create the rainbow spectrum. Of course, there were rainbows before the one that followed the deluge of the flood, but this one really meant something special to Noah and the other survivors. The Ka'bah shrine was there in Mecca before Allah revealed its purpose and meaning to Muhammad. There was bread before the time of Jesus, too, but it took on new meaning in the sacrament when he said, "This is my body." With the rainbow, Noah marveled at what he had previously taken for granted. That can happen to any of us when we realize what God has done to bring us through the flood. The signs of God are everywhere.

Genesis 10:1–6, 21, and 32 list the descendants of Noah through his three sons: Japheth, who was the father of Phoenician sailors and the peoples of Europe; Ham, who fathered Arab parts of the Middle East and all the nations of Africa; and Shem, the ancestor of Abraham, Moses, David, Jesus, and Muhammad, as well as the countries of Asia.

Some of the countries listed in the three Scriptures are impossible to identify, but the point is made that after the flood, all of humanity is related, and the divisions that followed are secondary to the underlying interrelatedness of people. The new worlds of North and South America and the lands "down under" were, of course, populated from Asia, Europe, and Africa, in mixtures that relate to their origins as one family, which we continue to rediscover with interest and joy.

All this can mean nothing to those who have never experienced the flood. Is there anyone who has not had everything swept away in the storm at some time? Has anyone never experienced the utter vulnerability of untimely illness, unwarranted suffering, betrayal, loss, disaster, ruin, unexpected misfortune, separation, tears, distress, bitter disappointment, or stupidity? Those who have experienced none of the above may pass go, collect two hundred dollars, and land on the mountaintop. The rest of us are huddled in the ark, where resources are limited, the stench is sometimes great, and fellow travellers get on our nerves day after day, but we trust in God to bring us through the storm. Again, the three Scriptures present epic themes that are as relevant to modern life as to the original context.

To experience the rainbow, we need both the rain and the light. Our personal prism of tears produces a rainbow, but only when there is faith, the light of love—God's love for us. Additionally light comes from our love for each other, both those we like and from all others, not just those who are good to us. We will never see the rainbow, except through tears, but, when we see it with the eyes of love, the whole world is beautiful, no matter what storms are raging or have raged.

Noah was 600 when the rain began to fall, or about 50 years old by modern calendar calculations. Like Abraham when he left Haran, Noah was ripe for a midlife crisis, and everything did come crashing down. Some individuals do have faith before midlife, but it is only in the second half of adult life that most of us really get things sorted out.

Things look very different after the deluge, but they are not so bad if you can see them through a rainbow of love. Noah built an altar and worshiped God—quite amazing for someone who had lost everything. We observe this instinct among the survivors of any modern disaster. There comes a time for each of us to make some kind of altar. The Qur'an is specific in its warnings that we should not wait too long.

In the Qur'an (Surah 11, often called the Book of Hud), Nooh appears suddenly as a prophet whose calling is to warn the people of his time about the consequences of their immorality: "O my people, I have been sent to you as a warning" (ayah 25). "Worship God alone and have no god but God. Otherwise, I fear for you the penalties of the Day of Judgment" (ayah 25).

The chiefs of the nonbelievers among his people derided him, saying: "We see that you are nothing more than a person like ourselves and that no one is following you except those who have already lost everything anyway. We think you and all who agree with you are liars" (ayah 27). Nooh replied: "If I do show you a clear sign from God, would you accept it? I tell you, I am not speaking up out of any hope for personal gain, and my prophecies are accepted on faith by those who know God. I could not prevent them from following the true path if I tried" (ayah 28).

The debate continued to go nowhere until the chiefs taunted Nooh to ask God to show the clear sign: "Nooh, you have been disputing with us in public for too long. If you are telling the truth about the wrath of God, bring it down upon us" (ayah 32). Nooh spoke first to them: "God will bring it on you when God decides. You should be talking to God, not me" (ayah 33). And then to God: "O Lord, when I try to lead my people in the right path, they run from it. When I give them advice, they stick their fingers in their ears. I beg them to ask for your forgiveness but they refuse. Bring your wrath upon them" (ayah 34).

Then follows the story of the building of the ark, largely presuming Muslim knowledge of the Bible story. In the Qur'an, the scoffers continue in their derision. Interestingly, the Qur'an also affirms some of the more obtuse details in passing, like the fact that the flood was caused by rain in a deluge but also what the Bible calls "the fountains of the deep" bursting forth.

The Bible emphasizes the rain. The Qur'an says the water "bubbled up from God's oven" in the center of the earth. Whether scientifically or metaphorically, there are truths to discover in all three traditions on the meaning of the observation that the origin of our troubles is partly from within. Does the wrath of God well up from inside each person as a result of our folly, or does it come to us from external sources, such as the folly we share? It is as the flood rises that perhaps the most interesting difference between the biblical and the Qur'anic accounts appears. The Qur'an does not dispute the truth of the Bible, but frequently adds details.

The story of another son of Noah who, in his youthful rebellion, refuses to get onboard the ark, is a most interesting instance of this pattern in ayah 42 of the same Surah:

So the ark floated with them on the waves that were towering like mountains. Nooh called out to his son who had separated himself from the rest of the family: "O my son! Embark with us and leave your friends, the unbelievers."

The son replied: "I will climb a mountain and it will save me from the water." Nooh said: "This day nothing can avoid the wrath of God except those upon whom He shows mercy." And the waves came between them and this son was among those overwhelmed in the flood. (ayah 43)

The name of that son was Canaan, according to the Hadith. In the Bible, Ham, another son of Noah, named his son Canaan, no doubt after his lost brother, so the name is not entirely unfamiliar to Jews and Christians. The land of Canaan is named for him also, as the land of those in the Bible and in the Qur'an who disobey and who are to be supplanted by the more obedient descendants of Noah.

The story of Noah's other son, Canaan, is a parable for our times when warnings go unheeded. It is the leitmotif for the stories of Cain, Ishmael, and Jacob, presented in the usual cryptic style of the Qur'an, but with a clarity equal to that of Jesus' parable of the Prodigal Son. All these stories of rebellion, freedom of choice, and failure to heed warnings are of a piece, a pattern, a midrash, but only the story of Canaan captures the complete poignancy of utter consequence. The other stories comprise one of the great biblical and Qur'anic scriptural themes, that of mercy, forgiveness and grace, but the pattern is not complete without the one somehow omitted from the Hebrew and Christian Scriptures. This could be the story most needed now by world civilization on the brink of self-destruction, before we are able to appropriate the grace we need.

Like Adam and Eve tasting the forbidden fruit, all of Noah's other rebellious sons—Cain, Ishmael, Jacob, the prodigal son, and atheists in the twentieth century—play a role in our faith development. They refuse to believe in the Old Tyrant in the Sky kind of god and they clear the decks for faith in the God Moses met in the burning bush; the God of Job's whirlwind; Elijah's still, small voice; Jacob's ladder; and Joseph's dream.

There is actually an obtuse reference to Canaan in the Bible that Jews and Christians have not recognized until now. A review of the story of the Curse of Ham near the end of the ninth chapter of Genesis is finally intelligible, once we know the story of Canaan.

And the sons of Noah, that went forth of the ark, were Shem, and Ham, and Japheth: and Ham is the father of Canaan. These are the three sons of Noah: and of them was the whole earth overspread. And Noah began to be an husbandman, and he planted a vineyard: And he drank of the wine, and was drunken; and he was uncovered within his tent. And Ham, the father of Canaan, saw the nakedness of his father, and told his two brethren without. And Shem and Japheth took a garment, and laid it upon both their shoulders, and went backward, and covered the nakedness of their father; and their faces were backward, and they saw not their father's nakedness. And Noah awoke from his wine, and knew what his younger son had done unto him. And he said, "Cursed be Canaan; a servant of servants shall he be unto his brethren." And he said, "Blessed be the LORD God of Shem; and Canaan shall be his servant. God shall enlarge Japheth, and he shall dwell in the tents of Shem; and Canaan shall be his servant." (Genesis 9:18–27)

Between his drunken state and his nakedness, it is unclear to biblical scholars what evidence of sinful activity caused Noah such acute embarrassment when one of his sons happened in upon him. It was Ham who discovered his father, but any parent can tell of times when, under pressure or in confusion, one might call whichever child by the name or names of the others. This is a recognized malapropism that happens in every family. Noah stuttered and spluttered the name of the wrong son, the one that was always on his mind ever since he drowned. He cursed "Canaan," but meant Ham.

Biblical editors and commentators, not knowing the story of Canaan, assumed he meant to curse Ham's son, Canaan, who is therefore mentioned, but was not present or involved in any way whatsoever. This has led to all kinds of red herring sermons, the most obvious being those about the sins of the fathers being visited upon their sons—which may be true and may be illustrated by other biblical passages, but not by this one.

Worse yet were the racist sermons carefully worked out on this misunderstanding of the text by the ministers of slave owners in America. Ham is actually an Egyptian word meaning black, a name for Egypt itself from earlier days when its population was more African in hue, as we see clearly in Psalm 78:51, Psalms 23 and 27, and Psalm 106:22. On this basis, for many years racist preachers justified slavery as related to the Curse of Ham—the Curse of Blacks in the Bible. It was Canaan that was cursed in the Bible story: not Canaan the son of Black, but the son Canaan, mentioned accidentally by Noah, aroused from drunken stupor and spluttering in embarrassment over being found in some possibly *in flagrante delicto* situation.

This interpretation of the curse of Ham may seem speculative to readers for whom this is all new information, but it is not nearly as speculative or as strained as all the traditional Jewish and Christian attempts to make sense of this passage down through the ages before the current rapprochement with Islam.

This episode provides an instance where knowledge of the Qur'an resolves a textual conundrum in the biblical text. There may be other such instances waiting for elucidation, once Qur'anic scholars are ready and able to truly join the discussion and share the quest. According to the Qur'an, Noah also had another descendant not found in the Bible. His name was Hud, and he was famous in ancient Middle East lore. He did not make it into the Judeo-Christian Scriptures because he became a prophet in Ad, the region of Southern Arabia now known as Yemen, where pilgrims still visit his grave at Hudhramaut (Hadramawt on some maps).

The people there, in both the Bible and the Qur'an, were known as Sabeans, and the Qur'an used them, along with Zoroastrians in India, as examples of how God has sent His prophets to all the peoples of the world. Both these groups have all but disappeared, but the inclusive position of the Qur'an remains as the model from which Jews and Christians can learn, as can modern Muslims.

The Qur'an is actually more all-embracing than the Bible, but that is not to say that Muslims live up to their Scriptures any more than Christians or Jews live up to theirs. The Scriptures show the way to safety for those prepared to heed the warnings from God, especially when the world seems to be falling apart.

Nooh is derided by the nonbelievers in the Qur'an, as was Jesus in the Christian Scriptures and as was Muhammad in his historical situation. Muhammad, who was informed of God's truth, came after Jesus, but Noah and the other rejected prophets were before him. The Qur'an preserves a few somewhat sophisticated twists that had been forgotten or lost, but if these characters seem as obtuse in the Qur'an as they do in the Bible, it is because they are the same characters presented in both sets of Scripture. As the Qur'an is read with full understanding only by those who know the biblical background, it is becoming increasingly obvious that understanding of the Bible can be dramatically enhanced by knowledge of the Qur'an. Commentators like Salman Rushdie and Reuven Firestone make us aware of how failing to appreciate each other's insight into scriptural motifs has limited our own appreciation over the centuries.

Jesus spoke of Noah in Luke 17:20–30, in reference to the Day of Judgment. In the same passage, he also speaks of Lot's era as another example of a time of Judgment. The Qur'an frequently links Nooh and Lut in connection with Judgment. When the Qur'an speaks of Nooh, Lut, and others, it is always presumed that we know for what they stand, just as modern listeners would understand if a modern writer described Noah's wayward son as a "Prodigal Son" figure. A further explanation would not be necessary. This is how smoothly the Qur'an fits with the Hebrew and Christian Scriptures.

The story of Noah has a high moral tone in the Qur'an. With his mission to offer warnings to sinners, Noah's own moral example is highlighted. The biblical account of him coming ashore to get drunk like a sailor after a sea voyage is not mentioned. Muslims find it objectionable that Jews and Christians can imagine such behavior on the part of one sent by God. In the Qur'an, Nooh is seen as a Godly messenger whose stern morality is tempered with love and grace. This is as clear an example as we might find of the difference in the way the Qur'an presents the Bible characters. In the Qur'an, the behavior of these characters is intended as a model for our own conduct, rather than as examples of redemption.

The Qur'anic story of Nooh's son, Canaan, is every parent's nightmare. Parents cannot control the lives of their children beyond a certain point, but they dread the consequences of their rebellious behavior. Nooh laments the loss of his son, but God does not permit him to accept the blame—a lesson some modern parents may need to learn again in order to move beyond "pop psychology." Again, the Qur'an takes its place in the timeless ambiance of these Scriptures.

Various metaphors may describe the relationship between the three religious traditions in Abraham's family. Foundation, temple, and dome are used in this investigation. But the overarching parable for our time is the story of Noah's other son, Canaan. Religion, in its moderate and mature form, is the ark we are constructing, or reconstructing, in the twenty-first century. Religious extremists have refused to get onboard. No one wants them to drown, but the ark is rising with the tide and must now set sail. The warnings focus on global warming, nonsustainable development in the West, AIDS and poverty in Africa, and especially the folly of war, with its unnecessary pain, suffering, and cost in lives and resources.

4

Towering Ambition

Babel/Babylon

Is it not the case that every time they make a Covenant some party among them throw it aside?—Nay most of them are faithless.

And when came to them an Apostle from Allah confirming what was with them, a party of the People of the Book threw away the Book of Allah behind their backs as if it had been something they did not know!

They followed what the evil ones gave out falsely against the power of Solomon; the blasphemers were not Solomon, but the evil ones teaching men magic and such things as came down at Babel to the angels Harut and Marut. But neither of these taught anyone such things without saying: "We are only for trial so do not blaspheme." They learned from them the means to sow discord between man and wife. But they could not thus harm anyone except by Allah's permission. And they learned what harmed them, not what profited them. And they knew that the buyers of magic would have no share in the happiness of the Hereafter. And vile was the price for which they did sell their souls, if they but knew! (Surah 2:100–103)

MUSLIM SCHOLARS all seem to agree that the above is a reference to the confusion at the Tower of Babel in the Qur'an, and the subsequent collapse of both the tower and the culture. The context seems to be a controversy in the time of King Solomon, compared to the earlier divisions in Babel, in which angels, or perhaps leaders of the confusion, were teaching blasphemy, division in the home, and magic.

The purpose of this quotation is to acknowledge the collage of images from the Bible and beyond in the Qur'an, from the social context of Muhammad's life through the voice of Allah to the ear and heart of the Prophet to recitation and eventual writing down of the Qur'an. These ech-

oes of the ancient Middle East even contain the names of two of the trouble-
makers at Babel—Harut and Marut. The confusion of lifestyles that went
along with their overarching blasphemy was based on the hubris associated
with the project and was personal as well as corporate. This material is a
prototype for Enron and WorldCom. It is so rich that we can be forgiven
for wondering where Muhammad got the details of the story that Allah so
deeply imbued with meanings that he was commanded to pass on.

The references to the Tower of Babel story in Surah 2, recurring in Egypt
and in every other corrupt and overambitious society, were no doubt
divinely inspired, every word in both rhythm and phrase. As for the role of
the prophet, Allah depended upon the fact that Muhammad already understood Arabic, the language of the revelation, for example. Perhaps Allah
also insured that Muhammad would know of Harut and Marut from conversations with Persian caravaners of the Zoroastrian faith who had their
own version of the story based on even earlier material from further east.
But first, fast-forward to the kind of trouble that makes news in our time:

In the year 2000 Pyramid Resorts International opened its largest-ever posh
resort hotel in Santo Rico. Though the island paradise has little in the way of
sanitary water or sewer, and the electrical system is hit and miss, the new Pyramid Resort Hotel had everything the Canadian, American, and European
tourists expected in a self-contained system. The forty-million-dollar structure
was, in fact, built to North American standards by workers on contract from
Texas.

The resort was staffed with experienced waiters, maids, and other staff
from all over the world, including chefs and Maitre d's from France. But the
owners and investors were disappointed that the rate of patrons returning the
next year was almost zero. So they contacted former patrons and the survey
said it was the discomfort at looking down into nearby slums that made them
decide to go elsewhere.

The solution was obvious and it was necessary to protect this huge investment at whatever cost. The owners commissioned their architects to design a
massive wall two hundred feet high, almost two miles in length on three sides
of the resort, leaving only the view of the sea. On the other three sides, the
windows faced hanging gardens cascading down the wall, with fountains and
beautiful statuary and terraced shapes designed by some of the world's best-
known sculptors. The wall cost nearly ten million dollars and took two years
to design and build, but it worked. People came back year after year. Even
riots in the nearby slum in 2004, which you may recall, failed to come to the
notice of the tourists. The investment was secure.

An international study into the causes of the riots failed to find any direct
link between the squalor and the opulence, but the International Development

Bank did agree to fund water, sewage treatment, and a new electric plant and agreed to encourage the use of local labor in these projects, including street lights, parks, and beautification. This was all at a budget of ten million dollars in loans from richer nations, the same amount as the cost of the wall. Three years later the Pyramid Resort, now in its seventh year of operation, is an amazing success as far as both patrons and investors are concerned. Work has yet to begin on the local improvements but there have been no further riots, not yet at least, and the government hopes to release a report on where the funds went sometime in 2010.

That apocryphal short story was drawn from news reports and true to the world situation. A long time ago the people of ancient Iraq (Babylon) decided to build a tower. Nineveh had its World Trade Center, and the Egyptians had the tallest pyramid in the world. Iraq had the money, so why not?

They set out to build a Ziggurat, a multistory tourist trap with a shrine on the top, just like the Ziggurats built in Mumbai, India, by the Zoroastrians, only bigger. (We get the word zigzag from the switchback path required to climb a ziggurat.) Everyone was invited to contribute and participate, at least at first. In this study, we have already noticed the intrinsic meaning attached to names of people and places, often giving a key clue to the meaning of the story. That is what we have also in the Tower of Babel, except that the pun on the word Babel does not need to be translated. Thanks to the Greeks, the pun works almost as well in English as in Hebrew and Chaldee (spoken in Iraq).

The Greeks liked the pun so much that they took the Chaldean word for confusion into their own language and passed it on to the rest of us. That word is *babel*, and it works as possibly the most famous joke in the history of the world. The Iraqis thought their great monument would reach the clouds and be known as the Gate of Heaven. The Chaldean word for gate is *babil* but, since the project collapsed in confusion or *babel*, people referred to it for years as the Tower of Babel, a pun on gate/confusion.

A big city did grow up around the famous ruins of the tower, even though the project was a monumental flop. People called the city "Babylon" as a joke, in much the same way as Toronto was known as "Hogtown" in its days as a farm market center (a term of affectionate derision remaining to this day). Babylon's name also stuck and Greek travellers liked the pun so much that it became part of their language and ours. That is where we got the English word *babble*, meaning confused talk.

The oldest version of the Tower of Babylon story is not in the Bible or the Qur'an. It comes from an ancient Assyrian tablet now in the British

Museum. "Babylon corruptly to sin went, and small and great mingled on the mound." Some unintelligible lines are followed by a reference to the god, probably Marduk: "In his anger also the secret counsel he poured out. He set his face to scatter them abroad. He gave a command to make strange their speech and their progress he impeded."

This is a very old story with a very modern meaning, especially among Jews, Christians, and Muslims, who all include it in their Scriptures. Today, we do not use hieroglyphics but are we any less confused, or is our communication better through video tape or cassette tape, e-mail or fax, TV satellite dish or cable, worldwide web or CD ROM, iPod, or TiVo? No, we still fail to communicate or to get the message, whether on a resort island or in a new World Trade Center which strains to touch the sky and symbolically make us a people who no longer need God.

In the Bible, the story is short, a mere nine verses, Genesis 11:1–9. The location is described in the text as the Plain of Shinar, because it predates the Babylonian Empire, now known as Iraq. In verse 4 they decide to make "a city and a tower." As the story of the collapse of the project proceeds, the text reveals in verse 9 that the name of the city is Babel, "because the Lord did there confuse them." The joke is right there in the Bible but, for those who need the joke explained, the Bible writer explains it.

The joke is written in neon lights, but, typical of the Hebrew version of any of these ancient tales, the moral is also there for those who are able to see it. God confused the Babylonians of old because of their false pride and because their project was founded on sinful ambition. The tower collapsed due to false motives. Is there a warning here for us?

God did not say, "Don't build" or "Don't build to the sky." God said, "Don't build for yourselves—build for others . . . build for My purposes, not your own. Consider the destiny I have for you and make a name for Me, if you need to make a name for somebody. Don't even think that your dreams can supplant Mine—I have a dream for all humanity, and don't you forget it."

For those who read this story in the Bible or the Qur'an, God obviously does not want unity among humans based on one language or on a super race of superior people. They failed to put God's purpose first and their dreams turned to dust almost as fast as the tragic collapse of the World Trade Center on September 11, 2001. As a world center of cutthroat capitalism, the World Trade Center did appear to some Muslims and others as a modern Tower of Babel in certain respects. It is still so hard to raise any question in this regard, since the trauma of its collapse is still so fresh in our hearts. The extreme paranoia that followed in parts of America is difficult for even Canadians and Europeans to understand, but it may be justified.

This is still possibly the best time to examine that picture, while the "shock and awe" of America's reaction is still reverberating around the world. As world leader and the only superpower, America deserves more attention and falls under more scrutiny than others in these regards. The WTC was the center where many had pension funds invested in a system that much of the rest of the world views with a mixture of envy and suspicion. Perhaps some questions still need to be asked about the successor to that tower. Is it built to serve humanity and to bring glory to God's dream, or to show the world who is really in charge?

The negative implication in this question is very uncomfortable, but the first reaction to the events of September 11th by some prominent American Christian fundamentalist leaders was to point to the collapse of the World Trade Center as "God's judgment on America." Soon after the terrorist attacks on the WTC and the Pentagon, Reverend Jerry Falwell appeared on TV on *The 700 Club* with Reverend Pat Robertson to say that "God continues to allow the enemies of America to give us what we probably deserve" because of America's sins. The transcript published in the *Washington Post* quotes Robertson replying in agreement, "Jerry, that's my feeling."

In the aftermath of 9/11, Falwell and Robertson quickly changed their tune in response to public outrage against their statements, but these prominent fundamentalist spokespersons unthinkingly articulated the position of Osama bin Laden and others who bring an extremist mentality to their understanding of the Scriptures.

Robertson is the fundamentalist spokesperson who preached that America is called by God to assassinate the democratically elected leader of Venezuela because he had a different vision than the American administration regarding the future of South and Central America (Reuters, August 24, 2005). He also expected God to smite the town of Dover, Pennsylvania, for electing a school board opposed to a fundamentalist understanding of instantaneous creation by intelligent design (CNN, November 10, 2005). The similarity of views among fundamentalists the world over has not escaped notice.

Robertson's website boasts that at nearly 80 years of age he can lift two thousand pounds on a gymnasium leg press, thanks to protein supplements he happens to be selling. The skepticism and cynicism of the American public is similar to the connection between selling of snake oil medicine and preaching the gospel on the old frontier. Moderate religious people are embarrassed at what is done and said by these charlatans in the name of religion, while those with only nominal religious beliefs are tempted to regard all religion in derision, thanks to the farcical appearance these proponents give to the faith.

Despite a string of failed prophecies in 2006, Pat Robertson completed his transition into laughing stock with his 2007 predictions of nuclear terror in the United States. This headline-grabbing announcement was presented on his news-and-talk TV program *The 700 Club* on January 2, 2007, based, as he said, on what "God told me." While such an event could happen in any year of the new century, the attempt of a judgmental preacher like Robertson to present a Moses-like intimacy with God discredits the American religious extremist position even further. After beginning the new century with seven years of deception and manipulation, Evangelicals in America have moved into what may be a biblical seven-year process of political maturation, with profound theological implications continuing to unfold.

The moderate majority of Americans initially allowed themselves to be swayed by Falwell's organization, the Moral Majority, and by Robertson's Christian Coalition in elections just before and after the turn of the new century. American religious extremists achieved ascendancy in the U.S. Congress in 1996 and narrowly tipped the balance in Presidential elections of 2000 and 2004. The War on Drugs, War on Crime, War on Abortion, War on Terrorism, and other "wars" all fit with their extremist and militant agendas. Despite a decade in power, the wars they waged have all failed because peace does not come through war.

The ambitions proclaimed in the 1997 neoconservative mission statement "The Project for the New American Century" turned into disappointment and recrimination as the crisis in Iraq grew. The idea of the "Project" was to project a fundamentalist vision of American power and influence around the world. By 2007, ten years later, "The Project for the New American Century" was reduced to a voicemail box and a stale website, leaving moderate Evangelicals to reassess their view of the world.

A Pew Research poll published on October 5, 2006, predicted results of the 2006 congressional elections, themselves a harbinger of what would happen in the Presidential election of 2008. The Pew research suggests the shift apparently came as some fundamentalists became more appropriately described as Evangelicals, and as increasing numbers of Evangelical Christians moved to the center of the political spectrum as part of the "new mainstream" of religion on America, a phenomenon we will examine later in another connection. At this point it is merely the political impact of this shift that matters, but we might set it in historical perspective.

At an earlier time, Methodism was thought of as an evangelical revival, but that movement matured into a church. To some extent this had been the pattern of the historic churches of the Protestant Reformation still earlier. Today, one hundred years after its beginning, the Pentecostal movement is well on its way to repeating the pattern.

Meanwhile, the failure of the extremist agenda is now apparent. By 2003, the percentage of citizens in prison in the U.S. surpassed even Russia as the highest rate in the world, exceeding figures for dictatorships like Cuba and Iraq, as well as authoritarian regimes like China and Egypt, all with no appreciable deterrent effect in the War on Crime. Similar observations can be made with respect to the War on Drugs. The militants in power can justify expenditures of millions of dollars for flying gunships used to harass Columbian farmers, when the front line in any action to combat drugs should be on American streets, not in enforcement but in prevention, remedial programs and the pursuit of fulfillment in life without drugs. Columbian farmers are not the source of America's drug problem and putting more Americans in jail is not the solution. A more mature religious culture may be part of the answer as significant elements of the Evangelical movement shifts from fundamentalism into the Protestant mainstream.

If the War on Crime was such a failure and the War on Drugs was so wrongheaded, the War on Terror was part of a similar pattern, with the number of terrorists increasing in proportion to the number of bombs dropped on civilians, who reacted more in shock than in awe. Western nations can seemingly raise any amount of money to fight wars against regimes they decide to change, but from Afghanistan to Nicaragua the aid for reconstruction is so meager that people are tempted to simply return the previous governments to power.

Religious extremists in America may not yet get it, but the moderate majority in America has seen this larger picture and the shift in political influence need only be small to effect major change. The world wants to see America comport itself according to the rule of law. America's friends have little doubt about the outcome.

A decade after achieving ascendancy, the Moral Majority has folded its tent and disappeared. The Christian Coalition, so vexatious for liberals and once dreaded by moderates, has seen its published revenues fall from $26 million in 1996 to just over $1 million in 2004 and on toward bankruptcy. With post-conservative moderates taking back control of the Republican Party and post-liberal moderates dominating the Democratic Party, government in the twenty-first century may have more to do with efficiency and consensus than ideology, or war on anything.

A question germane to this investigation remains. Why did so many fine American people fall under the spell of extremism? The answer must be more profound than mere reaction to extremism elsewhere, such as that responsible for the events of September 11th. The answer may be found partly in the fear of creeping secularism among those for whom their religion is paramount. We see this in a more detailed examination of the remarks of Jerry Falwell in his conversation with Pat Robertson on September 13, 2001, as widely published in the press and quoted on countless websites.

About the events of September 11th, Falwell said: "The abortionists have got to bear some burden for this because God will not be mocked. And when we destroy 40 million little innocent babies, we make God mad. I really believe that the pagans, and the abortionists, and the feminists, and the gays and the lesbians who are actively trying to make an alternative life-style, and the ACLU (American Civil Liberties Union), People for the American Way, all of them who have tried to secularize America, I point the finger in their face and say: you helped this happen."

These are not the words of bad people. These are the words of frightened people. There are parallels to these sentiments among the extremists in the Muslim world and elsewhere, and the solution is not found in charging American soldiers or politicians with war crimes, or in "hunting down" and "eliminating" the extremists elsewhere. Crimes must be prosecuted and justice must prevail, but the remedy is the rebalancing of society that is taking place in the renewal of moderate and mature religious instincts on Main Street, not among the fanatics but within the moderate majority. This is happening all over the world.

The situation in Europe is only different to the extent that the influence of secularism had become even more pervasive. Secularism may be bankrupt now, but the "fear" that engendered "right wing extremism," in the politics of the Netherlands with its assassinations, France with its riots, and Denmark with its cartoons was a fear of loosing some of the legitimate social advances of secular society. The Catholic Church in Poland and the Protestant Church in East Germany had almost single-handedly brought down the atheistic communist regimes. Those churches were, in some real sense, part and parcel of worldwide trends that include the resurgence of Islam among the immigrant communities in the suburban slums of Paris and the ghettos of Amsterdam. The religious "extremists" in those two cities are on a track parallel to the religious agenda of the friends of the late pope, who are now in power in Warsaw, and that of the East German pastor's daughter who became chancellor in Berlin.

The time has also come for the moderate majority to recover its voice in Europe, and that is happening among Catholics and Protestants, as well as Muslims and Jews. This involves a return to religion, but with a rejection of the more extreme manifestations of religion that were the reactions to overt secularism in Warsaw and Berlin as well as Paris and Amsterdam.

The situation in the Muslim world is much the same, with the wealthiest oil states experiencing the most rapid secularization and then drawing back. Post–World War II trends toward "Western" (read "secular") values were seen in divorce and in the "liberation" of women, the use of drugs and alcohol, the appearance of homosexual lifestyles, and the spread of lifestyle diseases. These developments led to the greatest reaction in places like Iran and Lybia, leading to the overthrow of Western-style (secular) governments and the implementation of "extremist" Islamic rule. These factors are in play in Saudi Arabia, Egypt, Afghanistan, and elsewhere in the Islamic world. They can only be moderated by the rise of moderate religious influences, a development that is underway throughout the Muslim world.

Israel too suffers from religious extremism, engendered by "fears" that relate to the experience of the Jewish people historically and recently. Secular answers have proven insufficient but religious fanaticism is not the solution. Moderate religious Jewish voices around the world are growing in influence and have begun to affect the political agenda, though they do not yet control it. In Israel, the religious extremists in the Likud Party and its allies are countered by the secularists in the Labour Party and its allies, but the way forward appears to lie with the centrist Kadima Party, in spite of the challenges remaining in the quest for final borders and lasting peace. Kadima has attracted activists from the peace movement and moderate politicians, as well as pragmatists and religious moderates, in a coalition that may be a worthy partner for moderates elsewhere if given a chance.

In spite of its fall from grace as a former super power, and despite its complicity in the misplaced targeting of Iraq in the War on Terror, the United Kingdom may be something of a model for others of good will. A democracy that has maintained the Monarchy—is Saudi Arabia listening? A World Empire that became a Commonwealth of Nations, right within the country itself, with half old-stock population and half new citizens in every major city—could France take note? English-speaking, with a Pentecostal babble, just like the world in the internet age—India's ticket to superpower status in the next era?

Even the Anglican Church is neither Protestant nor Catholic, or perhaps it is both in creative tension. Surrounded by Roman Catholic, Protestant, and other religious minorities, and in spite of major tensions and challenges within itself, the Anglican Church may be ready to fulfill a destiny to which it has long aspired—modeling unity in diversity for the whole Christian community and for the world. The popular and respected Bishop of Rochester, the Right Reverend Dr. Michael James Nazir-Ali embodies much of this within himself. This Pakistani-born immigrant wrote *Conviction and Conflict* (T&T Clark, 2006), which goes to the heart of the matters at hand.

After the World Trade Center fell, Americans did not disperse like the Babylonians of old. Rather, to their credit, Americans came together. They came together as Americans first, and increasingly together as part of the human community, despite some false starts in official circles. America's generous response to the 2004 Boxing Day tsunami, the earthquake in Pakistani Kashmir in 2005, and other post–9/11 situations may be a partial answer from America's moderate majority. The world and its Maker both may be more impressed with these generous actions than with the ineffectual bombing of the Taliban and other Al-Qaeda forces, the expensive bluster over Iraq's nonexistent weapons of mass destruction, and the sudden dedication to bringing "freedom" to Iraq, even while rejecting democratic outcomes elsewhere.

Hope remains that great good may yet come out of such tragedies. There are signs of increasing connections and communication between Muslims, Christians, Jews, and others. But a question remains as to whether a still bigger tower can do the trick, as around the world the race continues to see who will build the tallest. Are we all still under the spells of the secularists, Harut and Marut, with their magic, blasphemies, and discord?

In any event, in our time, the story of the destruction of the Tower of Babel has a tragically eerie echo in the now equally famous destruction of the World Trade Center. That icon of terror will remain fixed in the consciousness of the world. It is the response to this tragedy that must now be monitored. Ironically, in this age-old quest for communication and trust among Jews, Christians, and Muslims, many of the players on the modern stage are the same as in the other, more ancient scriptural story.

The Bible picked up that ancient story as an explanation for the different languages of the world, and set the stage for the story of restoration of communications at Pentecost in the Christian Scriptures (the Acts of the Apostles, chapter 2). That echo of the ancient Jewish first-harvest festival of Shavout prefigures the Islamic dream of a universal community. In a reversal of the Babel of confusion, at Pentecost, people of different cultures found the spirit of love to be such a universal force that they could communicate in spite of language difficulties. That is what the ancients needed; that is what people need in the twenty-first century.

The first steps in reaching this goal are religious. The agenda now is for Christians to live as if they believe their own Scriptures, for Jews to always remain more alive to the spirit of the Torah than to the letter of the Law, and for Muslims to again move beyond reciting the Qur'an to an understanding of its depths. Not that these laudable attributes of religion have been entirely missing, but to respond to the spiritual needs of the twenty-first century, Christians, Jews, and Muslims may need insights specifically from the scriptural traditions they hold in common. The starting place is not the conversion of others, but maintaining the integrity of our own scriptural traditions in this new broader context.

To do this, we must return to the question of how Jews and Christians got these stories, and to show how they came to Muhammad, even before God touched his heart with their meaning. So far, Muslim tradition is able to shed little light on such questions, but there are answers in that tradition waiting to be deciphered to the benefit of Muslim believers and their coreligionists alike, once the techniques of modern scholarship are applied.

We can get started in this exciting quest by noting a parallel development in the experience of Christians and Jews in the last century, a movement from a type of fundamentalism in which virtually the whole Judeo-Christian community has participated, with only the exceptions noted. A deeper understanding of the sources behind their Hebrew and Christian Scriptures has become widely accepted as part of God's way of communicating with his people. Both Jews and Christians have become the People of the Book in a more profound sense as a result.

For many centuries, through the Middle Ages and beyond, Jews and Christians believed that Moses wrote the first five books of the Bible, a pious tradition enhanced by the later addition of his name in the title of each book. These books are often called the Pentateuch, meaning "Five Scrolls." They form the essence of the Hebrew Torah and even the King James Authorized Version refers to them as the First, Second, Third, Fourth, and Fifth Books of Moses, though none of the Hebrew manuscripts bears such a title.

The Pentateuch itself does not give any indication that these books were written by Moses, and although the Book of Deuteronomy purports to be four speeches by Moses, the rest of this collection uniformly speaks of him in the third person as if he were not the writer. To illustrate, in Numbers 12:3 we read, "Now the man Moses was very meek, more than all men that were on the face of the earth." If Moses actually wrote that, he was certainly by no means meek. Either the statement is untrue or Moses himself did not write that verse. Or take Deuteronomy 34, where we have an account of

Moses' death and burial. We have heard of people who have written their own obituaries, but no one else has ever described their own funeral and remarked that his grave has been lost sight of "to this day." Moses could not have written this.

Biblical "criticism" or analysis is one of the world's most engaging detective stories. A medieval Jewish physician named Isaac ibn Yashush presented the problem to the court scholars of Muslim Spain. He pointed out that a list of Edomite kings appearing in Genesis 36 named monarchs who lived long after the biblical account of Moses' death. He suggested that this must have been written by someone who lived after Moses. A medieval Spanish rabbi, named Abraham ibn Ezra, gave Isaac the nickname "Isaac the Blunderer" and suggested that the book, written by ibn Yashush, should be burned.

Ibn Ezra, however, had doubts of his own, as could be found in his later writings. He alluded to a probable alternate author who wrote about Moses in the third person, described places that Moses had never been to, and used terms that Moses would not have known. He was not willing to make this claim outright though, for he wrote, "If you understand, you will recognize truth . . . and he who understands will keep silent."

The next to pick up the trail was a Protestant Reformer, Martin Luther's colleague Andreas Rudolf Bodenstein, known as Carlstat. He drew attention to Genesis 12:6, where we read that "the Canaanite was then in the land," obviously a part of Genesis written by someone after David had rid the area of the Canaanite inhabitants, who were still there when Moses would have been writing. Carlstat was followed by the Spanish Jesuit Pereira who raised a similar question about the story in Genesis 14:14, where Abraham pursues Lot's captors "as far as the city of Dan." He concluded this must have been written after the Hebrew conquest, since Dan was known as Laish in the time of Moses. This would be like a document purporting to be by one of the Dutch founders of New Amsterdam somehow calling the place New York, an absolute giveaway that the document came after the British conquest.

In 1651, the English scholar Thomas Hobbes came right out in his *Leviathan* with the conclusion that Moses could not possibly have written the Pentateuch. Another Jew, the Dutch philosopher Baruch Spinoza, and another Roman Catholic priest, Richard Simon, came to the conclusion that the Pentateuch was composed of several separate documents edited together, but did not realize that there could have been several separate writers. Until the middle of the eighteenth century, the pieces of the puzzle were being identified but no one was able to put them together.

Then in 1753, a French physician, Jean Astruc, poring over the evidence, noticed something about the Divine Names "God" (*Elohim* in Hebrew) and "Jehovah" (more correctly spelled as *Yehweh* and written as LORD in many English translations). The names were not used indiscriminately, but a block of verses using "God" would often be followed by a block using LORD. He was able to distinguish two major strands of material and scholars began to call these two authors E and J, for Elohim and Jehovah. They were different enough to indicate two authors or editors, and he later identified two more possible "sources" of documents that make up the Pentateuch as we know it.

Immediately after this conclusion was established, a number of things made sense for the first time. Why had Genesis 6:19 said that two of every sort of creature went into Noah's ark, when Genesis 7:2 said seven pairs of clean animals entered? How else do we explain that Abraham had trouble with the king of Gerar over his wife Sarah and that Isaac had the same trouble with the same king about his wife, Rebecca? Similarly, Abraham was involved in a dispute which led to a well being called Beer-Sheba in Genesis 21:31, and Isaac was involved in a dispute with the same result of the naming of the well Beer-Sheba in Genesis 26:33? And did Joseph's brothers sell him to Ishmaelites (Genesis 37:27) or did Midianite traders find him in the well and sell him in a transaction unknown to his brothers (Genesis 37:28)? These and dozens of other seeming discrepancies are easily resolved when we recognize that two or more tribal folk story versions are involved here in a richly textured fabric.

These tribal recollections, eventually written down and edited together, present God's Word as a many faceted diamond, with depth and beauty reflected from many angles. God's dealings with his people were consistent, however remembered, and God's people themselves had a role in the transmission of these gems out of the mists of prehistoric times and into the era of written literature of the most sacred kind.

The evidence is very strong that the text of the Qur'an did indeed come through only one fountain of revelation, one inspired Prophetic voice. But still God used a variety of sources in preparing his Prophet for these holy moments, and a variety of images with which Muhammad was familiar. An appreciation of these elements will lead not to a diminution of the Qur'an, as Muslims have traditionally feared, but to an enhancement of it. This is what happened in biblical scholarship, as we will see when we follow this detective story further. First let us continue to review the big picture of what happened to Noah's other son, Canaan, and God's plan of rescue and redemption for Noah's other sons, from Ishmael to the Prodigal Son, and from Bill Moyer to Salman Rushdie.

5

The Patriarch

Abraham/Ibrahim

To THIS POINT we have been retelling and examining stories that are not about the people of Israel. Nor are they stories of Jesus or Muslim tales of the life of the final prophet. These are universal stories, myths with meanings, prehistorical records, and legends reflecting on God's purpose in creation, the development of conscience, the dawn of civilization, the separation of consciousness from the subconscious, and the divisions between people. In the Bible, the universal stories conclude with the story of the Flood (supplemented by the Qur'anic verses about Noah's other son) and the Tower. The protagonists were "People of the Book," because they either submitted to God or they were becoming aware of their opportunity to do so.

The purpose of beginning with them, and highlighting Noah's other son, Canaan, was to step back from the plethora of books on Abraham and his dysfunctional family in every library and bookstore since September 11th. Studies in comparative religion and political bromides explaining the differences between these religions have not succeeded in enlightening us to sufficiently understand the situation in which we find ourselves, not only post–September 11th, but soon now a decade later as we reassess the first responses to that tragedy and others, both in wisdom and compassion, but also in panic and terror. With this more universal overview and more Scriptural perspective, and with the passage of time, America, Europe, the Middle East, and the world may be at last ready to move together in a more positive direction. Recent political developments are perhaps the harbingers of this development.

So then, out of the mists of universal prehistorical time comes a man not mythical, not legendary, but historical. And God said to him, "Through you all the families of the world will be blessed." In the twenty-first century, his physical and spiritual descendants, though they don't always get along, account for more than half the world's population.

Perhaps the final peace in the world will come through his half of the human race sharing the promise with the other half, and being taught some new aspects of God's reality by that other half. In some ways, the shadow of this man looms larger on the screen of history than the shadow of any other, even including Moses, Jesus, and Muhammed. This man was Abraham, and his shadow now covers the whole world—the half that descends from him and the half that must live with those descendents.

There is interest in Abraham these days because he is seen as a figure of possible reconciliation in the ancient family feud in which we are involved. Today, his stories are part of the shared heritage of the whole human family. From the standpoint of world culture, religious or secular (if there is still a secular culture anywhere), anyone ignorant of these Jewish, Christian, and Muslim stories is almost incredibly uninformed. These stories are central to the dramatic unfolding of human history in the present era. Yet public school systems in the West are still afraid to touch these essential elements that affect the destiny of at least half or, in some ways, all the world.

It appears that religion is mandated to play a greater role in world affairs in the twenty-first century than the twentieth century. Moreover, Greek mythology, Roman legends, European, Aboriginal, Chinese, and Indian anthologies notwithstanding, it is becoming increasingly difficult to be an educated person in this world without a full knowledge and appreciation of this material from Abraham's family, as a believer or not.

Abraham's father was from present-day Iraq, as reported in the Torah, the Gospel, and the Qur'an. He moved from Ur of the Chaldees to Syria with his father's family, which eventually broke up and scattered. Abraham, the son we know best, moved through Canaan, Palestine, Egypt, and contiguous territories before beginning his own extended family, the one to which over half the people in the world now trace their spiritual DNA.

It was soon after the year 2000 BCE (Before the Common Era) that Abraham strode onto the stage of this unfolding human drama. Abraham lived approximately as many years before Jesus as we live after him. Perhaps the single most enduring image on this planet is the fact that, dysfunctional as it seems, Abraham's family is now entering its fifth millennium of exceptionally well-documented activity.

As mentioned, like many primitive or aboriginal peoples, the biblical personages up to this point calculated their ages by how many moons they had seen. The oldest person in the Bible was Methuselah, who lived to be 969 (moons, that is) or the ripe old age of 91, by our method. When we enter the age of recorded history with Abraham, we begin to use the Egyptian system of measuring age by crops. Along the Nile, to this day, there are two crops in each "year," so the ages of the people in Abraham's time make perfect sense if one always divides by two. Israel did not adopt the solar year as we know it until the era of the Babylonian captivity, over a thousand years later. It remains in use today throughout most of the world.

At the beginning of this saga, the hero is called Abram and his principal wife is known as Sarai. When they found favor with God, their names were changed to Abraham and Sarah by the addition of an H, a letter standing for holy, and effectively changing the literal meanings from "Respected Father" to "Father of Nations" and from "My Princess" to "Everyone's Princess." The Arabic form of the patriarch's name is Ibrahim, which we will use interchangeably, depending on the text under review. From the Hebrews, Avraham is an optional English spelling.

With Sarah, Abraham had one son, Isaac, late in marriage—Abraham being 50 and Sarah 45, in terms of solar years. Isaac was the father of Jacob, the one whose name became Israel, and from whom that nation descended. Abraham had other children in a large, "blended" family. In the Bible, a childless Sarah encouraged Abraham to have children and an heir with her slave, an Egyptian girl named Hagar. In the Qur'an, Hagar is presented as a legitimate wife of Abraham, and most Arabs trace their descent to her son Ishmael. Various Bible verses also refer to her as a "wife," and this is certainly a legitimate understanding.

After Sarah died, a larger number of children were born to Abraham and various concubines, and especially a young wife named Keturah. According to the Bible, these included six sons who became the tribal chiefs of Arabia itself, including the Midianites. Most of Abraham's children married into local Arab populations, but Isaac married his cousin back in Syria and Ishmael married an Egyptian. The Bible is more explicit about Abraham's descendants through Ishmael than many readers may have noticed. The Bible says:

> These are the descendants of Ishmael, Abraham's son, whom Hagar the Egyptian, Sarah's slave-girl, bore to Abraham. These are the names of the sons of Ishmael, named in the order of their birth: Nebaioth, the firstborn of Ishmael; and Kedar, Adbeel, Mibsam, Mishma, Dumah, Massa, Hadad, Tema, Jetur, Naphish, and Kedemah. These are the sons of Ishmael and these are their names, by their villages and by their encampments, twelve princes according to their tribes. This is the length of the life of Ishmael, one hundred thirty-seven years; he breathed his last and died, and was gathered to his people.

They settled from Havilah to Shur, which is from Egypt to Assyria; his descendants settled down in the midst of all the people. (Genesis 25:12–18)

Isaac's progeny are best known to the world through the male descendants of his son Jacob, who was renamed Israel:

Now the sons of Jacob were twelve. The sons of Leah: Reuben (Jacob's first-born), Simeon, Levi, Judah, Issachar, and Zebulun. The sons of Rachel: Joseph and Benjamin. The sons of Bilhah, Rachel's maid: Dan and Naphtali. The sons of Zilpah, Leah's maid: Gad and Asher. These were the sons of Jacob who were born to him in Paddan-aram. (Genesis 35:22b–26)

The "traditional family values" represented by this biblical model are anything but the model of the nuclear family upheld by some who believe they hold a "conservative" position on family values. In North America, typical biblical family structures might be found on TV exposé shows hosted by Geraldo Rivera and Jerry Springer, and such sprawling families continue to exist as something like the norm in some Muslim cultures.

The main difference between the biblical model and the typical Western family is the modern discarding of unwanted spouses. We will examine the phenomenon of the biblical/Muslim family more closely, with its integrated social structure, in a chapter on the story of Jacob (Israel), where the Covenant with Abraham is passed on.

Along with all the in-laws and outlaws, and the "half-this" and "step-that" relationships of this truly biblical family model, Abraham's impact on world history was principally through two lines. One of these lines led through Isaac to Jerusalem and Jesus; the other led through Ishmael to Mecca and Muhammad.

We will discover more about the major rival branches of Abraham's family as they appear in the three scriptural traditions, but for now we recognize Jewish, Christian, and Muslim descendants of Abraham and converts to Abraham's God as making up half the population of the world. It remains to be seen if all people of the earth can consider this family to be a blessing.

There are some unsavory human situations in the Bible where we get glimpses of Abraham as less than the model person presented in the Qur'an. The Bible presents a shameful incident when Abraham tells the Pharaoh that Sarah is his sister and lets the King of Egypt become intimate with her. He explains later, "You are so beautiful and I am old enough that Pharaoh would have me killed just to get you. Besides, you are my half-sister anyway, so play along while we are here in Egypt." It is obvious that Moses had not yet presented the Commandments of God.

We know the story of Abraham almost sacrificing his son on Mount Moriah—Isaac in the Bible, Ishmael in the Qur'an. Scholars suggest that this story is also a figurative depiction of the time when humans turned away from child sacrifice in response to God's Word, though many modern people still go on sacrificing their children to their own dreams. The Abraham chapters of Genesis record the first dreams in world literature, and analysts like Freud and Jung have pored over their interpretations. There are accounts of Abraham's nephew Lot going his own way, some shameful sexual episodes, abuse of women, and a wife who turned into a pillar of salt by looking to the past (lamenting what might have been). Do people still do that? These stories are obviously timeless, but these, rather than others, are told and retold because their words contain the Word of God. It is clear that their "warnings" about the consequences of ignoring God's purposes in creation and in human destiny apply to all times.

How Abraham and Sarah both laughed at God's promise when they could not see how a 45-year-old barren woman and a 50-year-old man were likely to have a child! They called him Laughter, or Isaac, when he was born. Abraham's relationship with Hagar and her offspring requires separate chapters in the context of this study.

God made a covenant with Abraham: "Walk before me and do what is right and I will be your God. I promise to be the God of your descendants forever." Everywhere they went to live, Abraham built an altar to God—at Shechem, at Bethel, at Beersheba, and at Mamre. The graves of Abraham, Sarah, and their children are still there, at a spot called Mechpelah, a field Abraham bought for the purpose when Sarah died. A mosque and a synagogue stand there today outside Hebron. You can see the tombs, as people have for centuries, though the family still quarrels over the deed to the site.

God also required a special token of obedience on the part of Abraham and his descendants: circumcision. The theories that this procedure prevents infection and that it enhances sexual performance have been in and out of vogue in medical circles ever since, but neither theory relates to Abraham's covenant with God. In fact, just as we live in a sex-fixated society, so did Abraham. Greek religion made a cult of sex. Baal worship in Palestine was a fertility ritual. Egyptian religion was a vast conduit for sexual license with little subterfuge about it. In India, sexual expression was regarded as a high form of spirituality. Unrestricted sexual activity was so rife in ancient society that disease, family instability, debilitation, and immorality were widespread. God's great experiment in civilization, freedom, creativity, and human responsibility was all in jeopardy through the abuse of one of God's most precious gifts. This helps explain the hyper-anxiety about sexual mores among Jews, Christians, and Muslims ever since—another family trait.

God simply made it clear to Abraham that service to God, and fulfillment of God's purpose, were to be the highest priorities and that, accordingly, something needed to be "cut." You can substitute anything else that gets between you and God. Abraham realized that God was insisting on something.

Like the rainbow, which had been around but took on a new meaning after the Flood, circumcision may have been practiced previously to a limited extent, but now it came to symbolize complete allegiance to God by confronting something that is a challenge to just about everyone. Circumcision can be understood as symbolizing the exclusive covenant relationship with God, as best described in a central incident in the life of Ibrahim as presented in the Qur'an.

In the rift between Abraham and his father, the Bible hints at what the Qur'an makes explicit: young Ibrahim's quest for an all-encompassing faith in an all-encompassing God. Even as a child, Ibrahim was offended by his father's business, the manufacture of idols and images of lesser gods. Perhaps because he saw them being manufactured, Ibrahim saw through them, but his father was angered at this son who delighted to ride on the back of Mighty Marduk—an idol just made and barely cool from the kiln.

On one occasion, when his folks were away at a festival, Ibrahim destroyed a collection of idols, except for the largest. When they accused him of vandalism, he pointed to the remaining big idol and said, "He must be the guilty one." He knew full well that he had put them in an impossible position unless they were ready to admit the impotence of the idol. That question always remains about the idols we serve.

Abraham is the Father of monotheism, or loyalty to "One God," and Moses rediscovers this truth at the burning bush, as God helps Moses focus on its meaning. History shows Nefertiti, another Semitic relative of Abraham, introducing the idea to her love-smitten husband, the future Pharaoh Akhenaten, shortly before the time of Moses. Competing loyalties and divided allegiances are among the problems that modern people face, with all the "gods" they serve. One must ask oneself why one has so little energy, and why one can never focus on what really matters. The ancients knew what was going on in the human heart, and Abraham was the first to address it so clearly.

In the story of Adam, we learned that one difference between the Bible and the Qur'an is that the Muslim text asserts that God created humans a little higher than the angels, as compared with the Judeo-Christian Scriptures, which present mortals as a little lower than angels, or "divinities." As explained previously, in the story of Noah, the gentle twist between the texts is the Qur'anic recollection of the story of Canaan, the rebellious son of Noah who "misses the boat," so to speak. In each case, the texts run parallel to each other with the deep meanings of the Word for all the People of the Book. The scriptural texts complement each other with additional information or massage each other with enrichment of understanding.

This pattern continues as we examine the stories of Abraham and the origins of his family in its various branches. In particular, while 90 percent of the text is in harmony, the Qur'an presents a version of the offering of Abraham's son that is slightly but significantly different in one detail. The Jewish version, traditionally accepted by Christians, recalls that Isaac was the one offered for sacrifice. In the revelation in the Qur'an, the son to be sacrificed was Ishmael. In the Qur'an, the Divinity often speaks in the plural—a royal or an editorial "we," as it is called. Ibrahim, still childless, is found in prayer at the beginning of this passage.

> "O my Lord! Grant me a righteous son!"
> So We gave him the good news of a boy ready to suffer and forbear. Then when the son reached the age of serious work with him he said: "O my son! I see in vision that I offer thee in sacrifice: now see what is thy view!" The son said: "O my father! Do as thou art commanded: thou will find me, if Allah so wills, as one practising Patience and Constancy!" (Surah 37:100–108)

In the Judeo-Christian Scriptures, Isaac is a very young boy when Abraham is faced with the demand that he be willing to sacrifice his son. He tags along, asking the usual childish questions, and getting the usual put-offs a parent often gives a child.

Ishmael is presented in both the Bible and Qur'an as a teenager by this time, which, in ancient culture, is virtually a young adult—the time when females can first bear children and males can first bear arms. In the Qur'anic version, we note Abraham discussing the agonizing matter with his son. How many of us today have such rapport with our teenagers on life's biggest questions? The answer, as recognized by the youth, was to trust God. Perhaps this is what is missing in our family discussions. Nowhere else in the Scriptures of this family do we find parent and child agonizing before God together in this way. Not even Jesus' story of the Prodigal Son contains this element.

> So when they had both submitted their wills to Allah, and He had laid Him prostrate on his forehead for sacrifice, We called out to him "O Ibrahim! Thou hast already fulfilled the vision!" Thus indeed do We reward those who do right. For this was obviously a trial and We ransomed him with a momentous

sacrifice. We left this blessing for him among generations to come in later times.

Muslims know that what God wants is for us to submit completely and freely to the will of Allah. Billy Graham preaches the same message to Christians, with the sacrifice of Jesus as the model and catalyst for our surrender. So far in our study, in both Bible and Qur'an, the characters have been holding something back, but the unique element in the Abraham story, in all versions, is his total submission to the will of God/Allah.

God creates Adam as his agent and messenger, but Adam chooses Eve and the forbidden fruit, often interpreted as sex. We know what havoc can be caused if sex comes between us and a complete response to God. Likewise, Noah, at least in the Bible, was inclined toward liquor. The Jewish Talmud speculates that, instead of rebuilding the earth, Noah became an alcoholic. Muslims prohibit alcoholic beverages and find this accusation abhorrent. But true in the literal sense or not, we know that liquor can be a way to avoid obedience and complete submission to God. He built the Ark to save himself, his family, and animal life but, according to the Bible, Noah was not prepared to devote his life thereafter to fulfilling God's purpose—an interpretation at odds with the Qur'an.

With Abraham, God tries again. God must have suspected that since he had a child at last, and the promise of a family destiny, Abraham would place family above God in his ultimate loyalty. Perhaps Abraham would be no more inclined than the others to surrender completely his own dreams to a covenant relationship with God. God gives choice to humans, and, at least in the Bible, Abraham was no saint in other respects. Both Adam and Noah had done more impressive things for God, but God's demand to Abraham was that he should be prepared to sacrifice his beloved son.

The test was not to see if Abraham would kill for God, as some have speculated. The test was to determine if Abraham was willing to sacrifice his life's dream of a family and the precious promise made to him regarding that family. That test comes to every human being. Are we willing to put God first, with no rival priority?

Though he was stunned and mystified by the demand, amazingly, Abraham passed the test. Then the dreaded sacrifice was not required. God actually does respect our dreams and, indeed, fulfills them when we are in a covenant relationship with Him. This is how Abraham became our father in faith. Saint Paul says, "Abraham trusted God." Abraham entrusted everything to God in a complete submission to God's will, even though he did not understand it or like it.

What irony! The progenitor of the greatest family on earth had to forswear the importance of the family. Abraham treated Sarah with special respect as his principal wife, according to the Bible. He also maintained responsibility for Hagar, the surrogate. He visited her and Ishmael in Arabia, where he and his son rebuilt the ancient Ka'bah, a square tabernacle around a black stone from heaven where Adam had worshipped. Ishmael fathered a huge family, and, ironically, many of them married Isaac's progeny. If ever there was a reconciliation in a family, it was when these rival sons and their dynasties reconciled at old Abraham's funeral as recorded in the Bible at Genesis 25:8.

Moses was among Abraham's descendants, as were Jesus and Muhammed. The followers of all three claim to be descendants of Abraham. Jews claim a literal descent and call Abraham Jewish, even before Moses began their religion. Jesus said Abraham was saved by faith in him, and in a letter to the Galatians, Saint Paul described how Christians inherit Abraham's promise by faith. Because he surrendered to God completely, it is obvious to Muslims that Abraham was Muslim, and they are his literal descendents, like the Jews. It may be time to realize that these claims are not incompatible.

The site of Abraham's tomb in Hebron is authentic, without doubt, as described in the Bible, though the contents of the tomb may be questioned. Tourists can drink water from his well in Beersheba. It is the same well that has been known and recognized all down through the centuries, not some newly discovered archaeological site and, though the water may be different, the presence of the well is still important in the community.

Christian Arab associations, like the Palestinian human rights organization *Sabeel*, arrange for visitors to stay in tents with Bedouins, not very different from Abraham's tent in our children's coloring books. The people are still much the same, though now they migrate from transmission line to transmission line to keep television and internet connections. What has changed in Abraham's family? Not very much, except that, at the beginning of the twenty-first century, for the first time, a majority of the world's population is now part of Abraham's family.

The online edition of *Encyclopaedia Britannica* reports that as the new millennium dawned in 2001, the population of the world reached 6.128 billion people. Of these, 14.484 million Jews are descended from the original followers of Moses, 2.019 billion people are followers of Christ, and 1.207 billion are followers of Muhammad. Abraham's family—Jewish, Christian, and Muslim—totalled 3.24 billion people or nearly 54 percent of the world's population at the beginning of the twentieth century. With the world Jewish population growing steadily, rapid growth in the younger

Christian churches of the developing world, and recent dramatic increases in Islam, Abraham's majority continues to rise with dramatic consequences that are now inescapable.

Fundamentalists of all stripes love to juggle these numbers and calculate who is "winning." Moderate Christians of the West, in particular, are uncomfortable with this "majority status" reality, and this leads to a danger that such influence may not be recognized or exercised in a responsible manner. Many moderate Christian and Jewish leaders appear to be oblivious to the dominant role of religion in our time, while moderates in the Muslim world are only beginning to find their voices. A warning to moderates may be in order.

The facts are inescapable. Modern Judaism has never been stronger since the founding of the State of Israel. The growth of Christianity is taking place throughout South America, sub-Saharan Africa, parts of Asia, and especially in China at a rate unprecedented in modern times. In addition to significant natural increase in traditionally Muslim countries, Islam is expanding rapidly in Europe (22 million and counting), North America (approaching 10 million), the former Soviet states of Russia, and the republics of Central Asia (60 million, many of whom have reasserted the affiliation recently).

These figures, available from many sources, do not even begin to consider the newest realities of the world, such as Turkey's preparation for membership in the European Union. This would swell Europe's Muslim population by some 70 million, to nearly 100 million, assuming the accession of Muslim Albania, Muslim Bosnia, and Muslim Kosovo in the meantime. Europe's careful integration of Turkey could provide a model for Abraham's family worldwide. Failure in this regard would have other consequences.

The consequences of the new global majority status for Abraham's family could work out well for everyone in the human family if only the members of Abraham's family were true to their calling to submit completely to God. So far, this has not been what the world has observed or experienced. The negative consequences of the failure to follow in Abraham's footsteps are enormous. All religions have roles to play in the evolution of human destiny, but the role of Abraham's family in the current era is clear. World peace will not come unless Abraham's children submit to God, at least in relationship with each other. Abraham let nothing stand between himself and God. Can his descendents afford to do less? If they fail, there are consequences for the whole world. The current signs are not particularly hopeful, but the agendas in synagogue, church, and mosque may now determine the course of world destiny as rarely before.

6

The Matriarch

Hagar/Hajra

THE NEXT TEXTS we will examine in detail focus on Hagar, a strong, amazing woman revered by Muslims. She appears in both Bible and Qur'an, and we will especially note her faith as the key to her ability to rise to the challenges inherent in her life as "the other woman" in Abraham's life.

From the Bible we already know Sarah's story well. Though it was a difficult subject then, and even more so in our anxiety over family values, both Bible and Qur'an have surprising things to say about the experiences of "the other woman" in Abraham's life. Again, we may learn something new from the juxtaposition of Bible and Qur'an. At least we may appreciate another twist in the complex web of relationships we are considering under the shadow of the tensions between these religious cultures in the ongoing family feud within Abraham's dysfunctional family.

The central Scripture in the story is found in the Hebrew collection at Genesis 16:7–16 and 21:9–21, with a period of fourteen years between these two episodes.

> The angel of the Lord found Hagar by a spring of water in the wilderness, the spring on the way to Shur. And he said, "Hagar, slave-girl of Sarai, where have you come from and where are you going?" She said, "I am running away from my mistress Sarai." The angel of the Lord said to her, "Return to your mistress, and submit to her." The angel of the Lord also said unto her, "I will so greatly multiply your offspring that they cannot be counted for multitude." And the angel of the Lord said, "Now you have conceived and will bear a son; you shall call him Ishmael [God Hears] for the Lord has given heed to your affliction.

He shall be a wild ass of a man, with his hand against everyone and everyone's hand against him; and he shall live at odds with all his kin." So she named the Lord who spoke to her, "You are El-roi [God Who Sees]"; for she said, "Have I really seen God and remained alive after seeing Him?" Therefore the well was called Beer-lahai-roi; it lies between Kadesh and Bered. Hagar bore a son; and Abram named his son, whom Hagar bore, Ishmael. Abram was eighty-six years old when Hagar bore him Ishmael. (Genesis 16:7–16)

Sarah saw the son of Hagar the Egyptian, whom she had borne to Abraham, playing with her son Isaac. So she said to Abraham, "Cast out this slave woman with her son; for the son of this slave woman shall not inherit along with my son Isaac." The matter was very distressing to Abraham on account of his son. But God said to Abraham, "Do not be distressed because of the boy and because of your slave woman; whatever Sarah says to you, do as she tells you, for it is through Isaac that offspring shall be named for you. As for the son of the slave woman, I will make a nation of him also, because he is your offspring." So Abraham rose early in the morning, and took bread and a skin of water, and gave it to Hagar, putting it on her shoulder, and sent her away, along with the child.

And she departed and wandered about in the wilderness of Beer-sheba. When the water in the skin was gone, she cast the child under one of the bushes. Then she went and sat down opposite him a good way off, about the distance of a bowshot; for she said, "Do not let me look on the death of the child." And as she sat opposite him, she lifted up her voice and wept.

And God heard the voice of the boy; and the angel of God called to Hagar from heaven and said to her, "What troubles you Hagar? Do not be afraid; for God has heard the voice of the boy where he is. Come, lift up the boy and hold him fast with your hand, for I will make a great nation of him." Then God opened her eyes and she saw a well of water. She went, and filled the skin with water, and gave the boy a drink. God was with the boy, and he grew up; he lived in the wilderness of Paran; and his mother got a wife for him from the land of Egypt. (Genesis 21:9–21)

Of course, what we have here is the Jewish version of the story. In his letter to the Galatians, Saint Paul presents the Christian interpretation, understanding Sarah's son Isaac as an archetype of "freedom" in Christ, and Hagar's son Ishmael as representing "slavery" under the law given on Mount Sinai. Needless to say, this is an interpretation favored by neither Jews nor Muslims.

The Muslim version is alluded to frequently in the Qur'an in verses about Ishmael that we will consider in depth next in a study of the roots of terrorism in the world and in the human heart. Muslim traditions about Hagar herself are also numerous, but more of them come from the collection of sayings of Muhammad in the Hadith than from the Qur'an. The Qur'an contains only words of God in the poetic form of inspiration recited by Muhammad, first to his wife and then written down by his followers. Muhammad's own sayings are also cherished by the faithful. While the prophet's personal sayings do not have the standing of Scripture in "The Book," which is limited to Torah, Gospel, and Qur'an, they do give a wealth of detail about stories in our shared heritage as retained in the popular culture of the Middle East outside Jewish, Christian, and Muslim Scripture.

In what was revealed to Muhammad, Hagar, the "other woman," is both long suffering and saintly. Even today, surrogates are used and cast aside, paid for their services and paid to abandon their maternal instincts. Hagar bore both the low status of the surrogate and the opprobrium as "the other woman." Abraham genuinely cared for her, as well as for their son, as related in both the Bible and the Qur'an. In the Islamic world, there is an understanding of her situation, as well as admiration for her loyalty to Abraham and her dedication to their child.

In his 2002 best-seller *Abraham*, Bruce Feiler of the *New York Times* provides an evenhanded analysis of Hagar's situation. He goes so far as to present her as a model of redemption, for men and for women. He draws a parallel between Sarah's abuse of Hagar and Pharaoh's abuse of Israel. The language in the two scriptural situations is uncanny in its similarity, and Feiler thinks it is no accident. He brings a depth of Jewish tradition to his new appreciation of the Muslim matriarch.

After crossing the Red Sea, Israel flees to the Wilderness of Shur, the very same spot in the desert where Hagar became intimate with God. Feiler compares Hagar with Moses and with Abraham. God reveals Himself to Abraham as El Shaddai, "God Almighty" (Genesis 12:1) and just as personally to Hagar as El Roi, "God Sees" what is happening to you (Genesis 16:13). Moses sees God's "back" and talks with God; Hagar sees an angel who addresses her with God's voice.

Abraham is promised that he will father as many descendants as the stars in the sky; Hagar is promised that she will mother more descendants than can be counted. If Abraham is a model patriarch, Hagar is a model matriarch, in spite of her low status. God's gracious dealing with Hagar, the other woman, has been neglected by Christians and Jews in spite of her story being recorded in their own Scriptures. Muslims remember her in their Hajj pilgrimages to Mecca when they trek frantically back and forth between two hilltops seven times, recalling Hagar's desperate scampering to and fro seeking water for her dying child. When she reached the very end of her resources, she finally let God provide. Is there anyone who does not need to hear this story? And should we not now scamper in support of the dying children of the world?

We cannot endorse the untenable position of the other woman in ancient culture or in our own but, still today, difficult situations emerge and God places Himself in the midst of it all. The Holy Spirit shows us what is ideal in marriage, but, as Jesus himself says, "the ideal cannot always be achieved by everyone" (Matthew 19:11).

There are wonderful marriages achieved through devotion and hard work, and there are impossible marriages characterized by exploitation and suffering. There are relationships of amazing grace outside marriage but there many situations just as terrible. Wives have both challenges and blessings, but "other women" also know love and suffer much. In life's imperfect situations, God is able and willing to stand by people in whatever dilemma. God stood by Sarah, unworthy as she was at times. God stood by Hagar in her situation, even though it was unacceptable. God will stand by us in these days of turmoil in family life when we exhibit the faith of this matriarch.

Throughout this investigation of the Hagarian story, there are hints of myths and materials from Middle Eastern sources in the margins and on the fringes of the biblical and Qur'anic texts. Christians and Jews may begin to appreciate how richly God has blessed all peoples and attempted to communicate with them as we return to the quest for understanding the biblical text in its original setting. The corollary is the desire for the Islamic community to bless the world by confidently becoming more forthcoming, mining the rich ore of its own priceless textual heritage and scriptural tradition.

While it was never quite a religion or a national/ethnic grouping, there was a longstanding movement of Hagarianism throughout the desert areas of the Middle East for many centuries between Hagar and Muhammad. We may now have little appreciation of what the Prophet did, as God's mouthpiece, in integrating that tradition into the new Muslim community. Salman Rushdie hints at Muhammad's identification with desert matriarchal societies in the foreword to this work, but it remains for Muslim feminists today to flesh out this tradition in appropriate ways.

Finally, in reference to Hagar, Muslims who have revered her should always be thrilled to learn that Jews and Christians, at one particular time and in one particular place, recognized her story as an inspiration. The story is told in *Fractured Families and Rebel Maidservants: The Biblical Hagar in Seventeenth-Century Dutch Art and Literature* by Christine Petra Sellin, the director of the art history program at Woodbury University in Burbank, California. This 2006 T&T Clark publication is an examination of the story of Hagar and Ishmael through the eyes of seventeenth-century Dutch painters.

Hagar was was a biblical personage of unique interest in the seventeenth-century Dutch Golden Age, as many versions of her story in the literature and art of that era demonstrate. She is treated with an unprecedented degree of sympathy, mercy, and dignity. Transforming the outcast into a symbol of redemption and a model of maternity was perhaps a reflection of the embryonic Dutch matron's role as the "other woman" in relation to a succession of European empires.

Hagar's own story was interpreted as a didactic domestic drama, touching on topics such as family break-ups, extramarital sex, rivalry between women over men, sibling rivalry, and struggles between husbands and wives and masters and servants. Her story fired the imagination because it offered Dutch artists the equivalent of a modern soap opera. But it also revealed what mattered most to the Dutch and perhaps lay at the heart of the fledgling Republic's success and survival.

This included the primacy of the family, an emphasis on domestic well-being, and the maintenance of ideal civic order, but with allowances for deviation from the norm still seen in modern Dutch culture. The paintings reflect that the Dutch developed a tenderness, understanding, and compassion for Hagar that the world had never seen before. Exiled in Scripture, cast off by Saint Paul, Hagar found refuge among the burghers of the Dutch Republic and she was given pride of place on the walls of their homes.

To return to parallel developments in Judeo-Christian scholarship, after Dr. Astruc, the task of unravelling the Pentateuch switched to reconstructing it. This is a pattern we may be about to observe in the Muslim community in the twenty-first century, once critical techniques are respectfully and reverently established among Islamic scholars. For Jews and Christians, this process involved a deepened appreciation for the ways in which God entrusted the transmission of his Word to the whole community of believers, as well as to its divinely inspired prophets and leaders, each in their definitive roles.

After Astruc came a productive period of ferment, especially in the Protestant theological schools of Germany. One scholar would put forward a hypothesis about the authorship of the Pentateuch, and this would be seized upon and attacked unmercifully by the remaining defenders of the Mosiac authorship on the one hand, and by rival scholars with new syntheses on the other. For over a century this sifting and refining went on with every jot and tittle coming under scrutiny by scholars who loved the Lord and cherished the words of Scripture, always seeking to broaden as well as deepen their understanding of every phrase.

Finally, in 1884 a great servant of God's Word named Julius Wellhausen built a careful word-by-word study of the whole issue, based on his revisions of an 1866 attempt by K. H. Graf. Known as the "Graf-Wellhausen Hypothesis," the "Four Document Theory," or simply the "Documentary Hypothesis," the conclusions of this study are accepted as a definitive turning point in the quest to understand the origins of the Pentateuch, at least in the seminaries of most Christian denominations and most of the colleges of Judaism.

Almost no one today agrees with all the fine details of this hypothesis as first propounded by Wellhausen, but the idea that the Pentateuch is composed of four documents, or now more properly, four "strands of material," has almost universal acceptance. Debates continue about the composition of each strand, whether it began as a document or an oral "campfire" tradition, who edited them together, and why. For purposes of this study we will stick to the classic presentation by Wellhausen because of its watershed status, while recognizing that creative research continues in a helpful way.

The evidence for the basic hypothesis is strong and obvious, once the key is available. Canada has two official languages, but if history had turned out differently and English had become predominant, for example, a national collection of heritage documents might still contain poems, songs, and other references to both God and *Dieu*. Any knowledgeable student of Canadian history would be able to separate out such documents and discover a consistent pattern of historical, spiritual, and cultural traditions from the French Canadian "tribe." That is basically what happened in biblical analysis when the J and E documents were first identified on the basis of the use of the divine names, Jehovah (or Yehweh in Hebrew) and Elohim.

Once the documentary hypothesis became established, two other strands of material began to leap off the pages. Were the roots of modern culture to be published today using examples from Shakespeare, Arnold Schwarzenegger, Billy Graham, and Martin Luther King Jr., all edited together by topic, almost anyone could pick out the Old English, the immigrant's grammatical style, the salvation agenda of the evangelist, and the poetic cadences of Afro-American aspirations. The four strands of material in the Pentateuch are almost that obvious, though each of them may have subtexts. After a few courses in Hebrew, the modern seminarian can peel away the encrusted layers of the Pentateuch with relative ease, revealing a virtual treasure chest of theological gems.

We have already identified J and E, and Astruc's theory stood up under rigorous examination, though there is continuing and expanding discussion about the nature and the agenda of each source before being blended into the whole. There is evidence that J is older, probably written down in the era around the year 900 BCE, using material that was then up to a thousand years old. J came from the southern tribes of Judah, as we can tell from its stories, while E has its origins around the campfires of Israel in the north. The heroes of E are northern and it refers to the holy mountain where Moses received the Ten Commandments as Mount Horeb, as compared to J with its southern heroes and references to the same events on the mountain it calls Mount Sinai.

No one has yet speculated on the precise identity of the author or group that put the original E material together. In modern best-seller *The Book of J*, America's great literary critic Harold Bloom asserts that J was written by just one writer, a collector of the sacred stories of the Hebrew south. He gives that writer the stature of Homer, Shakespeare, or Tolstoy, and he puts forth the revolutionary idea that J was very likely a woman, possibly a daughter of King David.

The dating of J to David's reign is reasonable, and the author was certainly someone who shared David's patriotic vision and nation-building agenda. It makes sense that at the time only a wealthy woman would have had the opportunity to write—the men were busy farming, politicking, and fighting wars. Moreover, the subject matter of J has far more to do with home life, families, cooking, sewing, and traditional feminine pursuits than anything in E, which appears to be a hundred years more recent in its written form and is styled as more of a folk compendium.

Bloom presents "J" as a writer with insight into human character as demonstrated in her poignant portrayals of Abraham with both Sarah and Hagar, as well as her portraits of such characters as Rachel, Rebecca, and Tamar (more women than usual), Joseph, Moses, and especially Jehovah. *The Book of J* not only offers a plausible identification of the Bible's first author, and one of its greatest, but it also presents the panoply of her genius.

Another author wrote or edited the material now known as the Book of Deuteronomy, as established by other scholars between Astruc and Wellhausen, and traditionally identified by the letter D. It is generally regarded as the law book "found" in the temple in 621 BCE during the renovations sponsored by the young reformer King Josiah. This was some three hundred years after J—about the time the people needed a more concise summary of the teachings of Moses to get them back on track. D has a style and even a theological emphasis all its own, and it is perhaps the easiest of the four documents for students of Hebrew to identify.

Finally, running through all the other books of the Pentateuch, there is a fourth obvious and distinguishable stratum of material in a more highly polished style of Hebrew than either J or E. This stratum uses Elohim as the name for God all through Genesis and only switches to Jehovah at Exodus 6:2, when God reveals that name to Moses. This final document, prior to the blending of the four, is full of such theological sensitivities and is greatly interested in matters of ritual and ceremony. It records genealogies and statistics, both of which have theological significance, and its whole tone reflects a mature and lofty theology. This source supplies most of the second half of Exodus, including the description of the Tabernacle sanctuary, and all of Leviticus, with its instructions for worship. It is referred to as the Priestly Source and given the initial P to refer to the group of theological scholars who produced it.

Welhausen thought that the JEDP documents or, more correctly, "sources" were then combined by the Priestly Source, the last of the four, possibly a team working during the Babylonian Captivity (597–538 BCE). More recent speculation puts the final edit into the hands of just one person, possibly just after the return of the Jews to Jerusalem. This would have been possible under endowments provided by the Persian King Cyrus to the likes of Ezra. This worthy priest was determined to codify the life of Israel, seizing the moment to integrate all Hebrew traditions into one law, one Torah. The style used by the writer of the books of Ezra and Nehemiah bears a strong resemblance to the final editorial touches added to the text of the Pentateuch, especially in the small editorial changes to Deuteronomy, which stand out like sore thumbs in comparison to the mass of that material.

This review of the classic Documentary Hypothesis alludes to its ongoing evaluation. While there are rival hypotheses, and scholars of every decade propose new wrinkles, this bedrock thesis was a turning point for Jews and Christians in their appreciation of the richness of Scripture. It is an example of the greater depths to be plumbed with the aid of critical techniques.

Do such insights lie beneath the surface of the Qur'an? Will they someday provide equally rich insights into the Divine agenda in revelation? As we shall see, the Muslim community has a rich devotional practice in which the verses of the Qur'an are mined for every nuance of spiritual gold that is close to the surface. It is not unreasonable that, without diminishing the role of Muhammad as the vehicle of God's revelation, critical analysis may produce results of value to Muslims as well as to Christians and Jews and the whole world. Muhammad's role and the purity of the revelation, direct from God through the angel Gabriel, may be appreciated all the more when this greater depth of connection with the experiences and the quest of all people in the text of the Qur'an is recognized.

The People of the Book themselves are not merely hearers and believers, but also sources and conduits of God's grace, as may become apparent when Islamic scholars around the world take up this quest.

7

The Archer's Jihad

Ishmael/Ismail

THE AMERICAN NOVELIST Herman Melville opens *Moby Dick*, his land-mark study of alienation, with the famous words, "Call me Ishmael." This investigation of Abraham's Arab son Ishmael, as he appears in both the Bible and the Qur'an, will also be something of a study in alienation—the alienation of Ishmael and the alienation of the Arab world. Only in that context can we consider a second theme in this chapter: that of "striving" or *jihad*.

One of the greatest literary examples of personal striving, as an example of group striving, is the English novel, *Wuthering Heights*, by Emily Brontë. From her vantage point in the rectory, this clergyman's daughter was a keen observer of the class struggle during the industrial revolution in England, when hardworking laborers and resourceful individuals were able to amass wealth, challenge the privileges of the aristocracy, and even take over pre-viously inherited positions. Heathcliffe succeeds in gaining control of the manor, but at the cost of losing his soul to the same corrupt bitterness he sought to overcome. Ishmael has sometime experienced the same pain asso-ciated with advances in status.

Ishmael is the ancestor of the Arab peoples. Ishmael is described in the Judeo-Christian Scriptures as a "wild ass" living in the desert. Every Muslim reader finds this offensive as a description of one whom they revere as the Lord of the desert and a prophet of God. Yet, for reasons perhaps beyond his control, his hand was against all his kin in the family of Abraham, and their hands were against him. We do not know if the biblical depiction of his situation is contemporary with the events of his life, or if it is a slightly later commentary in the records of this dysfunctional family. The fact remains that, in both ancient times and early in the Christian era, the Arabs were as alienated from the rest of Abraham's descendants as they are today. The results of this alienation have always been tragic.

If such an observation is true, this is a challenge to Arabs (and their Muslim extension of the family), and to Jews (and their Christian extension), to get over it and move on. In this era, under the shadow of war, we may be living out the challenge of these Scriptures; at the very least, we should be more cognizant of the warnings in this regard.

We have lived through the Cold War between communism and capitalism, which nearly destroyed civilization as we know it, and which was at the crisis point for forty years. Some of us have lived through the civil rights eras, each one being forty years of tension: the Christian persecution of Jews was a major contributor to war in Europe; French–English tensions threatened to split the practically perfect country of Canada; and Black–White racism menaced the noble American experiment in the quest for human rights. Forty years was also the symbolically approximated time of the apartheid era in South Africa, and perhaps there are other examples of "The Forty Years Wars."

The Bible often uses the symbolic figure of forty years as the time it takes to work through such issues as apartheid, communism, Nazism, civil rights, or at least to make it through the critical destructive phases of such turmoil. This may be an oversimplification, yet it would seem that we are in the early years of a crisis that may well split the world and demand our attention, resources, and energies for the next forty years. We already know how it is supposed to turn out, but this may be an even greater challenge than those listed above. We may need Torah, Gospel, and Qur'an to see us through if we hope to avoid ruination in a total denigration of human destiny.

Three months before 9/11, Lansing United Church in Toronto was privileged to have Dr. Eyad El Sarraj on the pulpit. Dr. El Surraj is the widely acclaimed Palestinian psychiatrist sometimes seen on television news talking about the traumatic impact war has on children. This was before the war in Afghanistan and before Iraq II, but in the midst of the Palestinian *intifada* protesting the expansion of Jewish settlements in the Palestinian territories. El Surraj became a close advisor to President Abbas during and following the Israeli evacuation of Gaza, and he remains influential in the cause for peace in the current negotiations toward a final settlement of this seemingly intractable conflict.

Dr. El Sarraj, a Muslim, is as evenhanded in psychiatric medicine as the Jew Bruce Feiler is in historical religion. El Sarraj points out that Jewish children growing up in terror of suicide bombers are as traumatized as Palestinian kids under the bombs of Israel. In both cases, the incidence of bedwetting in children until their teenage years is nine times the American and European average. In the teen years, the results of the trauma begin to manifest themselves in other, more outwardly threatening ways. By adulthood, the trauma-induced pathology of killing may be ingrained. Dr. El Surraj believes the insight and inspiration from stories of forgiveness in Torah, Gospel, and Qur'an may be the key to the therapeutic understanding we need now more desperately than at any time in the history of Abraham's family. This may be as true for America and Europe as it is for Israel and the Middle East.

Ishmael's adult behavior as a wild ass, alienated from everyone, is an understandable reaction to the childhood trauma of being placed under the knife on an altar by his father (as in the Qur'an), or being abandoned to die in the desert by his mother (as in the Bible). There are many things worth questioning in these images, but they may contain a truth we need to recognize. Muslims believe Ishmael accepted the situation with equanimity, but recent reactions of some of the descendants of Ishmael point in the opposite direction. The terrorism of extremists has its roots in the history of traumatized people.

Jews, too, have been traumatized, sometimes reacting with either equanimity or resignation. However, their fierce reactions to the horrors of the twentieth-century Holocaust are perhaps more in the spirit of *jihad*, the striving never to forget and never to let it happen again. Israel remains armed to the teeth, and not without reason, but we need to somehow find a better way to move on.

Christians have suffered persecution at various times, under Roman Emperors, Soviet Dictators, and even in parts of Indonesia today. The spirit of *jihad* can be compared to the Christian understanding of bearing the cross. In Mark's gospel, Jesus said, "Whoever desires to come after me, let him deny himself and take up his cross and follow me. Whoever desires to save his life will lose it, but whoever loses his life for my sake and the gospel, will save it. For what will it profit a man if he gains the whole world and loses his own soul" (Mark 8:34). Christians are not unacquainted with suffering, including both its consequences and its required response.

The Scriptures address individual trauma, which is why we personally benefit so immensely from them, but they also address the corporate traumas outlined above. Historically, Arabs were alienated from all the surrounding cultures until Muhammad gave them faith and human dignity. Somehow, it has taken until now for the rest of the family to address the rehabilitation of our cousins and to recognize the powerful regeneration of morality and the valuable contribution Ishmael's descendants have made to world culture. Some of us have not yet gotten it.

Meanwhile, can we be surprised that Ishmael became an archer (an individual "lone-wolf" terrorist), according to the Bible, and that the descendants of Ishmael became the scourge of the last of the Roman Legion in ancient times, repelling the crusaders from Europe in the Middle Ages and resisting the forces of Western modernity, and some of its false values, in recent years? The major scriptural accounts of Ishmael's childhood traumas were presented previously in the stories of his parents, Abraham and Hagar. In addition, Ishmael has more gentle and beloved appearances in Scripture, such as at his father's funeral, as mentioned, and kindly references to him in the Qur'an, with which many are not as familiar. As Allah instructed Muhammad:

> Also mention in The Book the story of Ismail: He was strictly true to what he promised and he was an apostle and a prophet. He used to enjoin on his people Prayer and Charity and he was most acceptable in the sight of his Lord. (Surah 19:54–55)

But in the modern context, it is that facet of Ishmael's story of *jihad* that requires even more scrutiny. This is an area of great misunderstanding between Muslims and the rest of the family of Abraham. Understood correctly, it is also an area where Jews and Christians may yet take great comfort, or at least feel a greater sense of affinity with their Muslim cousins.

As mentioned, the word *jihad* means "striving" and, like other things Islamic, the concept has been hijacked by extremists in our time and picked up by the media in a twisted form. True striving in a positive direction is what moderate Muslims all over the world are promoting these days. Except for extremists, this is what most characterizes Muslims living in North America and Europe as a dynamic part of the wider community. They study hard, they work hard, and they are eager to contribute fully as citizens in their chosen countries, albeit, like most of us, on their own terms, or at least while being true to themselves. With all the tensions brought about by the minority of Muslim extremists in Europe, the Middle East, and Asia, and the so-called homegrown terrorists in North America and Europe, it is so essential that the striving of moderate elements be understood and supported.

The 1997 edition of the *Oxford Dictionary of World Religions* offers one of the clearest definitions of jihad:

JIHAD—"striving in the cause of God," is usually translated as "holy struggle," but this is misleading. Jihad is divided into two categories, the greater and the lesser. The greater jihad is the warfare within oneself against any evil or temptation. The lesser jihad is the defence of Islam, or of a Muslim country or community, against aggression. It may be a jihad of the pen or of the tongue. If it involves conflict, it is strictly regulated, and can only be defensive.

Thus Muhammad said: "In avenging injuries inflicted on us, do not harm non-belligerents in their homes, spare the weakness of women, do not injure infants at the breast, nor those who are sick. Do not destroy the houses of those who offer no resistance, and do not destroy their means of subsistence, neither their fruit trees nor their palms."

Jihad cannot be undertaken to convert others because there "cannot be compulsion in religion" (Surah 2:256). If these regulations seem on occasion to be ignored, that failure is an offence to be answered on "the Day of Judgement."

The striving described in this next verse from the Qur'an is *jihad*, and the "apostle" of *jihad* is identified by Muslim scholars as Ishmael:

> And strive in His cause, as ye ought to strive, with sincerity and under discipline: He has chosen you and has opened the way for you through religion; it is the cult of your father Abraham. It is He Who has named you Muslims, both before and in this Revelation; that the Apostle of Jihad may be a witness for you and ye be witnesses for mankind! So establish regular Prayer, give regular Charity and hold fast to Allah! He is your Protector, the Best to protect and the Best to help! (Surah 22:78)

Everyone must strive to surmount whatever challenges come to them, for challenges come to prince and pauper alike, to those born of privilege and to the disadvantaged. The only difference between human beings is the way in which we strive. Do we strive bitterly, on our own, hoping to survive and to get on top of life by force of willpower, or even force of arms, or whatever leverage we can bring to bear? Or do we strive joyously, in partnership with God, not needing always to win in order to experience victory over those things within ourselves that would bring us down? The essence of Muslim faith is to submit or surrender to God, and then, and only then, to strive. Otherwise, the striving becomes perverted with personal agendas instead of yielding to the will of God. Muslims are not alone in this fault.

The Muslim philosopher who popularized the notion that modern circumstances require a *jihad* that is both bitter and communal is Sayyid Qutb. The Egyptian pronunciation of his name is as tight and difficult as it looks, but the Pakistani and some Asian versions of the name Qutb are not far

from "Key-tab" to Western ears. We should get used to it in one version or
another, since his name may be as important in the twenty-first century as
was that of Marx in the twentieth. Dr. Ayman al-Zawahiri, Osama bin Lad-
en's second in command, has been regarded in certain media as the ideological brains behind the Al-Qaeda movement, but he is a lightweight compared
to Sayyid Qutb of the Muslim Brotherhood, with his influence on Hamas in
Palestine and Hezbollah in Lebanon. Qutb's thirty-volume commentary, *In
the Shade of the Qur'an*, is a Muslim classic. But, in *Milestones*, written
from his Egyptian prison cell prior to his execution in 1966, Qutb was as
bitter toward Arab ruling classes cooperating with colonial masters and
multinational corporations as he was toward those imperial and corporate
powers themselves. He blamed both for the exploited state of Arabs, then a
simple pious people, cheated by their own leaders and misled also by Christians and Jews, who perverted their own religions for economic gain.

Qutb recalled how Islam integrated science and spirituality between the
seventh and the eleventh centuries, before betrayal by its leaders, and how
Europe picked up the pieces, separating secular and spiritual elements to
dominate and ruin the world. The March 23, 2003, edition of the *New York
Times Magazine* articulates the view that Qutb's philosophy is the true
source of whatever semblance of doctrine the extremist groups may claim
in their *jihad*, a struggle they call holy war.

Qutb called for striving against sin and for a more wholesome life than
modern secular European and American societies offer. His calls have been
answered by angry young men crashing airplanes into New York skyscrap-
ers, blowing up London's subways, torching Paris by night, and waging
what they see as holy war to free Palestine and Chechnya, to regain the
wealth of energy resources, and to right the wrongs of history.

Except in exceptional circumstances, violent striving is a perversion of
Islam, even if many of the grievances are legitimate, because *jihad* is a positive religious teaching. But who would not be tempted to extremism if
threatened by the knife of your own father or if dying of thirst in the desert?
This is the story of Ishmael as the individual example of what the corporate
Arab branch of the family has experienced through history at the hands of
their own leaders and others. Who can forget the dramatic portrayal of
these realities in the British book, *The Seven Pillars of Wisdom* by Lord T. E.
Lawrence, or by *Lawrence of Arabia* in the American movie of that name,
featuring Peter O'Toole and Omar Sharif? It was originally titled *Revolt in
the Desert*:

Feisel (Omar Sharif): I fear they hunger for Arabia.
Lawrence (Peter O'Toole): Then you must deny it to them.

These were Hollywood's prophetic utterances fifty years ago.

Remedy began with Muhammad, but it has been mercurial ever since. There have been great advances in the Muslim world but also horrendous reversals, until we come to the impasse we face today. Things will either continue to get worse, or we may be at a turning point for the better. For the latter, Muslims will need to return to the spiritual roots of *jihad*, as so many Muslim scholars are urging. At the same time, Jews and Christians need to face the traditional Muslim contention that they have perverted their own religions, an assertion illustrated by Qutb's accusation that they have done so by the split of culture into secular and sacred life. It is a critique of Western culture that must be addressed, a process that will require religious moderates to take themselves and their spiritual responsibilities more seriously. Church and state should perhaps remain separated, but the dichotomy of secular and sacred is under review in Western culture as never before.

Muslim extremists sometimes say that Christians and Jews in the Western world live in beautiful houses with broken families, while Muslims in the East live in broken houses with beautiful families. That may be an oversimplification, but the suggestion is that, among Christians and Jews, high mortgage rates and high divorce rates are somehow linked. At the same time, modern Muslim critics, like the brilliant American jurist Khaled Abou El Fadl, assert that low divorce rates among Muslims can be attributed to harsh domestic restrictions, which also come at a price. These spiritual debates are sharp even around issues like which form of polygamy causes greatest harm to the family, the *contemporaneous* polygamy of families in the East or the *serial* polygamy of the West.

So, we may yet get the mortgage paid, but at a price we cannot afford if we neglect the family meanwhile. We all have challenges in our lives, every one of us. It is in the nature of human experience. Our family faith teaches us to strive, not bitterly, as did Heathcliffe, but with the devotion that the Qur'an recalls, and as illustrated by the story of Ishmael as we know it.

Today, we are invited to join in the *jihad*, to strive for what is right in God's sight. Our purpose in examining biblical figures as they appear in the Qur'an is not merely to understand the Muslim world in its turmoil and to appreciate its quest. It is for all of us to understand ourselves better from the well-rounded perspective of this faith journey by Abraham's family of Jews, Christians, and Muslims, dysfunctional though the family may often seem.

The archer's arrow does not come to rest when it is tired, but when its flight is completed. We long for that time to come, though we are still early in the forty years that may be needed. A time of turmoil and striving is often a time of renewal in personal life, sometimes in national life, and possibly throughout the world, even during this time of conflict. This is the meaning of the phrase in a popular song, "Let there be peace on earth, and let it begin with me." Let each one of us launch our own *jihad* in the renewal of our devotion to God.

8

The Hajj of Life

Lot/Lut

LOT AND HIS WIFE are almost comic characters in the Bible, except that, in Hebrew Scripture, Lot was a bad actor, a villain taking advantage of his Uncle Abraham, offering the sexual favors of his daughters to neighborhood hoodlums, drinking himself stupid, and indulging in incest with these same willing girls. This description of Lot appears almost unbearably insulting to Muslim readers, who regard him quite differently, as one sent by God to warn the people of Sodom and Gomorrah. The Jewish and Christian depiction of this prophet is especially distressful to Muslims for legitimate reasons that can still be found between the lines of Hebrew Scripture.

Fortunately for Lut, as his name appears in Arabic, the Qur'an retells his story in a more favorable light. Would this kind of retelling not be great for people like us? If only someone would come along and answer our critics by putting our stories in a better light. That is what Allah does in Allah's mercy. For Jews, this redemption experience comes through a corporate identity and, for Christians, whoever is "in Christ," assumes the identity of Jesus. With Lut, it is the sheer good fortune of devotion to a merciful God as recorded in the Qur'an.

This chapter is called the *Hajj* because Lut moves around, usually following Ibrahim, while Ibrahim is always getting his nephew out of trouble. Lut was possibly the first pilgrim to make it to Mecca after Ibrahim and Ishmael together restored the ancient shrine, known as the Ka'bah, from the Arabic word for "cube," where Aadam worshiped back in the mists of prehistory. Lut was the first to make the Hajj pilgrimage to this shrine, a pilgrimage all Muslims make at least once in their lives if they are physically able and can afford the journey. In the twenty-first century, about two million Muslims make that pilgrimage to Mecca each year during Ramadan to attend worship services and spiritual exercises. The power of this experience should never be underestimated, but what is it all about?

Muslims believe that Adam built this sanctuary and that it has been the center of worship for humanity from the beginning. Abraham and Ishmael had restored the shrine in their time, after it had become a ruin from neglect, misuse, and from previous natural disasters. Muhammad restored the shrine a second time, after it had been taken over for idol worship, with booths or side altars numbering 360, to be exact, in a circle around it.

To the Western mind this historical mythology seems a stretch, to say the least, but if Adam represents our corporate or communal ancestor, the Qa'bah may originate very far back. The proof is the 360 altars constructed on a circular track, called the *tawwaf*. Muhammad dismantled these altars in his purge of idolatry.

The number 360 is the number of degrees in a circle; it is engraved on the most ancient Aztec, Egyptian, and Chinese calendars as the number of days it used to take the Earth to orbit the Sun. The division of the circle into 360 degrees in these ancient, widely separated cultures is one of the hints from the earliest prehistoric civilizations that the earth survived a near miss by a giant comet, possibly Venus. Pushed back by magnetic repulsion, the earth may have wobbled into a new orbit just slightly farther out into the solar system, so that it now takes 365 days to circle the sun instead of the 360. This figure has been ingrained in humanity's definition of a circle since time immemorial. Few people and fewer buildings would have survived such an apocalyptic event, though it was mosques, temples, and churches that best withstood the 2004 tsunami in the Pacific Ocean, as did the Qa'bah, so long ago.

Documents would not have survived the tidal waves associated with such a wobble, but stone calendars might, from huge ones like Stonehenge in its current state, to tiny ones, of which there are many in museums around the world. The fact that the earliest calendars of 360 days had a counterpart in the architecture of the Qa'bah with its 360 altars attests to its prehistoric antiquity. The fact that worshipers on the Hajj pilgrimage still circle the tawwaf track seven times in the direction of the sun suggests that the connection with the sun is also ancient. The Qa'bah may very well be the most ancient shrine in the world, and we can indeed ascribe its origins to our corporate ancestor Adam, or mankind.

As mentioned, Lut, possibly the first "muslim" visitor to the shrine reestablished by his uncle, Ibrahim, and his cousin Ismail, is a bad actor, as he is presented in the Bible. In the Qur'an, Lut is rehabilitated, or else he is truly a patriarch, prophet, and apostle in his own right. If that is the case, the Bible may be guilty of deliberate slander, which is a distinct possibility. The Bible, after all, is not only a book about the lovely aspects of life. Its "sweetness and light" come in the context of human corruption and trouble, including deception that is well documented, even in the case of Lot's uncle. We may believe that every word of the Bible is true for the purpose it represents, but that does not mean that everyone quoted in the Bible is telling the truth. Sometimes, the Bible identifies the outright lies, identifying the liars, as when Abraham lied about Sarah being his sister. In other passages, the lies simply stand on their own, as a true reflection of what God has to deal with. Lot's reputation is a case in point, but the Bible paints the human situation "warts and all," even when some of the warts are on the authors of the source material rather than the subject.

The Bible is not intended as either a whitewash or a slander. It is the story of human corruption and God's redemption of all, including the writers. Sometimes, the writers were unaware of corrupting their own material, as Muslims have charged, but even that is part of the human situation with which God deals. In the case of Lot, the writers would have been very much aware of the hatchet job they were doing.

It would appear that Lot, as a prominent relative of Abraham, was too famous to be ignored in ancient times. The Bible points out that he was the leader of "the righteous remnant" that God agreed to spare—evidence in his favor. As the ancestor of Israel's enemies, nothing good is said about him in the Bible, while nothing bad is said about him in the Qur'an. The fact that he assimilated toward the Arab side of the family did nothing for his reputation among the Jews by the time these stories were being written down in the biblical account. Accordingly, at this point we are forced to recognize that, just as there are divisive issues between the Hebrew and Christian Scriptures, there are also divergences and differences between the Bible and the Qur'an that cannot be reconciled. To acknowledge this is not to say that one or the other is of no value, but this understanding can help us appreciate what kinds of holy books we may be reading, and may teach us how to understand God's Word and apply it in our own lives. So, let us look at the texts concerning Lot or Lut in which two very different pictures emerge of a biblical figure who appears prominently in the Qur'an.

The story, as elaborated in the Bible, begins with the angels who visited Abraham and Sarah, announcing that, despite their advancing years, they would soon have a child, as promised by God. These angels are handsome characters who now reveal that their next assignment is the destruction of the wicked cities of Sodom and Gomorrah, because of the vile sins perpetrated there.

Abraham's nephew lives in Sodom with his family, so Abraham prays that the Lord not permit the innocent to perish with the guilty. After some discussion, God agrees, even if only ten such people can be found. According to the Bible, the nephew had duped Abraham earlier, but the uncle evidently thought otherwise, or believed that Lot had reformed and lived a moral life. God's judgment concurs as God continues to regard Lot as "righteous," in both scriptural accounts, despite what the Bible says about him.

That evening, the heavenly visitors appeared to Lot at the Sodom city gate on the flats next to the Dead Sea. Lot invited them home and presented a banquet. In a city famous for wanton homosexual licentiousness, a gang of Sodomites surrounded the house demanding a chance to have sexual intercourse with these handsome dandies. In Middle Eastern style, Lot is loyal to his guests, but in the Bible he goes to ridiculous lengths to protect his reputation in this regard. He offers his virgin daughters for their pleasure instead, but the angels intervene and strike the intruders blind.

We come then to the episode where Lot flees with his family, just as the fire and brimstone begin to rain from heaven. They escape to a nearby town, except for Lot's wife, who lingers with longing regret for the city and the people she loved. She becomes "preserved" with that lifeless culture as a pillar of salt. Lot proceeds from the town to live in the safety of a cave in the hills, but he and his daughters are social pariahs. The girls eventually figure that no one will ever marry them, and they need heirs to care for them when Lot dies. So, they get their father drunk on successive evenings and they became pregnant by incest. They give birth to sons named Moab and Ammi, the ancestors of Israel's enemies through the ages, even down to the present era, in which they are parts of Jordan facing Israel across the river.

If we examine all the wars between Israel and its neighbors in ancient times, the enemies faced by the Hebrews down through the centuries so often seem to include those pesky Moabites and Ammonites, the descendants of Lot. The meanings of their biblical names are deliberate insults: "Bad Seeds" and "Children of Incest." It then comes as no surprise that Lot, impossible to ignore, comes off badly in the Hebrew account. If anything was more despised than wanton homosexuality, it was incest. The story was intended not only to discredit Lot, but also to cast Israel's Arab neighbors in the least favorable light, a deliberate slur on traditional enemies who claimed descent from the righteous prophet Lot.

The same general story is found in the Qur'an, except it presents Lut in an entirely favorable light, moving to those Cities of the Plain to share the faith and to issue warnings about their manner of life, no particular sins being specified. The outline of his story is presented seven times (Surahs 7,

15, 26, 27, 29, 37, 54). He is the innocent soul whom Abraham asks God to spare.

In the Qur'an, when the intruders demand sexual favors from the visitors, Lot chides them and says they should get married to avoid this wanton lifestyle. When he offers his daughters, it is not for pleasure, but for arranged marriages with neighbors he knows. In the Qur'an, Lut's whole purpose in life was to warn the People of the Plain of the consequences of their wickedness, and to ask that they submit to one all-sufficient God.

Like Nooh before him, Lut was destined to be a prophet and an apostle to a doomed people who would vanish from the face of the earth in their obstinate refusal of God's grace. Lut's own wife turned back and became the proverbial pillar of salt, as represented by a chemical formation seen today by tourists at the edge of the Dead Sea. This particular body of water has always been known among local Arabs as the Sea of Lut, and it is so known today.

One formation often visited by tourists has always been called *bint Lut* by the local Arab population, though that does not fit well with the story in either Scripture, as it translates as "Lot's daughter" rather than "Lot's wife." The Qur'an and the Bible agree on that one, but these are timeless stories with many versions outside either Scripture tradition.

Sermons about the danger of fixation on the past, by preachers in every generation and in all three traditions—rabbis, ministers, and imams—have been based on Lot's wife. The physical phenomenon that accounted for the destruction of these cities is usually understood as a meteor shower, another sign of God's Word in harmony with God's natural order. In the Qur'an, Lut is constantly referred to as a warner who preached a message of repentance. This is in line with the Qur'an's concern for Judgment and our need for God's compassion and mercy. Jesus used the story of Lot in a favorable way to illustrate his own second coming, which Muslims also await. Perhaps this more favorable image from Christian Scriptures is the truth about Lot, since the proof of Abraham's respect for him and God's own favor also survives in the biblical text. The Gospel appears to agree more with the Qur'an than the Torah in this instance.

What is the truth? These days we see certain Muslim mullahs preaching death to America and the Jews. Certain Christian televangelists have compared Muslim preachers in Iraq calling for the people to "slit the throats of the invaders" with the message of Jesus to "love your enemies." Their point is that one religion is good, and the other is bad, though the side dropping the biggest bombs is hard pressed to show how it is done in love.

The Christian extremists want the golden rule of religion applied to

Christians (the world should understand that they really love the enemies they are bombing) but not applied to Muslims (who may have been calling on people to defend their women and children). The golden rule is, in this context, that we should give the kind of favorable interpretation to the religion of others that we would hope they extend to us. Let us look briefly at the Qur'an in this light, and then examine the Bible again before deciding how to reconcile the seeming discrepancies in the time of Lot, or Lut, and then in our own time.

———— ⌀ ————

The language of the Arabic Qur'an is among the most beautiful ever recited, as Christians and Jews are beginning to discover at the increasing number of interfaith activities around the world. The only thing that compares with the Qur'an are certain sections of the Bible in a beloved translation. The Lord Is My Shepherd and the Lord's Prayer make sense in any translation, but the beauty of language is found only in the King James Authorised Version.

It is like that also with the Christmas story of the one "wrapped in swaddling clothes and lying in a manger," or Saint Paul's Hymn to Love: "Though I speak with the tongues of men and of angels, and have not love, I am become as sounding brass, or a clanging cymbal." Even with the availability of more accurate translations of both the Hebrew and Christian Scriptures, the people at a funeral prefer to recite the beloved traditional texts of the Twenty-Third Psalm and the Lord's Prayer, and woe to the preacher who insists on using the more prosaic modern versions that fail to reverberate in the soul.

This may be as close as we can come to understanding the Muslim affection for the very words of the Qur'an, and the determination not to lose that feeling by translating it. Jews and Christians can hardly be expected to realize it, but it would appear that, when recited in Arabic, the whole of the Qur'an has that combination of melody and power that they associate with only a few of their own Scriptures.

Muhammad was illiterate, but he was a deeply religious person who was sincerely concerned about the corruption and brutality of his society. After years of keeping his sanity by solitary meditation in his favorite cave retreat, he practically fainted when God gave him his first psalm/poem of spiritual truth and judgment. He knew he was inspired, and that this was not something that he made up himself, but something from God. Still trembling, he remembered the little verse and recited it to his family when he got home. They, too, realized immediately this was not just their beloved husband and father talking, but that the beauty and power of his words had to be from God. They loved his little verse and kept it. His wife's Christian cousin was the first to assert that this was from the God of the Hebrew Prophets.

The Qur'an is made up of 114 such utterances or psalms given by God, usually through the voice of the angel Gabriel. These experiences came to Muhammad over a period of twenty-three years, often unexpectedly, sometimes months, or even years apart. Each one is validated in its authenticity by its own impact on the hearers. The influence of this collection of oracular prophecies has been so immense that its content sometimes seems secondary to its beauty. The contents are getting more scrutiny these days than ever before in history, by Muslims and others, especially Jews and Christians, but critics and those seeking to understand.

At first, modern Westerners were inclined to treat the Qur'an as a quaint, even esoteric, rehashing of some of the main stories of the Bible, whitewashing the believing characters and tarring the unbelievers with stern judgment. Could it be that believers are treated with the grace we all need, while unbelievers get "tough love," as a timely warning about the consequences of their actions? Let us judge as favorably as possible.

The Bible, for its part, really is almost as jumbled as Muslims say it is, as a much edited community document in which historical authors and inspired poets alike, along with editors, compilers, committees of rabbis and councils of bishops, translators, publishers, and even readers contribute to the fabric of the story. To most Christians and Jews, this takes nothing from its authenticity as a living Word that can only be fully appreciated with the aid of both scholars and personal openness to the guidance of the Holy Spirit in the heart of the reader.

Jews and Christians believe the authorship, editing, selection of books for the official list, copying, translation, publication, and reading all happens under guidance of God's Spirit, and that God's Word shines through these inspired words. If biblical characters are painted "warts and all," even the unworthy motives of some contributors are part of the divine-human dialogue through which God's Word is spoken personally in the heart of each believer. God's Word comes as part of our faith quest as People of the Book.

Christians believe the Bible represents God's *Word* to them. Muslims believe the Qur'an presents the *words* of God. Jews sometimes say, "That all depends . . ." and perhaps these positions are not incompatible. There are indeed Christians who believe the Bible contains the literal words of God, rather than an inspired dialogue in which the reader also has a part. These days one increasingly reads of "progressive" Muslims who seek the deeper meanings in the text of the Qur'an by looking beneath the surface, a tradition that goes back to the earliest days of Islam.

Jews and Christians might benefit from an appreciation of the absolute style of the Qur'an. Something seems missing among the faithful when they believe the process is everything and the journey is more important than the destination. At the same time, is it possible that some aspects of biblical scholarship might be valuable to Muslims? That is not for anyone but them to say, but, as their self-confidence grows in the modern era, there could be breathtaking developments in understanding, of benefit to the whole family.

For example, the Bible contains the story of Esther and her uncle, persecuted in the Persian court by Haman, the Prime Minister. Muhammad thought he heard God say Haman was in the Egyptian court, not the Persian, though the evidence overwhelmingly supports integrity of the biblical account in this instance. No disrespect is intended in suggesting that perhaps Muhammad did not always catch the exact nuance of what God revealed to him. To put it gently, perhaps God intended the Qur'an to put "Haman" in quotes, as a figure type. Even stranger notions are possible.

For many years the world had two competing systems of measurement, Imperial and Metric. The Metric system is based on fingers and toes, a human division of everything into tens: weights, distances, temperatures, and coinage. The older Imperial System is based on the circle, measuring everything in numbers divisible into 360, whether an inch of fourths, eighths, sixteenths, and so on, a foot of twelve inches, a yard of thirty-six inches, pounds of sixteen ounces, or pounds, shillings, and pence. These systems competed in the Bible, as between Ten Commandments and twelve tribes and twelve disciples. Neither of them make total sense without a numbering system based on the concept of "zero," which the Arabic numbering system brought to the West from India and shared with Europe in the era of Muslim ascendancy.

Those who doubt the significance of all this should simply try to multiply some figures using Roman numerals. The point is that the Arabic numbering system in use throughout the world came into use following the intellectual stimulus of the Qur'an and Muslim culture. Someone needs to investigate the significance of numbers in the Qur'an itself, as the fountainhead of all this, and if this was brought from the Orient through Muhammad's caravan experience and Divine inspiration into the Qur'an, what else came with it?

All recent attempts to explain the Muslim use of the pagan Crescent Moon symbol are totally inadequate and without foundation beyond myth and legend. Is it possible that the Holy Qur'an, which establishes our relationship to the sun in its details about the Qa'bah, might somehow give the moon its place and significance? These examples of treasures yet to be revealed by unlocking the Qur'an pale in comparison to the greatest riddle of all. Muhammad felt compelled to have symbolic initials placed at the opening of many of the surahs. He knew they were from God, but nobody knows their meaning. Appearing like monograms embroidered on a sacred garment, these enigmatic inscriptions have puzzled Islamic scholars through the ages. It is universally agreed that they have, what Yusuf Ali, in his notes, calls "mystic meanings."

There are twenty-nine letters in the Arabic alphabet, fourteen of which appear in various combinations in these "Abreviated Letters" as they are known officially. The attempts at unravelling their meaning have been more puerile than the attempts to ascribe the Crescent Moon to a dream of one of the later Caliphs. When all the techniques of critical analysis are brought into the service of Qur'anic studies, the treasure hunt may yield no finer gems than those revealed in connection with these sacred monograms. This quest alone could reveal "secrets of the universe" of profound significance to Muslims, to Abraham's whole family and to all the world.

There may be no single presenter of biblical Scripture who had as much psychic awareness of God's revelation than did Muhammad. The Bible itself stands forever as containing God's Word to the People of the Book, as the Qur'an itself attests, a faithful Word in which all members have some part in transmitting. As Muhammad was the seal of the Prophets, perhaps the Qur'an is, in some sense, the seal of the Scriptures. Still, along with scholarship not yet employed, we need God's Spirit in reading it.

So the question remains, "Was Lot/Lut a good guy or a bad guy?" Major principles are involved, so how can good people disagree constructively, without denigrating each other? This is a question for us in our families and in our world at war. It is a question for us where we work, study, and play and a question for people in the synagogue, church, and mosque.

We do not have to agree, but we have to live together in harmony. Religious people in this particular family need to learn how to appreciate each other's position in the most generous way possible. We are to view the position of the other person in the most favorable light, instead of the deliberate denigration that has characterized these relationships at the level of popular culture. This point cannot be made too often. One may not necessarily accept the view of the other, but if each understands the position of the other, as the other would wish it understood, expanding horizons would enrich each and peace might be possible.

On this basis, we can even love each other, though we may not necessarily like what the other does. This is perhaps what Jesus meant when he said, "Love one another as I have loved you." He did not merely say, "Love one another," but "Love one another in the way that I have loved you." There is no indication that Jesus loved only those with whom he agreed or those whose actions he liked. On the contrary, he loved "sinners" with a transforming poignancy that involved no lowering of standards, but achieved a new and higher level of relationship, which the world needs. Nowhere is this required more than in the study of the Scriptures.

9

The Covenant

Yaqub/Jacob

FOLLOWING THE UNIVERSAL STORIES, we have considered Abraham and what it was that distinguished him from Adam, Noah, and others who resisted forming an absolute covenant with God, as Abraham did. Hagar and Ishmael are recognized as matriarch and founder of the Arab nations. Isaac plays a cameo role for Jews and Muslims. Even Christians, who see his near sacrifice as a paradigm for the cross of Christ, might concede that this is a typological role that might have been fulfilled by Ishmael and has been fulfilled by others.

So, we will next consider the covenant as exemplified in Jacob, Isaac's son, the patriarch whose name became Israel, and we will consider his son Joseph. They set the pattern of faith for the people of Israel in the desert years and during their sojourn in Egypt (concluding with Moses, to whom God spoke and revealed the fine points of the covenant). Jacob is a perfect example of a less than perfect person who works out the ramifications of this covenant in practical terms and is blessed by God. We use the biblical account as the basis of this investigation.

The value of giving particular attention to Jacob's story is more than the covenant he personifies (in a way we could all learn from), and more than the fact that he becomes Israel (and his direct descendants become the nation). Important as these things are, his story is especially instructive in this particular study because it represents biblical material equally familiar to Jews (ancient and modern), Christians, and Muslims and to modern children of the three traditions. Jacob could have lived when he did or in a more recent era, such as the time of Christ or in Afghanistan today. To gain a full appreciation of the Bible characters as they appear in the Qur'an we will

branches of Abraham's family. Active members of synagogue, church, and mosque do not wait for the latest tsunami to make good on this aspect of their covenant with God.

Within the United Church of Canada, for example, the total net amount raised by congregations per year is approximately $365 million, or about a million dollars a day, according to the latest Year Book. This is from a medium-sized church in a medium-sized country like Canada, where Abraham's whole family raises $70 million a week for charitable work in some fifty thousand synagogues, churches, and mosques. Abraham's family in Canada represents only 1 percent of Abraham's family worldwide. Anyone can do the rest of the math. So much for the question of the practical impact of this covenant. So much for the demise of religion.

Jacob's dream of a ladder up and down between heaven and earth has been analyzed by modern psychiatrists. If you dream of a car, a ship, or a plane, any analyst will likely suggest you are going somewhere, not to a different place, but that there is movement in your life. A ladder or staircase may indicate an elevation of your understanding, your spirit. Jacob was at a moment of spiritual momentum, though he was not quite ready to handle it. Yet, he never forgot the promises he made, nor the promises God made to him.

The family has not forgotten either. Jews and Christians both sing the psalm on their Sabbath: "O God of Bethel, by whose hand, your people still are fed. Who through this earthly pilgrimage hast all your servants led." Muslims are also familiar with it and, as their worship increasingly incorporates vernacular languages and other rhythms, this is one of the common scriptural songs all three sometimes sing together at interfaith worship services.

At last Jacob reaches Haran in Syria, where his uncle lives. He sees a band of shepherds gathering their flocks around a well and asks if they know Laban. They reply that they do and, "Look, here comes his daughter Rachel with his flock." These shepherds, like Rachel, are all women, like Bedouin shepherds today. They cannot move the stone over the well, so Jacob impresses them, especially Rachel, by helping out. Rachel is a beauty and Jacob suddenly remembers the second reason for his visit; it is true love at first sight. He too is attractive, and, when he identifies himself, she responds and together they go off to meet her father who is eager to get a relative as a husband for his daughter. It keeps the money in the family and maintains good bloodlines, or so they used to think. Elizabeth II is a cousin of her husband Philip, on both sides of her family. In Western culture it is usually aristocratic families that have maintained such conservative traditions down to our time. Though the marriage of cousins is not unheard of in parts of America, it is rare. Muslims still frequently marry within the family in many parts of the world for the same reasons as European aristocrats.

In Uncle Laban Jacob had met his match. He had two daughters: "Leah had lovely eyes, but Rachel was shapely and beautiful." Laban agreed that young Jacob could marry the lovely Rachel but only after joining the family and helping run the farm through the next seven crops. Jacob agreed and time flew by until a wedding date was set. They had a great feast with lots of drinking. With little ceremony at the end of the evening, a woman in the wedding *burka* was led to the wedding tent where she snuggled down with her drunk husband.

Except it was not Rachel! It was her sister with the lovely eyes. "Lovely eyes" is a back-handed compliment, like saying she had a nice personality. The next morning, Jacob had it out with his uncle, and Laban admitted his deception. "I had to get a husband for Leah, my eldest daughter, but just treat her as your wife for a week and then you can marry Rachel too. If you stay on as foreman for another seven crops, we will also share the profits from the farm."

To make this part of a long story short, in our modern weddings in this family of Abraham, there is a moment in the ceremony when the veil of the bride is removed to confirm who is really behind it. Moreover, ministers do not perform marriages if they believe the groom or the bride has been drinking. The first is now a custom; the second is the law.

Once Jacob and Laban began to split the profits, they got along even more poorly. Most of the profit was made by energetic young Jacob, but Laban was constantly changing the deal and tension mounted. Both daughters sided with their husband, even though they could not abide each other. When Laban was away on a three-day trip to distant pastures, the Bible says:

> Jacob got ready to go back to his father in the land of Canaan. He put his children and his wives on the camels, and drove all his flocks ahead of him, with everything that he had acquired. (Genesis 31:17–18)

Laban chased after them, claiming they had cleaned him out and even taken the company books and articles of incorporation, or the ancient equivalent, to no avail! Rachel even hid the documents (the divine symbols), under her skirt and claimed ritual reasons prevented any man from searching her. It was a terrible scene, but they got away. Now, heading back toward Canaan, or Palestine, Jacob heard that his brother Esau, the one he cheated years ago, was coming to meet him with four hundred armed men. Things were rapidly coming to a head.

"What was that deal I made with God again?" Jacob asks himself. It is not just that he has run out of options, since he had faced worse odds before. But Jacob is tired of the game and he knows there is more to life than sham and flim-flam, even when he wins. It is a thing called integrity. Jacob had seen it in his grandfather, Abraham, in his old age. He wanted it for himself, sooner now, rather than later. Jacob decided to face the music. He had crossed the Jabok River as a young man with nothing but a walking stick, but now he had hundreds of men and thousands of animals. He forded his caravans of animals, servants, wives, and children across the river. Then, he organized them into smaller units of droves and herds.

The men in charge each memorized a speech for Esau and his gang. When asked whose possessions and herds these were, they were to say, "They belong to your servant, Jacob. He sends them as a present to his master, Esau." Jacob sent them off in the morning with enough distance between each caravan that each time Esau would meet one group, the dust from another caravan would appear on the horizon. All day they came, and by evening Jacob sent a final group, including his wives, who were with him in this risky gambit.

Then, Jacob retreated, alone, back across the river to meditate. Jacob was on the right track and he knew it, but he was still nervous and asking himself if he had become soft, stupid, or both. Looking into the river, he saw the reflection of a man, and the Bible says Jacob wrestled with this man all night.

Perhaps he was the born and natural leader of this family that aspired to become a special nation, but he was wrong to gain the mandate by cheating and causing a quarrel between him and Esau that could ruin them all. Would Esau accept his humble surrender? Would Esau believe that Jacob now understood the ways of God and accept him back? Would Esau accept Jacob's leadership and maybe work with him, or would the four hundred pitch a battle that neither one could win in a decisive way? What other tricks, alliances, and resources had Esau mustered? Jacob knew he was smarter, but he also knew his brother was tougher. He asked himself a hundred times if he should have planned an offensive action against his brother.

Morning came, and the man with whom he wrestled would not let go. Was that man his own reflection in the water? Was it the image of God in him? Is this potentially the same thing? Most people have been to the Jabok River, at some point. If we properly understand these common Scriptures, it is with the image of God within ourselves that we must wrestle.

As the sun rose, Jacob knew he had seen the face of God in his own reflection in the river. He was physically lame from the struggle but, because he had hung onto his decision, he had a new identity. The One with whom he wrestled said:

> "Your name will no longer be Jacob. You have struggled with God and with human nature, and you have won. Your name will be Israel, the struggler who prevailed." (Genesis 32:28)

This new identity would last the rest of his lifetime and down through history, even for many who bore this name without understanding it. Some others believe a new struggle for this same integrity was waged on the cross on behalf of Israel and for all humanity who surrender in submission to God. Jacob/Israel was reconciled with his brother. God was with him, and he lived long and well with the love and respect of all who knew him.

In analyzing or critiquing the text, those reading in Hebrew will note the strands of material from J, E, and P intertwined throughout this story, cherished by both northern and southern tribes and in which the theological stakes are high. J uses the divine name Jehovah (Hebrew *Yehweh*) as usual, the E material sticks with *Elohim*, and P tries not to use the Lord's name in vain and so adopts the euphemism *Adonay*, meaning "Lord," whenever possible.

There came a time when the spirit of the P tradition became so strong in temple and synagogue, and especially in private conversation, that the name of *Yahweh*, revealed to Moses, was not to be pronounced at all, lest the commandment about using God's name in vain be transgressed. This was at about the time that diacritical marks, or vowel symbols, were being added to the Hebrew texts to aid in pronouncing words in an alphabet that has only consonants.

In the scrolls of the Torah, whenever the strict priests came to *Yahweh*, or *YHWH* in Hebrew, they added the vowel marks for *Adonay* instead, to remind people to avoid pronouncing *YHWH* and to use *Adonay*. This was not realized by the first Protestant translators of the Bible into European languages, who came up with an amalgamated word using the consonants of *YHWH* and the vowels of *Adonay* to produce a new name for God, *Jehovah* (J and Y being the same in many languages). The word Jehovah as a translation of *Yehweh* was an accidental invention of the Protestant Reformation that endured, to the amusement of the rabbis in Europe, but a name for God that has stuck among the devout.

This is a benign example of how the lack of critical abilities can lead to unfounded religious traditions, of which there are many in all faiths. About a hundred years ago a new sect of Christian "witnesses" proclaimed that not only is "Jehovah" a name for God, but that it is his only name! In fact, of all the names we use for God, Jehovah is the only one not actually found in the original Hebrew text of the Bible. Jews, Christians, and Muslims, who all love their texts of Scripture, can never be ill served by developing critical abilities and knowledge.

10

The Dream

Yusuf/Joseph

To MORE COMPLETELY understand the spirit of the Qur'an, it might be helpful to read one complete Surah in the modern Malik version. The Surah named Yusuf is accessible to the Western reader, because we know the story of Joseph so well, and it is presented in a familiar narrative format. Muslim legend has it that the whole story of Joseph was dictated to Muhammad in response to questions his Jewish allies were asking concerning the different stories about Joseph in Arabic culture. That distinguishes this information from other patriarchal material in the Qur'an, which presumes familiarity on the part of readers, either through the Bible or the Hadith.

While the text of the Qur'an account appears esoteric to the Western reader, we may assume that it is not quite as obtuse in the Arabic poetic original. The tone rings somewhat more spiritual than the more historical account in the Bible. This Surah, like many chapters of the Qur'an, opens with three monograms or epigraphs in Arabic script, transliterated here but never translated, in spite of endless speculation by Muslim scholars and Jungian philologists. In English they are often written out as syllables, just as V.S.N., the initials of a famous Nobel laureate in literature might be written as Vee Es En. In this case we have the Arabic letters A.L.R. written out as Alif L'am Ra, though we are none the wiser to their meaning as yet.

The frequent references to "signs" and the use of symbols in the Qur'an should be proof that, while these are taken to be the very words of God, they should not be taken literally. The Qur'an, of all books in the world, lends itself most to the layered meanings from the surface to the most profound depths. Indeed, the text of the Qur'an practically precludes the kind of literalism sometimes insisted upon by those needing to demonstrate the full extent of their devotion, much as in Jewish and Christian circles. As the text of this passage unfolds, the reader should keep in mind that, while Allah is One, he often speaks in the plural, the so-called royal or editorial we as used by the Pope, the Queen, or the editor of the *New York Times*.

While much of the Qu'ran is written in the style known to Christians in the Book of Revelation and to Jews in parts of David, and other parts have a psalmlike quality, Yusuf in the Qu'ran reads more like a biblical narrative.

Alif L'am Ra. These are the verses of the Book that make things clear. We have revealed this Qur'an in the Arabic language so that you [Arabs] may understand. We relate to you the best of stories through this Qur'an by Our revelation to you [O Muhammad], though before this you were one of those who did not know. This is the narrative of that time, when Yusuf [Joseph] said to his father: "O my father! In a dream I saw eleven stars, the sun and the moon—I saw them prostrate themselves before me!"

He replied: "My dear little son! Do not say any thing about this dream to your brothers, lest they plot an evil scheme against you; for Shaitan is an open enemy to human beings."

It will happen, as you have seen in your dream, that you will be chosen by your Rabb for His work. He will teach you how to interpret visions, and will perfect His favor upon you and the children of Ya'qoob [Jacob], as He perfected it upon your forefathers Ibrahim [Abraham] and Ishaq [Isaac] before you. Surely your Rabb is Knowledgeable, Wise. Indeed in the story of Yusuf and his brothers, there are signs for inquirers.

This is how the story begins: his step-brothers held a meeting and said to one another: "This Yusuf and his brother [Benjamin] are loved more by our father than us, even though we are a group of ten and can help him more than them. In fact, our father is clearly mistaken. Let us kill Yusuf or throw him out to some far-off land so that the attention of our father turns exclusively towards us, after that, we may again become righteous people!"

At this one of them said: "Do not kill Yusuf, but if you must, throw him into some dark well, so that he may be picked up by some passing by caravan."

After this meeting, they asked their father: "O our father! Why is it that you do not trust us with Yusuf, though we are his sincere well-wishers? Send him with us tomorrow, that he may play and enjoy himself. We shall take good care of him."

Their father said: "I will be worried if you take him away, for I fear lest a wolf should eat him up while you are off your guard."

They said: "If a wolf could eat him despite our number, then surely we would be worthless people!"

When after such persistence they were able to take him away, they resolved to throw him into a dark well. We revealed this [to Yusuf]: "A time will come when you will admonish them about this act of theirs, now they do not perceive its consequences."

At nightfall they return to their father, weeping. They said: "Father! We went off to compete in racing with one another, and left Yusuf by our belongings, and a wolf ate him! But you will not believe us even though we are telling the truth."

As proof they brought his shirt stained with false blood. "No!" he cried, "Your souls have tempted you to evil. I need good patience! Allah Alone can help me bear the loss you are speaking of."

On the other side, a caravan passed by, and sent a water carrier who let down his bucket into the well. Seeing Yusuf in it, he shouted with joy: "Good news! I found a young boy." They concealed him like trade merchandise. But Allah knew what they did. They [brought him to Egypt and] sold him for a petty price, a few dirhams [silver coins], they had such a low estimation of him.

The Egyptian who bought Yusuf said to his wife: "Be kind to him. He may prove useful to us, or we may adopt him as a son." Thus We established Yusuf in the land and arranged to teach him the understanding of affairs. Allah has full power over His affairs; though most people do not know.

When he reached maturity, We bestowed on him wisdom and knowledge.

Thus do We reward the righteous. Now, the lady of the house [his master's wife] attempted to seduce him. She bolted the doors and said: "Come!" He replied: "May Allah protect me from this! My lord has provided me with good residence. Should I betray his trust? Such wrongdoers shall not prosper." She advanced toward him, and he would have advanced towards her had he not seen a sign from his Rabb. Thus did We shielded him from indecency and immodesty, for he was one of Our chosen, a sincere devotee.

They both rushed to the door. In order to stop him she caught his shirt, and as a result she ripped his shirt from behind. At the door they met her husband. Seeing him she cried: "What punishment does someone who intended evil against your wife deserve except imprisonment or a painful chastisement?"

Yusuf said: "It was she who attempted to seduce me." At this—one accusing the other—one member of her own family bore witness saying: "If his shirt is ripped from the front, then she is speaking the truth and he is lying. But if it is ripped from behind, then he is speaking the truth and she is lying."

So when he [her husband] saw that Yusuf's shirt was ripped from behind, he said to her: "It is one of the tricks of you women! Your trick was mighty indeed! O Yusuf, say no more about this, and you [O my wife] seek forgiveness for your sins, for you were indeed the wrongdoer."

The women of the city began to talk about this incident, saying: "The wife of Al-Aziz has seduced her young slave, for she has fallen madly in love with him. In fact, we see her in manifest error."

When she heard about these remarks, she invited them and prepared for them a banquet, and gave each of them a knife. When they were engaged in cutting fruit, she asked Yusuf to come out before them. When they saw him, they were so amazed that they cut their hands and exclaimed spontaneously: "Good Lord! He is no human being; he is but a noble angel."

She said: "Well, this is he about whom you blamed me. No doubt I seduced him, but he escaped. If he doesn't do what I say, he will certainly be thrown into prison and be disgraced."

Yusuf said: "O my Rabb! I would rather go to prison than that to which they invite me; and unless You ward off their cunning snare from me, I may, in my youthful folly, feel inclined towards them and become one of the ignorant."

Thereupon his Rabb granted his prayer and warded off their cunning snare from him; surely He hears all and knows all.

Still, even after all the evidence they had seen [of his innocence and the guilt of their women], they thought it proper to send him to prison for a while. Two young men also entered the prison along with him. One day one of them said: "I saw in a dream that I was pressing wine." The other said: "I saw in a dream that I was carrying bread on my head, of which birds were eating." Tell us the interpretation of these dreams, for we see that you are a man of virtue.

Yusuf replied: "I will, with Allah's permission, tell you the interpretation of these dreams before you are served the food you eat, this is part of the knowledge which my Rabb has taught me. In fact, I have forsaken the faith of those people who do not believe in Allah and even deny the hereafter."

"I follow the faith of my forefathers Ibrahim [Abraham], Ishaq [Isaac] and Ya'qoob [Jacob]. It is not fitting that we attribute any partners with Allah. It is the grace of Allah on us and on mankind [that He has not made us the servants of anyone else other than Himself], yet most of the people are not grateful. O my fellow inmates! Tell me what is better; many different lords or one Allah, the Irresistible? Those you serve besides Him are nothing but mere names which you and your forefathers have invented, for which Allah has revealed no sanction. The Command belongs to none but Allah, Who has commanded that you worship none but Him. That is the true faith, yet most of the people do not know."

"O my fellow inmates! [Here is the interpretation of your dreams], one of you will be released and serve wine to your lord (the king of Egypt); and the other will be crucified and the birds will eat from his head. That's how your cases will be decided concerning which you inquired [that is the answer to your question]."

Then, to the one who he thought would be released, he said: "Mention me to your lord." But Shaitan made him forget to mention [Yusuf] to his lord, so he remained in the prison a few more years.

One day the king of Egypt said: "I saw seven fat cows in my dream which were eaten up by seven lean cows, likewise I saw seven green ears of corn and seven others that were dried up. O chiefs! Tell me the meaning of my dream if you can interpret the dreams."

They replied: "Confused nightmares! We are not skilled in the interpretation of dreams."

Thereupon one of the two inmates who was released remembered Yusuf after all that time, and he said: "I will tell you its interpretation; just send me to Yusuf in the prison." He came to Yusuf in the prison and said: "O Yusuf the truthful one! Tell us the meaning of the dream of seven fat cows which are eaten up by seven lean ones and of seven green ears of corn and seven others dried up: so that I may return to the people and let them know the meaning of this dream."

He replied: "You will cultivate for seven consecutive years. During this time you should leave the corn you reap in the ear, except what may be sufficient for your food. Then, after that period, there will come upon you seven hard years which will eat away all that you had stored except a little which you may have specifically set aside. After that period will come a year of abundant rain, in which the people will squeeze the juice."

The king said: "Bring this man to me." When the messenger came to Yusuf, he said: "Go back to your lord and ask him about the case of those women who cut their hands. Indeed my Rabb has full knowledge of their snare."

The king questioned those women, saying: "What do you say about the incident when you attempted to seduce Yusuf?" They replied: "God forbid! We know of no evil on his part." The 'Aziz's wife said: "Now that the truth has come to light, it was I who attempted to seduce him. In fact he is absolutely truthful."

Yusuf said, "By this inquiry I meant to let him [Al-Aziz] know that I did not betray him in his absence, and that Allah does not let the snare of the treacherous succeed. Not that I am free from sin—man's soul is prone to evil, except the one to whom my Rabb has shown mercy, certainly my Rabb is Forgiving, Merciful."

The king said: "Bring him to me; I will take him for my special service." When Yusuf had a talk with the King, he said: "From now on, you have an honorable place with us, and you will enjoy our full confidence."

Yusuf said: "Place me over all the resources of the land. Certainly I know how to manage; I have the necessary knowledge."

Thus We established Yusuf in the land to live therein in any way he wished. We bestow Our mercy on whom We please and We do not let the reward of good people go to waste. Yet the reward in the hereafter will be even better for those who believe and are righteous.

Several years later when the famine started and there was no food available outside of Egypt, Yusuf's brothers came to Egypt for food and entered his office. He recognized them but they did not recognize him. When he had given them their due provisions and they were about to leave, he said: "Bring your half brother to me next time. Do you not see that I give full measure and provide the best hospitality? But if you do not bring him, you shall have no grain, nor shall you even come near me again."

They replied: "We shall certainly try our best to bring him from his father. This we will surely do."

Yusuf told his servants to put his brother's money into their saddlebags secretly so that they should know about it only when they reach their family, so that they may come back again.

When Yusuf's brothers returned to their father, they said: "Father! Grain is henceforth denied us unless we take our stepbrother with us; please send our brother with us so that we may get our measure; we take full responsibility for his safety."

He said: "Should I trust you with him as I once trusted you with his brother? Allah is the best protector and He is the Most Merciful of the mercy-givers."

When they opened their baggage, they discovered that their money had been returned to them. "Father!" They cried with joy, "What more can we ask for? Here is our money returned back to us. We will buy more food for our family, we will take good care of our brother and obtain an extra camel load of grain. This way, it will be easy to add another camel load of grain."

Ya'qoob [Jacob] replied: "I will never send him with you until you pledge in the name of Allah that you will surely bring him back to me unless you become helpless." And when they had given their pledge, he said: "Allah is the Witness over the pledge you made."

Then he said, "My sons! Do not enter the capital city of Egypt through one gate, enter from the different gates. Not that I can avail you aught against Allah; this advice is just a precaution, because none can accurately judge except Allah. In Him do I put my trust and in Him let all the reliant put their trust."

When they entered the city as their father had advised them, it did not avail them against the will of Allah. Of course, Ya'qoob did his best to avert the fear he had in his heart. Indeed he possessed the knowledge which We had given him, but most people do not know.

When they entered to Yusuf, he called his brother [Benjamin] alone to himself, and said: "In fact, I am your brother [Yusuf], now you need not grieve at what they have been doing."

While Yusuf was arranging the loading of their provisions, he put the royal drinking cup into his brother's pack. Later on a crier called out: "O people of the caravan! You must be thieves."

They turned back and asked: "What have you lost?"

The royal servants said: "We have lost the King's drinking cup. [The leader of the royal servants added] and the one who brings it, will be awarded a camel-load of corn, I guarantee it."

Yusuf's brothers said: "By Allah! You should know, by our behavior during our stay here, that we did not come here to make mischief in the land and we are no thieves."

The royal servants said: "What should be the punishment of the thief, if you are liars?"

They replied: "The punishment of he in whose pack you find the royal cup will be to make him your bondsman, that's how we punish wrongdoers."

After this Yusuf first began to search the packs of his step-brothers before the pack of his own brother [Benjamin]. Finally he took it out of his brother's pack. Thus We directed Yusuf. He could not seize his brother under the King's law; but Allah willed otherwise. We exalt in ranks whom We please, He is the One Whose knowledge is far greater than the knowledge of all others.

At this accusation, his brothers remarked: "This is not strange if he has committed a theft—for his brother also committed a theft before him." Hearing this, Yusuf suppressed his feelings and did not reveal anything to them—he simply whispered to himself: "What a bad people you are! You are accusing me of something, the truth of which Allah knows best."

They said: "O noble prince! He [Benjamin] has a very aged father who may not be able to survive without him, so please take one of us instead of him. We see that you are one of those who do good to others."

Yusuf replied: "God forbid that we should seize other than the one with whom we found our property: if we did so then indeed we would be unjust."

When they lost their hope of moving Yusuf, they went aside to confer in private. The eldest of them said: "You know that your father had taken a solemn pledge in the name of Allah, and you also know how you fell short of your duty with respect to Yusuf. Therefore, I am not going to leave this land until my father gives me permission or Allah decide for me, and He is the best of all judges."

"Go back to your father and tell him, 'Father, your son committed theft. We did not see him stealing, we testify only to what we know. How could we guard against the unforeseen?'"

"You may enquire from the people of the city where we lodged and the caravan in which we travelled that we are indeed telling the truth."

When they went back and told all this to their father, "No!" cried their father. "Your souls have contrived a story for you. Well, I will bear this too with good patience. Maybe Allah will bring them all back to me; indeed He is the Knowledgable, the Wise."

He turned his face away from them, crying: "Alas for Yusuf!" His eyes became white with grief, and he became sorely oppressed with grief.

They said: "By Allah! It appears that you will not cease to remember Yusuf until you ruin your health or kill yourself."

He said: "I complain of my distress and grief to Allah Alone and I know from Allah what you do not know."

"O my sons! Go and search for Yusuf and his brother. Never give up hope of Allah's mercy; in fact none despairs of Allah's mercy except the unbelieving people."

When they went back to Egypt and entered Yusuf's office, they said: "Noble prince! We and our family are in great distress, we have hardly any money, please give us full quota and also some charity. Surely Allah rewards the charitable."

Hearing this, Yusuf, who could contain himself no longer, replied: "Do you know what you did to Yusuf and his brother while acting out of ignorance?"

This took them by surprise, and they cried: "What! Are you really Yusuf?" He said: "Yes! I am Yusuf and this is my brother. Allah has indeed been gracious to us. In fact as for the righteous and patient; Allah really does not let the reward of the righteous be wasted."

They said: "By Allah! Certainly Allah has preferred you over us. We have indeed been guilty."

Yusuf said: "There is no blame on you today. May Allah forgive you! He is the most Merciful of those who show mercy! Go, take this shirt of mine and cast it over the face of my father, he will recover his sight. Then come back to me with all the members of your family."

When the caravan started [from Egypt] their father [who was in Ken'an] said: "Certainly I feel the scent of Yusuf, even though you may think I am out of my mind." The people, who heard him, said: "By Allah! You are still suffering from your old illusion."

But when the bearer of the good news arrived, he cast the shirt of Yusuf over his face and he regained his sight. Then he said: "Didn't I tell you that I know from Allah what you do not know?"

They said: "Father! Pray for the forgiveness for our sins. We have indeed done wrong."

He replied: "Soon I will ask my Rabb for your forgiveness; surely He is the One who is the Forgiving, the Merciful."

When they came to Yusuf, he asked his parents to lodge with himself, and said: "Now enter the city. Allah willing, you will live here in peace."

After entering the city he helped his parents to seats on the throne, and they all fell down in prostration before him. "This," said Yusuf to his father, "is the interpretation of my dream which I dreamt long before. My Rabb has really made it come true. It was His grace that He took me out of prison and brought you all here from the desert even though Shaitan had stirred up strife between me and my brothers. For sure my Rabb fulfills His plan in mysterious ways. Surely He is the One Who is the Knowledgable, the Wise.

"O Rabb! You have indeed given me a kingdom and taught me the interpretation of dreams. O, the Creator of the heavens and the earth, You are my Protector in this world and in the hereafter, make me die as a Muslim and admit me among the righteous."

"O Muhammad, this story which We have revealed to you is a tale of the unseen; for you were not there with [the brothers of Yusuf] when they collectively conspired and schemed against him. Yet strive as you may, most men are not going to become believers, even though You do not demand any recompense for this information. This Qur'an is nothing but a reminder for all the people of the worlds. There are many signs in the heavens and the earth which they pass by; yet they pay no attention to them! As a result most of them who believe in Allah also commit shirk. Do they feel secure that Allah's scourge will not fall on them, or that the Hour of Doom will not come upon them suddenly while they do not suspect it? Tell them plainly: 'This is my way. I invite you to Allah with sure knowledge which I and my followers possess. Glory be to Allah, and I am not one of the mushrikin.'

"All the Rasools that We sent before you, O Muhammad, were human beings, to whom We sent Our Revelations after choosing them from the people of their town. Have these unbelievers not traveled through the land and seen what was the end of those who passed away before them? From their destiny you should know that the home of the hereafter is better for those who are righteous. Why don't you understand? Respite was granted until the Rasools gave up hope of their people and realized that they were being treated as liars, Our help came to them and We delivered those whom We pleased; and Our scourge was not averted from the criminal people. There is a lesson in these stories of former people for the men of common sense. This story of Yusuf revealed in the Qur'an is not an invented tale, but a confirmation of previous scriptures—a detailed exposition of all things, and is a guidance and blessing for the people who believe. (Surah 1–111)

Genesis, the first book of the Bible ends with these words:

Then Joseph asked his people to make a vow. "Promise me," he said, "that when God leads you to that land, you will take my body with you." So Joseph died in Egypt at the age of one hundred and ten. They embalmed his body and put it in a coffin. (Genesis 50:25–26)

Exodus 13:19 alludes to the belief that Moses and the Children of Israel took Joseph's remains with them when they left Egypt hundreds of years later—a verse which many scholars attribute to the priestly editors at a later date, added as an afterthought. In 1905, the tomb of an Egyptian official was discovered in the Valley of the Kings, normally reserved for royalty, a discovery that calls the biblical account into question.

The official, named Yusuf, and his wife are among the best-preserved mummies of all time, and their tomb furnishings were the most extensive until the discovery of King Tut's tomb seventeen years later. They were not royal, as determined by the pose and the jewelery, and the man appeared foreign in many important respects. The burial of a foreign commoner at this royal site seems justified by the inscription on his tomb: "Father of the Pharaoh." We know that Joseph's wives were Egyptian, and Hebrews neither embalmed nor used coffins in those days, unless they had Egyptian wives and were highly placed in Egyptian society.

Through the twentieth century, research at Cairo and Cambridge Universities continued the investigations into the identity of this remarkable corpse. In 1987, Harper and Row published the book *Stranger in the Valley of the Kings* by Ahmed Osman, which appears to establish beyond all reasonable doubt that we have found Joseph's body.

The Arab side of the family always maintained that Joseph was buried in Egypt, as both the Bible and the Qur'an record, and he holds an especially honored place in their history. The desire of both Jews and Muslims to claim his bones is no more surprising than for such an arcane old story to be revived as a musical by a Christian church organist, Andrew Lloyd Webber, presented on Broadway, and even practiced every winter in the gym at local high schools and synagogues and churches all over the world. How can all this be so when, according to the media and the public school curricula, these old religious stories have no relevance to modern life? Or is this story also part of the foundation of the modern world?

Pope John XXIII is reputed to have welcomed a delegation of Muslim leaders at the Second Vatican Council with the greeting, "I am Joseph, your brother," a story told at interfaith gatherings with fondness by Muslims. The sentiment was noble, and not as patronizing as it appears, since his first name, Giuseppe, is the Italian equivalent of Joseph. That was the beginning of an era of reconciliation, led in many ways by the Roman Catholic Church. He used the same greeting later with a delegation of Jews and these greetings were made into a movie, *I Am Joseph, Your Brother*, which is available from Roman Catholic distribution services.

The more recent approach of Pope John Paul II was to visit the Western Wall (sometimes called the Wailing Wall) in Jerusalem on March 26, 2000, not to observe, but to pray and to leave a note in a crack between the stones asking for forgiveness for the sins of Christians toward Jews. A year later, on May 6, 2001, this same pontiff was the first pope ever to attend prayers at a mosque, when he worshipped at the Omayyad Mosque in Damascus, where he greeted the people, "Dear Muslim Friends, As-salámu 'aláikum!"

11

The Foundation

Musa/Moses

BEDROCK MATERIALS for the moral foundation of Western civilization and aspects of the emerging world civilization were quarried from the primitive legal systems of Sumerian, Babylonian, Egyptian, and possibly Hittite sources. There are connections with the ethical endowments of related Indo-European cultures, and resemblances to the moral codes of other ancient cultures connected through Adam by migrations back in the mists of prehistory.

That universal moral foundation has roots in a quasi-covenant between God and Noah, took further form in the covenant God made with Abraham and his family, and was codified by God in the Commandments given to Moses on Mount Sinai. The divine law code known as the Ten Commandments is a distillation and a crystallization of what is required, at a minimum, in human relationships with God and with each other, in all places and at all times.

The "politically correct" desire to treat all citizens and their cultures fairly has led to controversy in the United States and elsewhere. Certain religious protagonists wish to display the Ten Commandments in public places, as if to gain precedence for one particular religious tradition of American values. Opponents object that to do so would offend those of other religions, though that charge seems to be led mainly by those who have fallen away from all religious practices and may wish not to be reminded of the rock from which they were hewn. Certainly the objections to the Ten Commandments rarely come from Hindus, Sikhs, or Buddhists, any more than from practicing Jews, Christians, or Muslims.

It is a simple matter to illustrate that the American legal system is not literally based on the Ten Commandments, several of which would be considered unconstitutional. Murder is against the law but adultery is not, in most states. Honoring one's parents is healthy and advisable, but swearing at them is not an indictable offense.

However, a general acknowledgment of the Ten Commandments is appropriate in some situations, not because of their association with current laws, but because they represent the essence of the ancient Jewish foundation of universal moral law, just as India claims precedence in the ethos of nonviolent action and Greece has an historic identification with Olympic ideals in sport.

As the philosophical basis for English Common Law and the French Civil Code, the Ten Commandments influenced the American Constitution, which was itself a model for the Japanese Constitution. Imbedded in the Swiss Civil Code, the Ten Commandments became the moral framework for the modern constitution of Turkey. The impact of this code throughout the Muslim world is profound, as another one-fifth of humanity seeks to strictly implement the principles of the Mosaic code, as attested frequently in the words of the Qur'an itself. It is reflected in Sharia Law, which might be more universally accepted if its relation to the Ten Commandments was developed, based on an interpretation of the Mosiac Commandments as provided by Allah to Muhammad, whose disciples continue to revere the letter of the law in the older version (regardless of more liberal developments elsewhere).

To all this we may add the direct lines of reference to the Ten Commandments in the systems of jurisprudence in more than one hundred modern countries that framed their independent constitutions on the basis of colonial experience under Britain, France, Spain, Portugal, and the Netherlands. Understandably, reference to the Ten Commandments is also in the constitution of the state of Israel. The words of the Ten Commandments are inscribed in the wood and stone of courtrooms and legislatures, from Manila through Nairobi and Cairo to Santiago, as well as Europe and America. Without denigrating other contributions to the emerging body of international law, it is no exaggeration to point to the Ten Commandments as critically foundational. The limits to this understanding are becoming clear, but the role and the value of these commandments cannot be denied.

In 2005, after lengthy hearings, the U.S. Supreme Court found a balance between displays intended as preferential and those which form part of the American landscape. In *McCreary County v. American Civil Liberties Union of Ky.*, the court ruled by a five-to-four vote that two courthouses in Kentucky could not display framed copies of the Ten Commandments on their walls, while a five-to-four majority decided in *Van Orden v. Perry* that it is constitutional for a six-foot monument inscribed with those same Ten Commandments to remain standing on the capitol grounds in Austin, Texas. If claims that the Ten Commandments are foundational in all these ways seem exaggerated to some, even the critics of this thesis might well concede "cornerstone" status to this Mosaic codification of the ancient covenant between Abraham and God. It may not fit smoothly into the secular context, but when humans began to respond to a formal code of ethics that had an external frame of reference (God saying "You do those things and I will do these things"), something fundamental happened on planet Earth.

Many codes have expressed this, including the Noahide Code, a somewhat strained attempt to find a universal code that is less specifically Jewish. But the Ten Commandments alone are acknowledged as representing this principle across continents and down through centuries. They are unique in that they summarize the codes that came before them and they endow those that come after them. The desire to enshrine them is more a proclamation that the secular context is insufficient in itself than any attempt to foist the religion of one group on others.

Religious people of all persuasions instinctively recognize this, and it is rarely they who raise objections. Within the family, Abraham, Isaac, Jacob, their wives, and the children of the covenant, most notably Moses, to whom God gave the codified Law, are all revered by Jews, Christians, and Muslims. With Christianity and Islam coming on the scene only in the so-called Common Era, the Jews alone were the custodians of that code for well over a millennium between Moses and Jesus, who summarized it, and for almost two millennia between Moses and Muhammad, who tells of it in the Qur'an.

It is widely recognized that Christianity sits on a Jewish foundation and Americans in particular frequently refer to a Judeo-Christian foundation of their new-world culture. It is not unreasonable to state that Western civilization has a Jewish moral foundation and the Ten Commandments are increasingly acknowledged as Judaism's inestimable contribution of the moral foundation to an emerging global culture.

Judaism's seeming vulnerability in the world might be countered by the recognition of this reality, with all the benefits that might accrue to the Jewish people if they had a more secure place in the human family. It is perhaps understandable that whoever brings a moral perspective is persecuted in a world never quite ready for moral life, but this oft-persecuted people is a very special community that should be cherished for its contribution in a more mature world. Hence this almost convoluted attempt at affirming the place of the Ten Commandments in world civilization. Securing the Jewish place in the fabric of world culture is business left over from twentieth-century horrors. We should simply get on with it in grateful appreciation, bringing to a close one of the most shabby aspects of the internecine conflicts within Abraham's family.

But the foundation is not everything. It is a starting point, not the whole structure, and not the conclusion of the matter. In a sense, the foundation is more like the basement, rather than the temple or the dome. Interpretation is required, and those who insist on taking the foundational code simply as it is are among the first to form little sects and cults around their own particular interpretations. Understood correctly, the Sharia is a divine abstract of the Law; the summary of the Law by Jesus is an interpretation; each person must work out his own ethical responsibilities in fear and trembling, as opposed to either merely obeying the Law or adopting the illusion that anything goes.

There are both personal and communal applications of the Law to be worked out in every age. The Ten Commandments are about fundamental relationships, but it is necessary for responsible believers to extend their application to the relationship between humans and their environment, for example, or between humans and their fellow creatures in the animal world. Even many who say they have moved "beyond belief" (rare birds in the twenty-first century) are merely insisting on moving on to application of these principles.

Muslims sometimes criticize Jews and Christians for neglecting the foundation and allowing it to fall into disrepair in their haste to build their own superstructures, the Chosen Nation or the Holy Church. Indeed, while the Christian Scriptures quote Jesus as saying that he came not to destroy the Law but to fulfill it, and while Gospels and Epistles alike acknowledge Moses as the great lawgiver, it is the Qur'an that gives greater place to the quest to recover the Law. The Qur'an holds Moses in the highest esteem and refers to him as the one to whom Allah gave the Law in its codified form. Later generations of Jews are blamed for falling away from the instructions given by God, as are the Christians, but the acknowledgment of the particular Jewish role is clear and can be built on today in Muslim-Jewish relations in particular.

This is an ongoing story. As indicated, "authorship" of the Ten Commandments is by God. Although God presented them first through Moses, our response has been influenced by his editors, compilers, translators, publishers, distributors, scholars, students, and readers. We also share in the story by writing our chapters as we journey through the Wilderness of Sin (an actual place named in the Bible). God is with us every step of the way.

In olden times it seemed that every five hundred or thousand years, someone was called by God to elucidate His Word in epic ways. Abraham, Moses, David, Jesus, and Muhammad would all seem to fit that description. Jacob and Joseph, Peter and Paul, and Abu Bakr and Ali are giants, but not quite in the same category. Neither is Homer or Plato, Shakespeare or Goethe, not even Marx, Freud, or Einstein, as much as they have contributed to or have affected humanity.

Few imagine that there is anyone alive in our time who will be remembered in three or four millennia. What then was so special about a man like Moses, the Lawgiver? The question is important enough for us to consider everything we know about his background from ancient Jewish and Egyptian sources, as well as later Christian and Muslim perspectives. As a new awareness of its value develops in the West, the Qur'an may be helpful in epitomizing the spiritual essence of the story, once critical abilities are developed in the reading of it. As noted in the story of Joseph, the details are essentially the same in Bible and Qur'an.

Traditional biblical interpolations suggest that there may have been four hundred years between Joseph and Moses. The time may be less, since it now begins to become difficult to be sure which type of calendar is in use. However, the change in the calendar happens just at the point where it hardly matters. The Hebrews grew in numbers by biological increase and intermarriage with other desert people moving into Egypt. They grew so numerous that the Egyptian population and its leadership felt threatened.

The mutually threatening relationship between these descendants of Israel and the Egyptian majority (descended from Ishmael) was as big in the news then as it is now. The exciting thing now is the possibility that, in our time, some of these old animosities might be resolved. Although much of the speculation on TV news seems dubious about the possibilities of a reconciliation, we may be on the brink of something historic. There must be an essential religious element in any solution of age-old problems. All of us may have a role to play in the absence of a Moses figure. We may be living at an historic turning point in these family relationships.

These ancient peoples, and many associated with them through Christianity and Islam, have one thing in common that is not found anywhere else in the world. They take monotheism, a belief in one God, as given. Most other religions have drifted toward belief in one God only in the twentieth century, when all their gods have been thought of as "faces of God." Even the Israelites of old had only been drifting in that direction. Until Moses, most used plural names for the Divinity, like *Elohim*, which literally means "gods," in their oldest stories.

Then something happened that changed everything; something that is still changing the former Soviet Union and China; something that may contain the only answer for Afghanistan and the Middle East; something that Europe and the Americas ignore at great peril. One God came in from the desert and His presence was announced to Pharaoh by Moses in a confrontation the world has never forgotten.

"Drifters" were sifting into Egypt like sand in a sandstorm. The Egyptian word for drifters, *Habiru*, was usually applied to all foreigners, not only the descendants of Israel, yet these Hebrews were the leading family in the slave ghetto. The term was an insult, but there were desert people joining Egyptian society at all levels—even marrying into the royal family. This situation is similar to modern cultures that need and yet sometimes resent both foreign laborers and foreign professionals—Mexicans in the United States; Eastern Europeans and Muslims from Turkey and North Africa in western Europe.

At about this time, Pharaoh Amenhotep III sent his 12-year-old son for a year of study in Matanni, northern Syria, as part of his education and preparation for rule over a vast empire. Fifteen-year-old Nefertiti, daughter of the King of Matanni, was sent along to be his companion and to help with language. Everything went according to plan, but given the importance of religion in Egypt, the young prince would have been mystified by the idea in this desert kingdom that there was but one God. He may have heard rumors of this idea among the drifter Habiru in Egypt, but had not previously given the matter much thought.

A few years later, the vassal king of Matanni proposed to the Pharaoh that they cement their alliance with a royal wedding. Amenhotep III discussed it with his respected first wife, Tye, who agreed that the beautiful Princess Nefertiti should indeed come as an additional young wife for the Pharaoh. She could assist with royal duties and help the queen with her aging husband, who was far too old and too repulsive for intimacy anyway. Even her son, the prince, urged the advancement of his young friend. "Mother, you can teach her everything. I can promise that she will be loyal to your interests."

Crown Prince and Drifter Princess were thrilled to be reunited in the Egyptian palace. Those not wanting foreigners called her kind Habiru behind her back, even though she was not descended from the Israelite slaves. They were Semitic distant cousins, with ideas of God found only in the desert. The city had gods of its own—too many gods—a characteristic of cities, even in our times.

Nefertiti was a beauty. Her famous bust is the most beautiful art treasure in the Berlin Museum to this day. Her story is told especially well in the 1975 "Archaeological Biography" *Nofretete* by Philipp Vandenberg, the noted author of *The Curse of the Pharaohs*, an investigation into the dozens of mysterious deaths connected with the opening of the tomb of King Tutankhamun.

Nefertiti was given the finest silks from India, as well as perfumes, furnishings of gold and transparent alabaster, and servants for every purpose. She amused the king, found favor with the queen, and loved the prince. She never lost the sincere simplicity that endeared her to the people. Nor did she lose that sense of a relationship with God, not the petty gods of fame and fortune, but the God of the desert places whom you could know only in your heart. This God was almost nameless, yet all pervasive; in all, under all, and behind everything. She thought a person could only know such a God in the desert, but she now experienced God in the city. Her prince would not ignore such spirituality. Nefertiti became the mother of monotheism in Western culture.

Two years later, Amenhotep III died, a great obese drunken glutton. His son was to be crowned Amenhotep IV, but he now represented a clean new lifestyle based on faith in a single God who had high standards for all of life, and who was represented symbolically by the sun, Aten. He took the name Akhenaten: "Pleasing God." A month later he married Nefertiti, and his mother, old Queen Tye, gave them all possible political and moral support. They shut down the temples and closed the cities of Memphis and Thebes, twin capitals of northern and southern Egypt. They built a new capital at Amarna, worshiped God, consolidated political control, and patronized the arts in a Camelot environment, like Washington in the Kennedy era or Ottawa under Trudeau.

But Akhenaten was not well and, moreover, had many enemies from the old regime. The family became paranoid about the line of succession. Akhenaten and Nefertiti had three daughters, a shaky succession to the throne. In contrast to formalized Egyptian art before and after this dynasty, we see the liberal spirit of this court in the famous picture of this royal family at play. In it, the king and queen bounce their daughters on their knees under the image of the sun and its rays, symbolizing God and His love. Tourists at the Cairo Meseum have made this picture a favorite, and copies are found around the world.

Powerful generals were running the country in the name of the sick Pharaoh, and photo opportunities did not make the throne secure. Old Queen Tye advised a political marriage of Ankesupaten, the eldest daughter, on the left in the picture, to Tutankamon, son of a powerful general, an old friend and ally. She hoped for a male heir from that marriage, but Ankesupaten was still a teenager, and "Tutmose," as King Tut would be known, was just 11 years old. No heirs were apparent, in spite of their best efforts, and the monarchy could collapse if Tut was not recognized or was murdered. Tut did indeed die, murdered or not, at 18 years of age, and his tomb, found in 1922, contained over a ton in golden furniture, and more valuable treasures than any other modern find to this day.

How did the regime survive to conduct such a burial and continue in power? What we have to this point is solid history, not biblical, but from Egyptian records that were stored in Tut's tomb, though the solution to this puzzle was first proposed by none other than Sigmund Freud, posing as "biblical scholar" in a 1937 monograph called *Moses and Monotheism* (his last significant work). Where could they find an heir, even just for appearances? Why would a princess adopt a Habiru baby hidden in the bulrushes? We just may have a snapshot of the adoptive mother of Moses in the royal photo, copies of which are available in Egyptian art galleries and souvenir shops everywhere.

The Bible tries to explain that Moses' name came from the Hebrew word *Mashah*, "to draw out," because he was drawn out of the water. But it was the Egyptian Princess who named him, so the name would be Egyptian, as Freud insists. If she wanted to make the point about an heir, she would likely have named him after the one pretending to be his father: Tutmose, or Moses for short. Scholars who now believe that the Hyksos and the Hebrews in Egypt were the same people have problems with this chronology, but it works quite well and serves to give us a realistic picture of palace intrigue and the kind of circumstances leading to the privileged upbringing and education of Moses. It even alludes to the spiritual dynamics of the brief Egyptian monotheistic court. By the time Moses was a young adult, Akhenaten had died, Tut had ruled briefly and died, and the two queens, Tye and Nefertiti, shared power through generals, but a cruel new pharaoh ruled.

When Moses had grown up, he went out to visit his people, the Hebrews, and he saw how they were forced to do hard labor. He even saw an Egyptian beating a Hebrew, one of Moses' own people. Moses looked all round, and when he saw that no one was watching, he killed the Egyptian and hid his body in the sand. The next day he went back and saw two Hebrew men fighting. He said to the one who was in the wrong, "Why are you beating up a fellow-Hebrew?" The man answered, "Who made you our ruler and judge? Are you going to kill me just as you killed that Egyptian?" Then Moses was afraid and said to himself, "People have found out what I have done." When the king heard about what had happened, he tried to have Moses killed, but Moses fled and went to live in the land of Midian. (Exodus 2:11–15)

Moses became a drifter again and, when he befriended some shepherd girls at a well (a midrash repeated from the experience of the earlier patriarchs), they took him home to their father, Jethro. Jethro took Moses on as foreman, gave him a daughter named Ladybird in marriage, and they had a son.

Moses had a lot of time to think out under the desert stars. He was born and bred for leadership. When he heard that the Pharaoh who had been looking for him had died, only to be replaced by one even more cruel, he could not stop thinking about the Hebrew slaves. They were like a nation within a nation, and some of them claimed a covenant of destiny with God. He must have been thinking, "God? Who is God? Where can any God be found in all this?"

Moses had heard from his own mother and from his adoptive grandmother, Nefertiti, that there is but one God, though all the lesser gods of Egypt had made a comeback since she and her idealistic young king had tried to sweep them out of the palace. He had not paid a lot of attention. Moses hardly knew the name of his grandmother's God, reminding us of some people today. Muslims have been recovering a dynamic sense of God for the last fifty years, and since the collapse of communism, Russians have begun to recover their memory of God. They are not the only ones. This desert God, trying to catch the attention of Moses, wants the attention of the modern world. After a century of secular "progress," Christendom is trying to adapt to this reality. Even China is taking notice, as are the secular Jews of New York City.

One day, while all these thoughts were heavy on his mind, both conscious and subconscious, Moses saw something in the desert that caused him to stop and think. It may have been a natural phenomenon, but it was the moment when he saw God as a reality, a force, a spirit of power with a plan. This God had the intent and the resources to move into Egypt—or in modern times Cairo, Kabul, Moscow, Toronto, Washington, or New York—to set the captives free and to be their God, a God adequate for any challenge or circumstance, ancient or modern, national or personal. Moses took the shoes off his feet, as he sensed he stood on holy ground, just as Jews and Christians do at a mosque when they go to show solidarity with their anxious Muslim neighbors in these similarly troubled times.

We all know about the burning bush. Was it a sunset, or the burnoff from a natural gas well? Was it the heart of Moses that God set on fire, expressed in concrete poetic imagery? It does not matter. There is no doubt in the world that God spoke to Moses, "loud and clear." Like the big bang of creation, the impact is still reverberating.

When God revealed his plan, Moses resisted as we all do: "Your

demands, God, are too great." . . . "My demands are your only hope." . . .
"But I am not a public speaker." . . . "Your brother Aaron will handle that
part." . . . "I am not a theologian." . . . "Your sister Miriam has all
that under control." . . . "I can't even tell the people your name." . . . And
God said:

> "I AM who I AM. This is what you must say to them: 'The one who is called
> I AM has sent me to you.' Tell the Israelites that I, the Lord, the God of their
> ancestors, the God of Abraham, Isaac and Jacob, have sent you to them. This
> is my name for ever; this is what all future generations are to call me." (Exo-
> dus 3:14–15)

I AM, "*Ehyeh Yehweh*" in Hebrew, is usually rendered inadequately in
English as LORD or GOD, from the Old German, *Gott*. The verb *hayah*,
"to be," is at the root of this name, and translators have tried everything: "I
Am Who I Am," "I Am What Will Be," "I Am the Essence of All," "I Am
Existence," "I Am the Source of Life," "I Am All There Is," "I Am in What
Is Happening."

In this noun/verb we can connect consciously with the basis of life in the
universe and its meaning. For many people, the word *God* has lost its power
through over-familiarity and its use "in vain." Sixty years ago, soon after
World War II, German theologian Paul Tillich proposed at Harvard University that the world stop using the word *God* for a generation and substitute
the phrase "Ground of Our Being" until we had recaptured the essence of
its meaning; but, of course, that did not catch on despite the I AM ring to it.

This God who is Lord of everything—over all, in all, under all, behind
all—may confront us more easily in the desert, at our grandparents' farm,
or at the cottage, but this God insists on coming in from the desert to invade
the city and to pervade our lives. At this point in the Bible story, we have
become prepared for the societal changes that come next, not only in
ancient Egypt, but what is supposed to happen in modern Kabul, Moscow,
London, Toronto, and Washington when God is identified. One suspects
that Pharaoh is quite unprepared, since "the powers that be" always need
the people of God to confront them at such moments.

We do not know the city gods as well by their Egyptian names, but they
will be confronted in the plagues. We know these symbolic gods somewhat
better by their Greek and Roman names. Many modern people fail to make
the connection, but their lives are just as easily dominated by Mamon, the
god of money; Bacchus, the god of wine; Eros, the god of sex; and Asclepius,
the god whose cult is physical health. People make generous offerings to

these gods and goddesses: Venus, the goddess of beauty; Athena, the goddess of learning; and Mars, the god of war.

What happened in the Moses event was the "burning" realization that there was truly only One God. Following Moses, we realize that life is meaningful only when we serve that One with heart, soul, mind, and strength. Moses' ancestors had intuitive sayings about this, and had taught their understandings in the stories told by this slave people in Moses' time— stories still told today. Those who will not listen are Canaan's modern brothers and sisters and the warnings about their fate should be heeded in the fields of the environment, material possessions, and religious extremism, whether in fundamentalism or atheism.

The force of impact from Moses' encounter with God in the burning bush overturned the Pharaoh, freed the slaves, and gave people of faith the courage to flee into the desert. This happened as the earth itself was rocking and reeling in a tsunami-like upheaval of the Red Sea that favored the naked poor over the landlords in their teetering palaces. Atlantis sank, Santorini rose from the floor of the Mediterranean, and the Red Sea drained and then refilled. God spoke and the people heard His voice. God said "I AM and you can be."

For purposes of instruction and meditation, the Qur'an lists the following in scattered, random order: Moses' birth and concealment in the bulrushes (in a "floating chest"); the roles of his sister and mother; his youth in the palace; loyalty to the Hebrew people; murder on their behalf; betrayal by them; flight to the desert; shepherding career; marriage; the burning bush; the call to ministry; objections, Aaron's role; confrontations with Pharaoh; competitions with magicians; plagues; exodus; pursuit; Red Sea crossing; desert pilgrimage; manna and quail; water from the rock; rebellions; revelation of the Law at Mount Sinai; the Golden Calf; sighting of the Promised Land; spies; blessing the people; and one final submission to God. The whole story of Moses is there, in the typical Qur'anic format to which non-Muslims are slowly becoming accustomed.

The burning bush revelation of God's nature to Moses was the most significant event in his life, and it changed everything. The revelation of the Law on Sinai was the distillation of that experience and all that followed, in a format that could be simply and easily taught to the people. That codified version of Moses' encounter with God has always been easier to communicate, but perhaps more difficult to obey. People still need the direct personal encounter with God I AM. The foundation for each person's life and for the life of the world was made concrete and "set in stone" on Mount Sinai, but to be effectual, it still needs to be rooted in a personal covenant

with I AM, as well as in the corporate, communal expression of that covenant in public worship.

It was We who revealed the Law to Musa. Therein was guidance and light.
The Jews have been judged by its standards, by their prophets who bowed in
submission to the will of Allah, by their Rabbis and by their Doctors of the
Law. For to them was entrusted the protection of Allah's Book, and they were
witnesses to its creation. (Surah 5:47)

And in their footsteps we sent 'Isa, the son of Maryam, confirming the Law
that had come before him. We sent the Gospel. Therein was guidance and
light, and confirmation of the Law, a guidance and an admonition to those
who fear Allah. (Surah 5:50)

And to thee [Muhammad] We sent the Scripture in truth, confirming Scriptures that came before you, to guard it all in safety. So judge between them by
what Allah hath revealed and not by their vain desires, diverging from the
truth that has come to thee. (Surah 5:51)

To each among you We have prescribed a Law and an open way. If Allah had
so willed, He would have made you a single people, but His plan is to test you
in what He has given you. So strive in virtues as in a race. The goal for all of
you is Allah. It is He that will show you the truth of the matters in which ye
dispute. (Surah 5:51)

I AM thy Lord! (Surah 20:12)

I AM God! (Surah 20:14)

I AM Allah! (Surah 28:30)

12

Three Kings

Saul, David, Solomon/Talut, Dawoud, Sulaimon

Art thou not aware of those elders of the children of Israel after the time of
Musa? They said unto a prophet [Samuel] of theirs, "Raise up a king for us,
[and] we shall fight in Allah's cause."

Said he, "Would you, perchance, refrain from fighting if fighting is
ordained for you?"

They answered, "And why should we not fight in Allah's cause when we
and our children have been driven from our homelands?"

Yet when fighting was ordained for them, they did turn back, save for a
few of them, but Allah had full knowledge of the evil doers.

And their prophet said unto those elders, "Behold, now Allah has raised
up Talut [Saul] to be your king."

They said, "How can he have dominion over us when we have a better
claim to dominion than he, and he has not [even] been endowed with abundant wealth?"

[The prophet] replied, "Behold, Allah has exalted him above you, and
endowed him abundantly with knowledge and bodily perfection. And Allah
bestows His dominion upon whom He wills: for Allah is infinite, all knowing."

And their prophet said unto them: "Behold, it shall be a sign of his [right-
ful] dominion that you will be granted a heart endowed by your Sustainer with
inner peace and with all that is enduring in the angel-borne heritage left
behind by the House of Musa and the House of Haroon [Aaron]. Herein,
behold there shall indeed be a sign for you if you are [truly] believers."

And when Talut set out with his forces, he said, "Behold, Allah will now
try you by a river: he who shall drink of it will not belong to me, whereas he
who shall refrain from tasting it—he, indeed, will belong to me; but forgiven
shall be he who shall scoop up but a single handful."

However, save for a few of them, they all drank [their fill] of it. And as soon as he and those who kept faith with him had crossed the river, the others said, "No strength have we today [to stand up] against Galoot [Goliath] and his forces!"

[Yet] those who knew with certainty that they were destined to meet Allah, replied: "How often has a small host overcome a great host by Allah's leave! For Allah is with those who are patient in adversity."

And when they came face to face with Galoot and his forces, they prayed: "O our Sustainer! Shower us with patience in adversity, and make firm our steps, and succour us against the people who deny the truth!"

And thereupon, by Allah's leave, they routed them. And Dawoud [David] slew Galoot; and Allah bestowed upon him dominion, and wisdom, and imparted to him the knowledge of whatever He willed.

And if Allah had not enabled the people to defend themselves against one another, corruption would surely overwhelm the earth; but Allah is limitless in His bounty unto all the worlds. (Surah 2:246–251, Asad Version, amended re names)

IS THIS MATERIAL from the Qur'an a faint echo of stories we have in more detail and more accurately in the Bible? Or does this recall a more ancient account than any of the manuscripts possessed by Jews and Christians, a corrective offered by God through Muhammad? Or is this divine poetry with spiritual images that, understood deeply, might touch our hearts and guide our minds? A further hint on how the Qur'an may be appreciated will come in a subsequent chapter when we consider more fully the possibility of its figures presenting "types" of characters and ideas. Meanwhile, let us compare this summary with the tone in the material found in the Jewish texts.

Samuel (Shammil in the Hadith) was the prophet in question, of course. Samuel began his work in a period of lawless confusion. By the end of his time, Israel had become a unified nation on the brink of its greatest era of all time under monarchs handpicked by Samuel. The Israelites wanted a king, so that they might be like other nations. Samuel's first instinct was to protest that their whole purpose as a nation was to become a new kind of nation, not like all the others. He knew that kings often demand an allegiance that belongs only to God, a prescient anticipation that could be fulfilled only by the Messiah as the King of Kings, but the people insisted. Samuel prayed about it before God and then went back to the people again.

He said, "These will be the manner of the king who will reign over you; he will take your sons and appoint them for himself, to his chariots and to be his horsemen, and some shall run before his chariots. And he will appoint him captains over thousands and captains over fifties, and will set them to clear his ground, and to reap his harvest, and to make his instruments of war and the instruments of his chariots. And he will take your daughters to be confectioners, and to be cooks and to be bakers. He will take your fields, and your vineyards and your olive yards, even the best of them, and give them to his servants. And he will take the tenth of your seed, and of your vineyards, and give them to his officers, and to his servants. And he will take your menservants, and your maidservants, and your goodliest young men, and your asses, and put them to his work. He will take the tenth of your sheep; and ye shall be his servants. And ye shall cry out in that day because of your king which ye shall have chosen you; and the Lord will not hear you in that day."

Again they demanded a king. Again Samuel prayed about it and this time the Lord said to him, "Harken unto their voice, and make them a king." (Samuel 8:11–18)

For a first king over Israel, Saul (Talut) was not a bad choice, in the beginning anyway. He was from the smallest tribe, the tribe of Benjamin, so it was a smart choice politically. He was very tall and somewhat handsome, so he looked like a king. He drove away the Philistines and was lucky in battle. Napoleon once said that he would much prefer a commander-in-chief who was lucky over one who was smart, and the Bible never accused Saul of being smart. Sadly though, it was not long before everything Samuel predicted had come true, and worse.

Saul had been "anointed" to show he was under authority before God, and Samuel had warned him that the proof of his loyalty to God was that he should never fight for plunder or loot, but only defend Israel. When Saul began to enrich the royal treasury at the expense of Israel's neighbors, Samuel knew that the idea of becoming like other nations was in full flight. He condemned King Saul, decreed that God would find a worthy replacement, and headed for the hills to sulk, to pray, and to meditate on the future.

The search was on for a new king, even while Saul entrenched his position on the throne. Samuel realized that someone was needed, someone young enough to train in the ways of the Lord, again acceptable politically, probably attractive in the sense of having what we call charisma, but most especially this time, one who had a sense of humility before God.

And the Lord said unto Samuel, "How long wilt thou mourn for Saul, seeing I have rejected him from reigning over Israel? Fill thine horn with oil, and go. I will send thee to Jesse, the Bethlehemite, for I have provided me a king among his sons." And Samuel said, "How can I go? If Saul hears of it, he will kill me." And the Lord said, "Take an heifer with thee, and say, 'I am come to sacrifice to the Lord.' And call Jesse to the sacrifice and I will shew thee what thou shalt do: and thou shalt anoint unto me him whom I name unto thee."

And Samuel did that which the Lord spake, and came to Bethlehem, and the elders of the town trembled at his coming, and said, "Comest thou peaceably?" And he said, "Peaceably; I am come to sacrifice unto the Lord. Sanctify yourselves and come with me to the sacrifice." And he sanctified Jesse and his sons, and called them to the sacrifice. And it came to pass, that when they were come, that he looked on Eliab, and said, "Surely the Lord's anointed is before Him."

But the Lord said unto Samuel, "Look not on his countenance, or on the height of his stature, because I have refused him. For the Lord seeth not as man seeth; for man looketh on the outward appearance but the Lord looketh on the heart." Then Jesse called Abinadab, and made him pass before Samuel, and he said, "Neither hath the Lord chosen this." Then Jesse made Shummah to pass by, and he said, "Neither hath the Lord chosen this." Again, Jesse made seven of his sons to pass before Samuel, and Samuel said unto Jesse, "The Lord hath not chosen these."

And Samuel said unto Jesse, "Are here all your children?" And he said, "There remaineth yet the youngest, and, behold he keepeth the sheep." And Samuel said unto Jesse, "Send and fetch him, for we will not sit down until he come hither." And he sent and brought him in. Now he was ruddy, and withal of a beautiful countenance, and goodly to look to. And the Lord said, "Arise, anoint him, for this is he." Then Samuel took the horn of oil, and anointed him in the midst of his brethren, and the Spirit of the Lord came upon David from that day forward. (I Samuel 16)

The story of David and Goliath, as presented in I Samuel 17, is one of the best-known and most-loved vignettes in world literature. Christians and Jews all know it by heart, as do Muslims who know the characters as Dawoud and Galoot, so the details are not necessary, except for the spiritual emphasis that David brought to the situation.

And he took his staff in his hand, and chose him five smooth stones out of the brook . . . and his sling was in his hand as he drew near the Philistine. . . . And the Philistine said unto David, "Am I a dog, that thou comest to me with sticks?" Then said David to the Philistine, "Thou comest to me with a sword, but I come to thee in the name of the Lord of hosts, the God of the armies of Israel, whom thou hast defied. This day will the Lord deliver thee into my hand; that all the earth may know that there is a God in Israel."(I Samuel 17:40–46)

Muslims correctly insist that the order of the text is somewhat jumbled. This is because I Samuel comes from several sources edited together, and, as happens in other parts of the Bible, the editing is not always in order. For example, in verses just before the selection above from chapter 17, it is clear that Saul met David for the first time when the young boy took his slingshot onto the battlefield, but the next time he met David is actually several pages earlier, in chapter 16. Here David is already a little older and goes to the palace to play the harp for old King Saul during some of his manic-depressive episodes.

This teenager—athlete, musician, shepherd, military hero, and poet— already knew that it was God who had guided old Samuel to anoint him as the successor to Saul. He knew enough even then to leave the timing of that entirely in the hands of God. He kept quiet while he served the mad king and he even became true best friends with Saul's son, Prince Jonathan. The people of Israel turned David into a national hero, and he fled from the jealous king only to find his popular following increasing.

In the ensuing story, the warlords and rebels chasing around through caves is reminiscent of the landscape of Afghanistan we see on television, and the tone of the story reflects the code of honor that we might find only in such a culture.

And it came to pass, when Saul was returned from following the Philistines, that it was told him, saying, "Behold, David is in the wilderness of Engedi." Then Saul took three thousand chosen men out of all Israel, and went to seek David and his men upon the rocks of the wild goats. And he came to the sheepcotes by the way, where was a cave; and Saul went in to relieve himself in the very cave where David and his men were hid. And the men of David said unto him, "Behold, this is the day of which the LORD said unto thee, I will deliver thine enemy into thine hand, that thou mayest do to him as it shall seem good unto thee." Then David moved stealthily up behind the king, and slit off a piece of Saul's robe privily. And David whispered to his men, "The LORD forbid that I should do harm unto my master, the LORD'S anointed, to stretch forth mine hand against him, seeing he is the anointed of the LORD." So David restrained his servants with these words, and suffered them not to rise against Saul. Then Saul rose up out of the cave, and went on his way.

David also arose, and went out of the cave, and cried after Saul, saying, "My lord the king." When Saul looked back, David stooped with his face to the earth, and bowed himself. And David said to Saul, "Wherefore hearest thou men's words, saying, 'Behold, David seeketh thy hurt? Behold, this day the LORD delivered thee into mine hand in the cave: and some bade me kill thee: but I spared thee; and I said, I will not put forth mine hand against my lord; for he is the LORD'S anointed.' Moreover, my father, see the fringe of thy robe in my hand. Since I cut off the fringe of thy robe, and killed thee not, know thou and see that there is neither evil nor transgression in mine hand, and I have not sinned against thee; yet thou huntest my soul to take it."

"The LORD judge between me and thee, and the LORD avenge me of

thee: but mine hand shall not be upon thee. As saith the proverb of the
ancients, 'Wickedness proceedeth from the wicked': but mine hand shall not
be upon thee. After whom is the king of Israel come out? after whom dost
thou pursue? after a dead dog, after a flea. The LORD therefore be judge,
and judge between me and thee, and see, and plead my cause, and deliver me
out of thine hand."

And it came to pass, when David had made an end of speaking these words
unto Saul, that Saul said, "Is this thy voice, my son David?" And Saul lifted
up his voice, and wept. And he said to David, "Thou art more righteous than
I: for thou hast rewarded me good, whereas I have rewarded thee evil. And
thou hast shewed this day how that thou hast dealt well with me: forasmuch
as when the LORD had delivered me into thine hand, thou killedst me not.
For if a man find his enemy, will he let him go well away?"

"Wherefore the LORD reward thee good for that thou hast done unto me
this day. And now, behold, I know well that thou shalt surely be king after
me, and that the kingdom of Israel shall be established in thine hand. Swear
now therefore unto me by the LORD, that thou wilt not cut off my seed after
me, and that thou wilt not destroy my name out of my father's house." And
David sware unto Saul. And Saul went home; but David and his men remained
in their stronghold. (1 Samuel 24:1–22)

Abraham, Moses, and David are unique in the Scriptures in that they are
named after no one and no one is named after them. As the patriarch of
the family of Israel, the founder of the Hebrew religion, and the king who
established the Jewish nation, we recall them as patriarch, prophet, and pol-
itician, each leaving an indelible mark. David practically defines the ideal of
kingship in Israel and is also unique in prefiguring the lordship of Jesus
Christ in the understanding of Christians.

Jesus was a descendant of David among a people intuitively longing for
an Anointed One, a Messiah, or a Christ figure, and sometimes even articulating that instinct. Muhammad is not descended from David, in spite of
David's mixed Hebrew and Arab ancestry. Muhammad's line came from the
branch of the family established by Ishmael.

In the course of time, David succeeded Saul and led Israel to its pinnacle
of greatness as a nation. Yet there is also something of Canaan in him,
Noah's other son who would not heed the warnings. His stealing of another
man's wives (perhaps echoed in the Qur'an in the parable of the ewes), his
battles, his anguish at the death of an infant son, the execution of his own
beloved but rebellious son, and his ultimate and profound loyalty to God
are all reflected in the psalms David wrote.

Countless millions can recite portions of the Psalms of David by heart
today. The Bible asserts that David composed all the Psalms (some written

down by temple functionaries or by Solomon) but the Qur'an makes a "correction" here, attributing most of them to "Seth." Seth is an ancestor of David as the progenitor of the Messianic line, and possibly represents that most ancient literature, a proto-articulation anticipating that messianic intuition which was the Middle East's most profound instinct. Perhaps David did give voice to ancient melody, but David's own songs also rang true. Jews, Christians, and Muslims all see something prefiguring the Messiah in him.

David saw to the anointing of his youngest son, Solomon, by Zadok, the first High Priest in Jerusalem, though the ceremony took place out in the hill country at Gihon, where the monarchy had its roots, and where there was the most loyal political support. The royal succession went smoothly to Solomon, who indeed became a king like those of other nations. He was an oriental potentate with three hundred wives and seven hundred concubines, a public relations department that promoted his reputation for wisdom, a finance department that managed the treasury brilliantly, and a public works department that built splendid public buildings throughout the royal compound. This was at the top of a hill called Mount Zion in the heart of the capital city, Jerusalem, and it included the first permanent Temple since Israel had come in from the desert—superseding the shrines of the tribes.

Solomon's own actions in the religious sphere did uphold the role of a monarchy that is subservient to God, confirming both his wisdom and his devotion. However, he married an Egyptian daughter of the Pharaoh and allowed her to continue to worship her own gods, as did all of his wives and concubines, few of whom were Israelites. Their children, acceding to the throne, would change everything.

We catch something of the flavor of Solomon's reign from the Qur'an in a passage that preserves echoes of events merely hinted at in the Bible. This information may well have been part of the lore of the ancient Middle East, heard first as a rumor or folk tale by Muhammad, but articulated to him in the cave by the angel Gabriel as one of those psalm/poem revelations that he should recite. Its beauty in the Qur'an, as recited, is simply lost in translation.

And We verily gave knowledge unto Dawoud [David] and Sulaiman [Solomon], and they said: "Praise be to Allah, Who hath preferred us above many of His believing slaves!" And Sulaiman was Dawoud's heir. And he said: "O mankind! Lo! we have been taught the language of birds, and have been given [abundance] of all things. This surely is evident favor."

And there were gathered together unto Sulaiman his armies of the jinn spirits and humankind, and of the birds, and they were set in battle order; Till, when they reached the Valley of the Ants, an ant exclaimed: "O ants! Enter your dwellings lest Sulaiman and his armies crush you, unperceiving."

And [Sulaiman] smiled, laughing at her speech, and said: "My Lord, arouse me to be thankful for Thy favor wherewith Thou hast favored me and my parents, and to do good that shall be pleasing unto Thee, and include me in [the number of] Thy righteous slaves." And he sought among the birds and said: "How is it that I see not the hoopoe, or is he among the absent? I verily will punish him with hard punishment or I verily will slay him, or he verily shall bring me a plain excuse."

But he was not long in coming, and he said: "I have found out [a thing] that thou apprehendest not, and I come unto thee from Sheba with sure tidings. Lo! I found a woman ruling over them, and she hath been given [abundance] of all things, and hers is a mighty throne. I found her and her people worshipping the sun instead of Allah; and Shaitan maketh their works fair seeming unto them, and debarreth them from the way [of Truth], so that they go not aright: So that they worship not Allah, Who bringeth forth the hidden in the heavens and the earth, and knoweth what ye hide and what ye proclaim, Allah; there is no God save Him, the Lord of the tremendous Throne."[Sulaiman] said: "We shall see whether thou speakest truth or whether thou art of the liars. Go with this my letter and throw it down unto them; then turn away and see what [answer] they return."

[The Queen of Sheba] said [when she received the letter]: "O chieftains! Lo! there hath been thrown unto me a noble letter. Lo! it is from Sulaiman, and lo! it is: In the name of Allah the Beneficent, the Merciful; Exalt not yourselves against me, but come unto me as those who surrender."

She said: "O chieftains! Pronounce for me in my case. I decide no case till ye are present with me."

They said: "We are lords of might and lords of great prowess, but it is for thee to command; so consider what thou wilt command."

She said: "Lo! kings, when they enter a township, ruin it and make the honor of its people shame. Thus will they do. But lo! I am going to send a present unto them, and to see with what [answer] the messengers return."

So when [the envoy] came unto Sulaiman, [the King] said: "What! Would ye help me with wealth? But that which Allah hath given me is better than that which He hath given you. Nay it is ye [and not I] who exult in your gift. Return unto them. We verily shall come unto them with hosts that they cannot resist, and we shall drive them out from thence with shame, and they will be abased."

He said: "O chiefs! Which of you will bring me her throne before they come unto me, surrendering?" A stalwart of the Jinn said: "I will bring it thee before thou canst rise from thy place. Lo! I verily am strong and trusty for such work." One with whom was knowledge of the Scripture said: "I will bring it thee before thy gaze returneth unto thee." And when he saw it set in his presence, [Sulaiman] said: "This is of the bounty of my Lord, that He may try me whether I give thanks or am ungrateful. Whosoever giveth thanks he only giveth thanks for [the good of] his own soul: and whosoever is ungrateful [is ungrateful only to his own soul's hurt]. For lo! my Lord is Absolute in independence, Bountiful." He said: "Disguise her throne for her that we may see whether she will go aright or be of those not rightly guided."

So, when she came, it was said [unto her]: "Is thy throne like this?" She said: "[It is] as though it were the very one." And [Sulaiman said]: "We were given the knowledge before her and we had surrendered [to Allah]." And [all] that she was wont to worship instead of Allah hindered her, for she came of disbelieving folk.

It was said unto her: "Enter the hall." And when she saw it she deemed it a pool and bared her legs. [Sulaiman] said: "Lo! it is a hall, made smooth, of glass." She said: "My Lord! Lo! I have wronged myself, and I surrender with Sulaiman unto Allah, the Lord of the Worlds." (Surah 27:15–44, Pickthall Version, amended re names)

Are these hints of a desert people's recollections of the ancient meeting between Solomon and the Queen of Sheba (identified elsewhere in the Qur'an as Bilqis)? The Qur'an also has references to the copper mine exploits of Sulaimon, as mentioned in the Bible, as well as to his wise judgments.

Does Allah put all this in the inspired poems that He gives to Muhammad in the cave for a purpose? What do we make of a king who talks with the animals like Dr. Dolittle, or Saint Francis of Assisi, one who marshals spirits, humans, and birds, in ranks, in a palace surrounded by a moat of mirror glass like the glassy sea of Revelation? As the Qur'an is recited, the head of the Muslim believer swims in a sea of beautiful images.

Either we are in an unreal world of fantasy, as those who choose to lampoon Islam would have us believe, or else we are in the realm of divine images that may yet speak to the whole world in reference to ultimate things. The Qur'an begins to challenge not only platitudinous morality, but also conventional views of reality.

13

Women Who Have Names

Bilqis, Zulaika, Khadija, Fatima, Maryam, Asiya/Ruth

ACCORDING TO THE BIBLE, the Queen of Sheba (Ethiopia), was the one who visited Jerusalem, was briefly a consort of Solomon, and was the facilitator of social and commercial intercourse between Israel and Ethiopia. The Bible is, if anything, even more patriarchal than the Qur'an, and has not even acknowledged her name, Bilqis, as recorded in the Muslim Scripture.

Then too there was Zulaika, the powerful wife of Potiphar in the Bible, the "lady scorned" who had Joseph thrown into prison on trumped-up charges of rape. These are two examples of the names of women who are recognized in the Qur'an alone, and there are others. Bilqis and Zulaika are each featured on their own in other chapters, but the Jewish and Christian notion that Islam is somehow less respectful of women is a selective example of the pot calling the kettle black.

The Muslim community has four particular feminine role models who individually exemplify virtues any woman may attain and collectively portray a feminine idealism that Christians and Jews have so far failed to appreciate. At the same time, the Islamic expression of the ideal in any particular time or place may fall short of the model, just as so many Christian and Jewish virtues may be rare in practice. Two of these role models are outside our study of the Qur'an but may be mentioned because they are part of the corporate model presented in the Scripture.

Khadija was the wealthy businesswoman who became Muhammad's patron, wife, best friend, and advisor. *Fatima* was Muhammad's daughter and heir, who organized the religion during and after his life, a confidante and facilitator of the written record of her father's revelations. *Mary*, mother of Jesus, and Pharoah's wife *Asiya*, are scriptural and round out the list of the four women who together portray the feminine ideal in leadership roles in Muslim business, religion, family, and government.

There are also other women of God in the Qur'an whom we might recognize. Eve and Sarah loom large, Hagar is especially important, Hannah deserves mention, and there are others whose names are forgotten in the Judeo-Christian tradition, but the four ideal women listed above together define femininity in Muslim tradition.

Only Mary rivals Jesus in the time and the space dedicated to individuals in the Qur'an. Jesus is mentioned in fifteen different chapters of the Qur'an, and in ninety-three verses, where he is called the Messiah eleven times. Mary is mentioned in the Qur'an thirty-four times, as compared to nineteen references in the Christian Scriptures. They are by far the two persons most often mentioned in Muslim Scriptures. Like Jesus, Mary requires a chapter of her own in this study.

Finally, in terms of these initial introductions to leading Muslim women, we meet Asiya, a woman who appears unnamed in a cameo role in the Bible. She is prominent in the Qur'an, and worthy of a far greater place in modern consciousness. In the Qur'an, Asiya is identified as Pharaoh's wife; we may also know her as Pharaoh's daughter, before she and her husband ascend the throne. If the pharaohs and the pharaohs' wives appear more prominent in this study that Jews or Christians might expect, they might be reminded that in the Qur'an these are not only figures in their own rights, but also "types" who remain prominent in our world as political tyrants and popular celebrities.

In Egyptian history, Asiya's name is recorded as Ankesepaten, the daughter of the famous beauty Nefertiti, whose fame should more generally acknowledge her role in bringing monotheism into the Egyptian palace where Moses grew up. We considered her story in a previous chapter from the perspective of the Hebrew and Egyptian texts. Asiya's story is the same in the Qur'an and in Egyptian history, except that in the Scripture we see more of the leadership role exercised by this first lady.

We have noted how Nefertiti's daughter was married to King Tutankamun, too young to produce an heir; so "Tut's" wife, Asiya, desperate to produce a successor to secure the dynasty, seized on the chance to adopt secretly a seemingly abandoned Hebrew baby. After Tut's death, the young queen would be married to the next pharaoh, possibly the one confronted by Moses.

This fearless lady, identified in the Qur'an as Asiya, risked everything to stand for justice on behalf of the Hebrews and to witness for the veracity of the religious ideals she shared with her ancestors, her mother, her first husband, and her adopted son. In the Qur'an, all through the crisis of the Hebrew slave revolt, Asiya confronts the Pharaoh time and again. She appears to have been behind his decision to let God's people go. This story is only complete when seen from the well-rounded perspective of the three sources: the Hebrew Scriptures, the Egyptian records, and the Qur'an.

Asiya lays a foundation for feminism in Islam and, with Mary, Khadija, and Fatima, she paves the way for women like Megawati Putri, Benazir Bhutto, and Kalida Zia (in modern Indonesia, Pakistan, and Bangladesh respectively), all powerful female presidents of the largest Muslim states in the world.

The golden rule of religious relationships is to offer the other party the most generous appreciation of their tradition possible, just as you might hope they would offer to your heritage. Jews and Christians are not famous for following this dictum toward each other; it is perhaps easier to admire Buddhists and others who are not so close. And neither has extended this grace to the Muslim community, in spite of familial relations, nor has it been extended in return. The shadow of war may provide the impetus to extend the mutual appreciation that is long past due.

Nowhere is this lack of grace more apparent than in the negative assessments of one another by Jews, Christians, and Muslims on women's issues. For example, Jews and Christians decry Muslim polygamy. It is rare these days, and illegal in most Muslim countries, but in any case, polygamy at its worst may be no more demeaning than the "serial polygamy" widely practiced in America and Europe, and less ignoble than infidelity. Muslim extremists delight in pointing to the sexual perversions of Jerry Springer television shows and Western pornographic magazines as illustrations of Jewish and Christian sexual immorality, choosing to see the worst elements in the culture of freedom their cousins have nurtured.

Western society chooses to see the veil as a symbol of repression of women by Muslim men, while many Muslim women see the veil as status and dignity in a culture where it was adopted first by female members of the aristocratic families. Modern Western religious art continues to depict Mary wearing the veil as an almost instinctive acknowledgment of its correct imagery. The burka and other perhaps more extreme manifestations of the veil are debated as much within Islam as in the West, but Westerners should relax and realize that for most Muslim women who chose it, the veil simply denotes modesty. Such women are not necessarily submissive or restricted; many are highly trained professionals in practically every field.

Some Western women tend to see Muslim women as being repressed and exploited; many Muslim women see Western women as sexually aggressive, exhibitionist, and under social pressure to wear "special undergarments designed to exhibit their breasts," as is sometimes suggested by Muslim women at public forum debates on the veil and dress code controversy. Is gender role appreciation to be part of the twenty-first-century renaissance? Or should we strive next to liberate Catholic nuns and Amish women from the veil?

It was incomprehensible to Westerners that a majority in Afghanistan contemplates the Taliban with respect, until Western aid workers began to report anecdotal evidence that since the overthrow of the Taliban the incidences of rape and other forms of abuse have risen sharply. How can this be? Were we not given to understand that the Taliban themselves hold women in low esteem?

The truth is that the Taliban do indeed hold women in low esteem, but absolutely and strictly forbid sexual exploitation of this "weaker sex" on pain of death. With the Taliban gone from power, the theaters of Kabul are awash in "Western" pornography, prostitution is rife, and rape is common among a populace where men generally hold women in low regard and now have no restraints on their actions.

At the same time as these reports were coming out, the Pope issued a statement decrying the fact that worldwide trafficking in human flesh has reached proportions unequalled even in the years of African slaves being sent to America. The trafficking in children includes child laborers, boy soldiers, and girl prostitutes, all serving Western interests in cheap clothing and carpets, the "blood diamond" trade, and sex tourism. The adult trade in human flesh is seen in illegal migration of Asian prostitutes to America and Eastern European prostitutes to Western Europe. Westerners insist that these perversions are not typical of Western culture, but from Saudi Arabia to Indonesia, Muslims are inclined toward a strictness that precludes the spread of these aspects of Western culture to their countries. None of this is intended to justify the rage against Western ways and the extremist actions by a criminal minority of Muslims who have taken matters into their own hands. It may, however, help some Westerners to understand what, to many others in the world, is simply beyond comprehension.

The fact that HIV/AIDS is largely limited in Africa to the Sub-Saharan "Christian" areas of the continent, and is not at all widespread in Muslim countries, has been explained by the United Nations and Western agencies as "denial" or "insufficient information" and "a likely impending crisis," but at some point the Muslim "extremists" feel they have a point to make. It is perfectly legitimate for Western Christians and Jews to make the point that freedom involves risks, and that they have created a freed society that depends on personal maturity, rather than a restrictive society where morality is enforced. The spokesperson from the Taliban says, "Tell that to the boy soldiers and the little girl prostitutes who depend on Western patronage." The debate is worthy of our participation.

This human trafficking continues behind closed doors in London and New York, and it ill behooves one culture to insist that all cultures adopt their ways, as the prisoners in Abu Ghraib and Guantanamo Bay have discovered. These negative images are selective examples of the tendency of all parties to believe the worst about each other, but it sometimes helps to see how we are regarded by the other. Then with open eyes we may be more ready to see the unnecessarily negative bias in the view we hold of them.

Muslim men and women may actually have many difficult issues to resolve in the modern era, but negative impressions from the Western media begin with a negative bias. In the same way, Muslims develop a negative bias about the Western world as they find it hard to imagine, for example, why every city and town in Western society requires women's shelters to provide refuge from abusive men. Job's story was well preserved in the Hebrew Scriptures, and in it women are named and given inheritance rights, though Jewish women have questioned whether the status of Job's daughters has actually been maintained in either Scripture or history. Jesus recognized women in exciting ways through dialogue with the sisters Mary and Martha, companionship with Mary Magdalene, conversations with the "fallen" woman at the well, the rescue of the woman "taken in adultery," the honors he bestowed on his mother, and several other examples of mutual respect, rare in the Mediterranean world of his time and culture. Yet the disciples all turn out to be male, at least as reported in the Bible, and prominent female women mentioned by Saint Paul were all eclipsed in the patriarchal systems of the church.

In the Qur'an, Muhammad presents the divine will in a feminist perspective in the same progressive manner as we see it through Job or Jesus. It was remarkable for its time and it set down principles that can contribute to the quest of modern women and men, regardless of the historic and present experiences of Muslim women, which many decry as restrictive.

Muhammad's much disparaged "advance," in which women receive half the inheritance of men, for example, may be interpreted by those of goodwill as a provision that every person should receive status and inheritance in just proportion to needs and numbers. In Arabia of the seventh century CE, men were half as numerous as women, due to constant warfare, and men had twice the responsibility in a system where they may have had responsibility for two partners on average, plus sisters, mothers, and others. Moreover, a woman's wealth could not be touched or seized under any circumstance, a regulation far in advance of the situation in Europe at that time.

Modern women might say that the system needed changing, but it was changed within the context, and the principles for further change were established. Modern Islam is in the throes of a sharp debate between the eternal principles of the Qur'an and its expression in the context of its time, but many Muslims believe they have little to learn from the West. For every Wahabist "scholar" from Pakistan who teaches that all women are "inferior," though cherished, there is an Evangelical Christian "scholar" from Missouri teaching that only men are qualified to be heads of households and that they must be obeyed. For every Islamic stricture against women sitting behind the wheel in Saudi Arabian cars, there is a Baptist barrier preventing women from standing behind the pulpit somewhere in Texas, and a Roman Catholic barrier preventing women from standing before the altar anywhere in the world. Jewish communities have ultra-orthodox authorities that are a match for their Christian and Muslim counterparts in these regards, as witnessed by the prohibitions against women at the sacred Western Wall in Jerusalem. All three traditions have their Talibans and their Wahabists, but their lack of depth and wisdom is clear to most of the world, except for those who continue to follow them out of insecurity or other particular needs. Islam cannot be judged on this basis unless we agree that Christianity and Judaism be likewise judged.

The eternal principles found in Hebrew, Christian, and Muslim Scriptures all commend themselves and perhaps rank equally. In some cases they appear in embryonic form and sometimes they are more fully developed. The interpretation is the responsibility of the believer and the community as a whole. The excuses for failure in implementation are equally obscene in all three traditions, though one or the other may appear more culpable in any given century or culture.

At the same time, representatives of these traditions through the ages have often led the column of humanity's progress, whether the issue be the rights of women, race relations, or other areas of prophetic vision. Systems without God (atheistic communism on the left, secular humanism at the center, and pagan Nazism on the right) all reached their apex in the twentieth century, proclaimed their ideals and tried them out, but now appear to be in eclipse, with little to show for their efforts.

Western society has a long way to go to reach God's reign, but the good news is that God is with all people in truly effective ways in all situations, as we saw in the story of Hagar. Meanwhile, if there is to be a renaissance of Islamic culture in our time, it would be helpful if Western Christians and Jews could be open to a renaissance of true religious values in their own culture. "Women's liberation" has opened many doors to equality but has fallen far short in the quest for fulfillment it sought for both women and men. Can anything be learned from the Qur'an in this connection?

For example, there are just eight nations in the world with populations over 100 million. These are China, India, the United States, Indonesia, Brazil, Pakistan, Russia, and Bangladesh. Three of those are Muslim, and a fourth, India, has over 120,000 Muslims in its population. The four countries with over 100,000 Muslims are the only countries among the big eight where women have been elected as heads of governments. How could this be if women are not respected? A few nations of Christian background and the State of Israel have had female leaders, but of the eight countries with populations above 100 million, how long did it take for America to even consider the possibility of a woman as President? And the prospect is not even on the horizon in China, Russia, or Brazil. Are some so focused on the speck in the eye of a neighbor that they cannot see the stick in their own?

The role of Muslim women of God, from Asiya and Hagar to modern leaders, has been misunderstood. Perhaps men will always misunderstand women, and women sometimes misunderstand each other, but God always understands. The Scriptures of this whole family tradition may be mined for greater inspiration and guidance than any modern cultures have yet known. The process is under way in the Muslim world every bit as much as in the West, but perhaps approaching the matter from an entirely different perspective.

On September 18, 2006, Anousheh Ansari became, not the first female to journey into space, but the first female to do so and pay her own way. A business communications entrepreneur who left Iran because of restrictions on girls studying science after the 1979 Islamic revolution, she is an example of the paradox of our times: a Muslim woman, first in her field, but who had to come West to become everything of which she was capable. Meanwhile, twenty-five years after she left Iran, female students have become an absolute majority in all Iranian universities. We are in a time of dramatic change.

We have already noted the scriptural examples of Arab-Jewish intermarriages and other interconnections in the time of Adam through Noah, as well as the wives of Abraham and his mixed extended household. The Arab wives of Esau, Judah, Joseph, Moses, and many of the Judges may be noted as among the formulating factors in the faith family of Israel. Arab Ishmael revered his Hebrew father just as the Jewish patriarchs revered their Arab mothers. Perhaps even Moses first became aware of the monotheistic reality of God from his upbringing by the deeply spiritual women in the Egyptian palace, his mother, Nefertiti, and Asyia, who all helped to prepare him for his burning bush moment.

We can extend this pattern by concluding this aspect of our investigation with one of the most beloved stories in the Hebrew Scriptures. Ruth was the Arabic great-grandmother of King David and one of the notable Arab ancestors of Israel. Her notability was not in the realm of military victory, like that of Jewish Deborah or her Arab accomplice, Jael. Ruth was not a great poet like Miriam, nor did she talk much with God, like Hagar. She was not even married to one of the Patriarchs or one of the pharaohs. Ruth was simply an Arab woman of decency, loyalty, and grace, whose love story we have never forgotten and whose style might be a key to modern needs for reconciliation.

The scene opens in Moab, which is part of the modern nation of Jordan. In a famine or economic recession in Israel, some Jewish families moved into Arab communities to find work. One such family was that of Elimelech and Naomi with their sons, Mahlon and Chilion. Elimelech died, but his Jewish sons had married two Arab girls, Ruth and Orpah, who were both very close to their Jewish mother-in-law. This was fortunate for Naomi, because ten years later, Mahlon and Chilion died and the three women were on their own.

Times continued to be difficult, but Naomi heard that things had improved in Israel and prepared to return to be near more prosperous family members. At first, both girls announced their intention to go with Naomi. At her mother-in-law's insistence, Orpah turned back to rejoin her own family, but nothing could deter Ruth from accompanying Naomi, to care for her. Her words of loyalty have given rise to poignant songs and poems in every age, the more so when we recall that Ruth was both an in-law and an Arab. By following Naomi, Ruth left behind all reasonable hope of remarriage and personal security in order to care for her Jewish mother-in-law in a strange land.

They survived on scraps and gleanings for some time until Naomi realized and told Ruth that the rich farmer who gave them food was a relative who just might recognize some obligation to the widow of his cousin's son. "He is a good man, but in harvest season he likes to drink and to spend the night in the barn. My dear, perhaps you should spend a night there with him, and see if you two might not be somehow right for each other. He is a good man and there is no better woman than you, in my opinion." The rest of the story appears in the Bible:

So Ruth went to the threshing-place and did just what her mother-in-law had told her. When Boaz had finished eating and drinking, he was in a good mood. He went to the pile of barley and lay down to sleep. Ruth slipped over quietly, lifted the covers, and lay down at his feet. During the night he woke up suddenly, turned over, and was surprised to find a woman lying at his feet. "Who are you?" he asked. "It is Ruth, sir," she answered. "You are a close relative and you are responsible for taking care of me, so please marry me."

"The Lord bless you," he said. "You are showing even greater family loyalty in what you are doing now than in what you did for your mother-in-law. You might have gone looking for a young man, either rich or poor, but you didn't. Now don't worry Ruth. I will do everything you ask; as everyone in town knows, you are a fine woman.

"It is true that I am a close relative and am responsible for you, but there is a man who is a closer relative than I am. Stay with me the rest of the night, and in the morning we will find out whether or not he will take responsibility for you. If so, well and good; if not, I swear by the living Lord that I will take the responsibility. Now lie down and stay here until morning."

So she lay there at his feet, but she got up before it was light enough for her to be seen, because Boaz did not want anyone to know that she had been there. (Ruth 3:6–14)

The next day, Boaz was true to his word. If one wants to know the difference between a traditional Middle Eastern society and modern Western ways, or the difference between life in Afghanistan today and life in Toronto, it is suggested that one read the next chapter from one's own Bible. One social system may not be better or worse than the other, but they are so different. Western people might learn a little respect for other ways, and there is nothing like our Bible to teach that lesson, especially the Book of Ruth.

The issue of intermarriage, racial or religious, would be the least concern on the mind of Boaz, no matter what others thought. It just happens, as we read in Matthew 1:5 as well as Joshua 6:23, that Boaz's father had married Rahab, the Arab prostitute of Jericho who entertained the Hebrew spies. So David, the greatest king of Israel, was Arab on two sides of his family tree . . . and so was his descendant Jesus, the Messiah for many Jews of his time, for Muslims in time to come, and for Christians beyond number in the world today.

A hundred thousand tourists recently saw the timeless drama of *Ruth* on the three-hundred-foot wraparound stage at the Millennium Theater in Lancaster, Pennsylvania. It appears that these stories are here to stay, the vaunted secularism of the last century notwithstanding.

The Book of Ruth was included for a reason in the Hebrew Scriptures, a collection of sacred writings compiled by the Council of Rabbis at Jamnia shortly before 100 CE. After the destruction of the Jerusalem Temple by the Romans in 70 CE, Jewish leaders decided against rebuilding. Instead, they provided a portable temple for their widely dispersed people. That portable temple was a book, known to Christians and Muslims as the Old Testament, but, of course, it stands supreme in the Jewish community as simply the Hebrew Scriptures or *Tanakh*.

Conservative rabbis at Jamnia had attempted to safeguard the Jewish community from assimilation by including the strictures against intermarriage by Ezra and Nehemiah, written in a similar era of uncertainty. This led the more liberal elements in the council to push for the inclusion of Ruth for balance, since, if even the great King David was both Arab and Jew, who should worry? This issue, like many others, has not gone away, but this comparative study of Scriptures may help modern members of this family keep things in perspective.

14

Cameo Appearances

Enoch/Idris, Job/Ayyub, Isaac/Ishaq, Joshua/Yusha,
Goliath/Galoot, Aaron/Haroon, Elijah/Illiyas, Ezekiel/Zul-Kifi,
Aman/Haman, Ezra/Uzair, Jonah/Yunus, and Children of
Isreal/Bani Israel

To SUGGEST THAT the following great characters of the Bible are featured in the Qur'an as "cameo appearances" is no insult to them. To describe them in this way helps us to understand further the nature of the Qur'an as an inspired book of material suitable for recitation and meditation. The whole of this form of Scripture is a collection of artfully worded cameos. There are a few exceptions, such as the longer narrative of the story of Joseph, though it, too, is terse and each *ayah*, or verse, can be used out of context as a basis for meditation.

The use of such material out of context is actually intended and approved. There is the presumption of additional knowledge furnished by the Hadith or, in the case of Muslim scholars, the Hebrew and Christian Scriptures, though the latter require careful exegesis because they are thought to be compilations from various sources, some of which have become jumbled.

The vast Muslim literature, and verbal traditions of meditation, and the study of the cameo passages of the Qur'an are well beyond the scope of this investigation. However, there are similar rabbinical traditions of treating texts as isolated sources of inspiration, and Christians, too, have a well-developed tradition of meditation on single verses in booklets such as *The Upper Room*, found in the households of many active church members.

What follows is a very select number of excerpts that may serve to help round out our survey of biblical characters in the Qur'an. In some cases, this is their only mention in the Qur'an. Others are mentioned many times in verses that convey only a slight shift in the focus of meditation. The comments are not intended as any kind of illustration of meditation style; they are merely intended to slightly augment the introduction of these particular characters.

Enoch/Idris

Also mention in the Book the case of Idris: he was a man of truth and sincerity and a prophet: And We raised him to a lofty station. (Surah 19:56–57)

Enoch is presented in Hebrew Scriptures as one who "walked with God." All three traditions record, without comment, that he was one of the few humans who physically left the earth to be received directly into heaven, the "lofty station." This would be an ample focus for meditation, and ayah 57 probably refers to that but, in the cameo presented in ayah 56, the focus could be on truth and sincerity.

Job/Ayyub

And remember Ayyub when he cried to his Lord "Truly distress has seized me but Thou art the Most Merciful of those that are merciful." So We listened to him: We removed the distress that was on him and We restored his people to him and doubled their number as a Grace from Ourselves and a thing for commemoration for all who serve Us. (Surah 21:83–84)

Job (Ayyub) is traditionally regarded as the oldest complete book in the Hebrew Scriptures, probably from a non-Jewish source, because it is set in the Orient at a time long before the Jewish religion. In Jewish and Christian circles, it epitomizes the intellectual discussion of the meaning of suffering, especially unwarranted suffering. Jungians speculate that it may be regarded as a dream (because Job's panic attack and all the other events could have happened in one night) in which God speaks, after which Job awakens to God's grace and mercy. Could a beautiful recitation of this cameo lend itself to meditation on the mercy of Allah?

Isaac/Ishaq

"Praise be to Allah who hath granted unto me in old age Ismail and Ishaq: for truly my Lord is He the Hearer of Prayer!" (Surah 14:39)

Isaac never appears on his own in the Qur'an and really does play a mere cameo role in both Hebrew and Christian Scriptures. Popular Jewish writer Rabbi Harold Kushner makes a convincing case that Isaac was quite possibly mentally retarded, and his success in maintaining the covenant may be seen as God's grace to one of limited ability. Meditation on this passage might center on relationships between estranged brothers, or on the listening ear of Allah.

Joseph's Brothers/Bani Israel

Now when they came into Joseph's presence he received his full brother to stay with him. He said to him: "Behold! I am thy own brother; so grieve not at aught of their doings." (Surah 12:69)

Now when the others saw no hope of his yielding they held a conference in private. The leader among them said: "Know ye not that your father did take an oath from you in Allah's name and how before this ye did fail in your duty with Joseph? Therefore will I not leave this land until my father permits me or Allah commands me; and He is the best to command." (Surah 12:80)

Joseph's brothers are not mentioned by name, but in them the rivalry between brothers reaches new heights, after all the issues between Cain and Abel (Qabeel and Habeel), Isaac and Ishmael (Ishaq and Ismail), and Jacob and Esau (Yaqub and Al-Eis). The first cameo is a clear reference to Benjamin, Joseph's "full brother," a worthy subject for meditation on brotherly loyalty and protection. The second reference is to Judah, according what we know from the Hebrew Scriptures, and might focus on taking personal responsibility.

Moses' Sister and Mother

The wife of Pharaoh said: "Here is a joy of the eye for me and for thee: slay him not. It may be that he will be of use to us or we may adopt him as a son." And they perceived not what they were doing! But there came to be a void in the heart of the mother of Musa: she was going almost to disclose his case had We not strengthened her heart with faith so that she might remain a firm believer. And she said to the sister of Musa "Follow him." So the sister watched him in the guise of a stranger and they knew not.

And We ordained that he refused suck at first until his sister came up and said: "Shall I point out to you the people of a house that will nourish and bring him up for you and be sincerely attached to him?"

Thus did We restore him to his mother that her eye might be comforted that she might not grieve and that she might know that the promise of Allah is true: but most of them do not understand. (Surah 28:9–13)

The wife of the new pharaoh in the Qur'an is the daughter of the old pharaoh in the Bible. She is the princess who rescued Moses and we will hear more of her role in a subsequent chapter.

Moses' mother and sister are not named here either, though Maryam's name appears later in the Qur'an when Mary, the mother of Jesus, is called "sister of Haroon," a very interesting allusion that strengthens our appreciation of the use of symbolic language or personality types throughout the Qur'an, especially for meditative purposes.

In this passage we have a brief narrative, as well as two or three topics for focused meditation, in each ayah: mercy, adoption, fulfilling God's will even in ignorance, heartache, strengthening, belief, obedience, predestination, nourishment, restoration, comfort, and justification to list a few, always intensified by the sweet wail of the poetic text.

Aaron/Haroon

Then he brought out of the fire before the people the image of a calf: it seemed to low: so they said, "This is your god and the god of Musa but Musa has forgotten!" Could they not see that it could not return them a word in answer, and that it had no power either to harm them or to do them good?

Haroon had already before this said to them: "O my people! ye are being tested in this: for verily your Lord is Allah, Most Gracious: so follow me and obey my command."

They had said: "We will not abandon this cult but we will devote ourselves to it until Musa returns to us."

Musa said: "O Haroon! what kept thee back when thou sawest them going wrong from following me? Didst thou then disobey my order?"

Haroon replied: "O son of my mother! seize me not by my beard nor by the hair of my head! Truly I feared lest thou shouldst say 'Thou hast caused a division among Bani Israel and thou didst not respect my word'!" (Surah 20:88–94)

Aaron is another of the cameo players who never appears on his own. He is always associated with Moses in the Qur'an, except briefly when Moses is on the mountain with God. Even that did not work out well for Aaron, though some of the details differ from the Hebrew text.

A good meditation on Aaron might center on the value of playing a supporting role or the folly of overreaching, as in this narrative.

Joshua/Yusha

But among their Allah-fearing men were two on whom Allah had bestowed His Grace: they said: "Assault them at the proper gate: when once ye are in, victory will be yours. But on Allah put your trust if ye have faith." (Surah 5:23)

The spies had checked out Jericho and some had cold feet, but Caleb and Joshua had faith in their God-given cause of establishing a homeland for the nation of runaway slaves.

In the Qur'an, the walls of Jericho do not fall in dramatic fashion, a subject of many Jewish debates and Christian sermons. Assaulting the proper gate might be an equally fitting theme in meditation for business or personal reasons.

Goliath/Galoot

249. They said: "This day we cannot cope with Galoot and his forces." But those who were convinced that they must meet Allah said: "How oft by Allah's will hath a small force vanquished a big one? Allah is with those who steadfastly persevere."

When they advanced to meet Galoot and his forces they prayed: "Our Lord! pour out constancy on us and make our steps firm; help us against those that reject faith."

By Allah's will they routed them: and Dawoud slew Galoot. (Surah 2:249–251)

What can we say, except that the big galoot was not a favorite in Hebrew, Christian, or Arabic texts? But it is a delight to realize where we get that phrase. Alternatively, Goliath is also rendered "Jaloot" in some translations, but "Galoot" is well established in the English language and comes from the North African pronunciation.

The story of David facing the giant is one of the best-known themes in world literature. Here Goliath appears in more of a communal context, with his "forces." There may be something upon which we could meditate in that reference to the forces of evil, which rarely appear alone.

Elijah/Illiyas

So also was Illiyas among those sent by us. "Behold," he said to his people. "Will ye not fear Allah? Will ye call upon Baal and forsake the Best of Creators, Allah your Lord and Cherisher, the Lord and Cherisher of your fathers of old?"

But they rejected him and they will certainly be called up for punishment. Except the sincere and devoted Servants of Allah among them. And We left this blessing for him among generations to come in later times: "Peace and salutation to such as Illiyas!" (Surah 37:123–130)

The prophet Elijah stands tall in the Hebrew Scriptures, appears with Moses (representing the Law and the Prophets) beside Jesus in the Transfiguration, and is mentioned in many Qur'an cameos that are suitable for meditation. The name Elijah means "God is God." The events of his life and ministry are depicted often in religious art, scenes such as ravens feeding him in the desert or his ascension to heaven through a whirlwind in a fiery chariot. His story is presented by the Jewish Christian Felix Mendelssohn in a supreme masterpiece, the musical oratorio *Elijah*, first performed in 1846.

In the aftermath of all the drama in the contest between Elijah and the prophets of Baal, Elijah took off south to Judah, where people still at least pretended to believe in God. After finding refuge in a desert cave, Elijah at last found God again, but not as he expected. This northern prophet was actually on Mount Horeb (elsewhere called Mount Sinai), at that time, where Moses received the Ten Commandments from God. How often do we walk on holy ground but behave as if sacred precincts are nothing special? Like Elijah, we want God to speak in earthquake, wind, and fire, but God so often whispers in a "still, small voice."

In Jewish expectations, the coming of the Messiah will be preceded by the Day of the Lord. The text of the Old Testament of Hebrew Scriptures concludes with the role of Elijah, whom Christians identify with John the Baptist.

Behold, I will send you Elijah the prophet before the coming of the great and dreadful day of the Lord: and he shall turn the heart of the fathers to the children, and the heart of the children to their fathers, lest I come and smite the earth with a curse. (Malachi 4:5–6)

The traditional Jewish belief that Elijah will herald the arrival of the Messiah is shown today in the rites of the Passover celebration, which many Christians and Muslims are attending these days as special guests in Jewish homes. At the Passover Seder, recalled now at Holy Week services in many churches, a cup of wine is placed on the table for this prophet. A door is left open in anticipation that he might choose this day and this gathering to proclaim the arrival of the Messiah, for the first time for some, or the second coming for others, or the end of time for all.

Ezekiel/Zul-Kifl

And remember Ismail, Idris and Zul-kifl, all men of constancy and *patience*. (Surah 21:85)

Or take the similitude of Zul-Kifl who passed by a place all in ruins. He said: "Oh! how shall Allah bring it ever to life after this its death?" But Allah caused him to die for a hundred years then raised him up again. He said: "How long didst thou tarry thus?" He said: "Perhaps a day or part of a day." He said: "Nay thou hast tarried thus a hundred years; but look at thy food and thy drink; they show no signs of age; and look at thy donkey. We make of thee a Sign unto the people, so look further at the bones, how We bring them together and clothe them with flesh!" When this was shown clearly to him he said: "I know that Allah hath power over all things." (Surah 2:259)

The name of Ezekiel in the Bible appears as Zul-Kifl, or Dhul-Kifl in various parts of the Muslim world (usually the latter among Arabs but, more frequently, the former in North America, where a preponderance of Muslims are non-Arab). This passage is a divine recollection of stories about which we all know, thanks to the children's song about "The toe bone connected to the foot bone, the foot bone connected to the ankle bone, the ankle bone connected to the shin bone . . . now hear the Word of the Lord."

When the State of Israel was re-established in 1949, the story of Ezekiel and the Valley of Dry Bones was told and retold with emphasis on what the Lord would require in answer to the question, "Can these Bones Live Again?" The theme has universal application and is being brought out again these days in the sermons of Imams in reference to the proposed State of Palestine, as estranged brothers seek peace again.

Aman/Haman

Pharaoh said: "O Chiefs! no god do I know for you but myself: therefore O Haman! light me a kiln to bake bricks out of clay and build me a lofty palace that I may mount up to the god of Musa: but as far as I am concerned I think Musa is a liar!" (Surah 28:38)

For Jews and Christians, the puzzling thing about Haman in the Qur'an is that he is not the Persian Prime Minister who hates Jews, but the Egyptian Prime Minister or Vizier with much the same agenda. (In the Jewish Apocrypha he is called Aman.) The fact that the same ayah asks Haman to build a tower that reaches to heaven indicates a mixing of biblical images from several sources. Haman appears several times in this manner, but that only means that, in the Qur'an, God is using "types" of characters. The central parable in this study is a use of the image of Canaan, Noah's other son, as a scriptural type of rebel, anticipating the fall of humanity in Adam and Eve and seen again in Cain, Jacob, Ishmael, and the Prodigal Son, and experienced today be individuals and nations. The Qur'an frequently refers to the fact that its words are but "signs" or "similitudes."

Calling the mother of Jesus "the sister of Aaron" is a similar symbolic use of a name. The Egyptian vizier was "a Haman," and we should know what that means. Literalists may dispute it, reading only the surface meanings of the Qur'an, without depth. Christians and Jews have always had minorities with that agenda. They usually found sects of their own, study the Bible for a generation or several, and come back to the more profound understandings on their own, believing they have discovered the secret meaning, at last.

Ezra/Uzair

The Jews call Uzair a son of Allah. (Surah 9:30)

When the first of the warnings came to pass We sent against you Our servants given to terrible warfare: They entered the very inmost parts of your homes; and it was a warning completely fulfilled. Then did We grant you the Return as against them: We gave you increase in resources and sons and made you the more numerous in manpower. (Surah 17:5–6)

Ezra is not a major figure in the Qur'an, and the first cameo here, from Surah 9, is merely of interest in the Qur'an's running reminder that God does not have sons, or, that sonship is an inappropriate description of even one so clearly anointed as Jesus, born as a result of God's fiat.

The second cameo, from Surah 17, is of perhaps greater interest, as the subject of sermons at Juma (Friday Prayers) in mosques around the world these days. Ezra is important in the whole story of Abraham's family because he reconstituted Judaism following the Babylonian captivity and he supervised the Return. Muslims cannot help but meditate on this passage, and on its parallels in the Hebrew Scriptures, at this time when some kind of right of return is being negotiated by the Palestinian people. The question being asked is, "Where is Ezra when we need him?"

Jonah/Yunus

So also was Jonah among those sent by us. When he ran away like slave from captivity to the ship fully laden. He agreed to cast lots and he was condemned:

Then the big Fish did swallow him and he had done acts worthy of blame. Had it not been that he repented and glorified Allah He would certainly have remained inside the Fish till the Day of Resurrection. But We cast him forth on the naked shore in a state of sickness and We caused to grow over him a spreading plant of the Gourd kind and We sent him on a mission to a hundred thousand men or more. And they believed; so We permitted them to enjoy their life for a while. (Surah 37:139–148)

Jonah is read annually by Jews in the synagogue service of Yom Kippur, the Day of Atonement. Jonah is also featured in the Christian Scriptures, where Jesus compared Jonah's three days in the belly of the great fish to his own impending three days in the tomb.

Few stories in any of our shared Scriptures lend themselves so completely to symbolic interpretation as does Jonah's. We all get swallowed up by false dreams, debts, temptations, and false priorities. The narrative cameo above is full of signs and symbols: "like a slave" . . . "the ship fully laden" . . . "to cast lots" . . . "swallowed" . . . "cast on the naked shore" . . . "in a state of sickness" . . . "a spreading plant" . . . as the Qur'an continues in imagery, the beauty of which can only be guessed by those unfamiliar with the sound of the text recited in Arabic.

The Reverend Dr. Lancelot Andrews, one of the chief translators of the King James Version of the Bible, once preached 365 sermons on Jonah in one year in a college chapel. The Qur'an is a rich source of reflection on God's Word. The examples given here are directly related to the stories of characters we can identify as appearing in the Qur'an as well as the Bible. Muslims also have a whole tradition of meditation on beloved scriptural verses, known as "duas."

Perhaps seeking the deeper levels should not be so difficult with the Qur'an, because, as noted, every page reminds the reader that much here is sign and symbol. While the whole of Islam is inclined to meditate on the deeper meanings, one group in particular, the Sufis, have cultivated the practice of the deeper focus.

Jews employ various rabbinical traditions of interpretation, and Christians have developed "form criticism" and other techniques of scriptural analysis that open the text to deeper levels of spiritual interpretation. Because the text of the Qur'an is possibly the world's best example of Marshall McLuhan's dictum "the medium is the message," it is often erroneously assumed that Muslims are literalists. Such is not the case at all. The sounds of the recitation are intended to lift the worshiper into an ecstasy in which the content of the passage is sometimes almost incidental to the meaning of the experience.

The study of what are called "contexts" is the Muslim method of extending the application of Qur'anic texts to situations not actually described. Likewise, seeming disparities in the text of the Qur'an are dealt with by the Muslim scholarly technique known as abrogation, in which earlier revelations may be superseded or clarified by later texts. The Qur'an reference to this is found where Allah speaks:

> We do not abrogate any of Our verses of the Qur'an or cause it to be forgotten, except when We substitute it with something better or similar; do you not know that Allah has full power over everything? (Surah 2:106, Malik Version)

This practice of abrogation is a reference to progressive revelation in which Allah, through Gabriel, dictated revised versions of part of the Qur'an to improve upon those He gave earlier as Muhammad grew in his ability to comprehend.

These methods of explanation, supplemented by more modern techniques such as the character type application, give Muslim scholars at least as much responsibility as their Jewish and Christian counterparts, though Muslim scholars prefer to speak of "application," rather than "criticism" of the Scriptures.

However, it may be conceded that in the Muslim community these studies at the higher level of application are the preserve of scholars and not the practice of the students learning to recite the sacred text in the fundamentalist madrasah schools, which may be as literalist as any fundamentalist Christian Bible college.

15

The Mother of Jesus

Mary/Maryam

IN THE QUR'AN, we learn much of what the ancient Middle East believed about Mary, or Maryam, and a fair amount also about her parents, the grandparents of Jesus. The name of Jesus in Arabic is 'Isa (pronounced E-sah). The grandparents, Imran and Hannah (Joachim and Anna or Saint Ann in English), also appear in early Christian literature, but they are only confirmed in Scripture from Muslim sources. Further critical studies could be of immense value to Christian believers as well as Muslims and even Jewish scholars specializing in that era.

We learn from the Qur'an that the parents of Maryam, Imran and Hannah, were sincere and devoted Jews. They had hoped for the birth of a son, a boy whom they could dedicate to priestly service, but when Mary was born they dedicated her anyway, a first for those days. The priestly uncle of Mary, Zakariya (Zechariah), sponsored her vocation in God's service. The Qur'an details her purity, symbolized by her virginity as a young girl, and her role in carrying the son that would be honored throughout the world. It has only been since 1936 that Christian churches began ordaining women again, and female rabbis are an even more recent advance. For Muslim women now leading prayers and assuming clerical roles in some places, Mary's priestly vocation in the Qu'ran is a latent but potent validation.

Like Aadam, Maryam's child was created by the grace of God and without mortal paternity. In Islam, as in Christianity, Maryam is demure and submissive to God, but strong in her own right and courageously supportive of 'Isa (Jesus). From the Qur'an we learn many details of Maryam's confinement prior to giving birth to 'Isa, in some respects more than we learn in the few verses recorded in the Bible. Many of the events surrounding the

163

birth of 'Isa are so well known to Christian and even Jewish readers that we will let the Qur'an tell us more about the experience of Maryam and her family in its own words (using the familiar Yusuf Ali English translation as the basis of several verses, with a mixture of Arabic and Anglicized names added from various other translations).

> Behold, the wife of Imran said, "O my Lord, I do dedicate unto Thee what is in my womb for Thy special service. Accept this of me, for Thou hearest and knowest all things."
>
> When she was delivered, she said, "O my Lord, behold, I am delivered of a female child." And God knew best what she had brought forth. "And nowise is the male like the female. I have named her Mary, and I commend her and her offspring to Thy protection from the Evil One, the Rejected."
>
> Right graciously did her Lord accept her. He made her grow in purity and beauty; to the care of Zakariya was she assigned. (Surah 3:35–37)

> Relate in the Book the story of Mary, when she withdrew from her family to a place in the east. She placed a screen to screen herself from them. Then We sent to her our angel, and he appeared before her as a man in all respects.
>
> She said, "I seek refuge from thee to God Most Gracious. Come not near if thou dost fear God."
>
> He said, "Nay, I am only a messenger from thy Lord, to announce to thee the gift of a holy son.
>
> She said, "How shall I have a son, seeing that no man has touched me, and I am not unchaste?"
>
> He said, "So it will be. Thy Lord saith, 'That is easy for Me, and We wish to appoint him as a sign unto men and a mercy from Us. It is a matter so decreed.'"
>
> So she conceived him, and she retired with him to a remote place. The pangs of childbirth drove her to the trunk of a palm-tree. She cried in her anguish, "Ah, would that I had died before this! Would that I had been a thing forgotten and out of sight."
>
> But a voice cried to her from beneath the palm-tree, "Grieve not, for thy Lord hath provided a rivulet beneath thee. And shake toward thyself the palm-tree; it will let fall fresh ripe dates upon thee. So eat and drink and dry thine eye. And if thou dost see any man, say 'I have vowed a fast to God Most Gracious, and this day I will enter into no talk with any human being.'"
>
> At length she brought forth the babe to her people, carrying him in her arms. They said, "O Mary, truly an amazing thing hast thou brought." (Surah 19:16–27)

Others were not so sure, and began to deride her unmarried state. The insults begin with a reference to her name, the same as the sister of Moses and Aaron (Musa and Haroon in many translations), and a reference to the reputation of her own parents. "O sister of Haroon, thy father was not a man of evil, nor was thy mother unchaste."

(Implying the question, "So why are you so?")

> But she merely pointed to the babe. They said, "How can we get an answer from one who is a child in the cradle?"
>
> And 'Isa said, "I am indeed a servant of God. He hath given me a revelation and made me a prophet. He hath made me blessed, wheresoever I be, and hath enjoined on me Prayer and Chastity as long as I live. He made me kind to my mother and not overbearing or miserable. So peace is upon me the day I was born, the day that I die, and the day that I shall be raised up to life again."
> (Surah 19:28–33)

Such clear references to the resurrection as a "type" of God's redemptive activity may cause some Christians to think more deeply about their own understanding, though Muslims regard this and similar passages as references to the second coming of Jesus.

There are also stories of Maryam and 'Isa during his infancy and childhood, preserved in the lore of the ancient Middle East and revealed to Muhammad as authentic stories with profound meaning. The baby 'Isa in the Qur'an is quite remarkable, he is even able to speak from the manger. As we have seen, when people condemned Maryam for having a baby without a husband, the baby 'Isa spoke up as if to defend her virtue in relation to God's miracle. Muslims believe that his infant speech was a miracle of the same order as his birth without a male parent, both being "signs" of his messianic destiny.

To Jews, these stories may be of the same order of myth as the Christian birth stories of Jesus, though many of these also coordinate nicely with certain of the prophecies concerning the birth of the Jewish Messiah. Christians are encouraged to consider these stories in the Qur'an alongside those they grew up with, but not to enter into any competition as to who has the higher view of Jesus as a baby, or the more "accurate" story of Mary, for that matter. All these similitudes are profound beyond measure.

In addition to the birth stories, Jesus, Son of Mary, or 'Isa Ibn Maryam, as he is called in Arabic, also did many other remarkable things as a child in the Qur'an.

> And God will teach Him the Book and Wisdom, the Law and the Gospel, and appoint Him an apostle to the Children of Israel, with this message:
> "I have come to you with a sign from your Lord. If I make for you out of

clay, as it were, the figure of a bird, and breathe into it, it becomes a bird by God's leave. And I heal those born blind and the lepers, and I quicken the dead by God's leave. Surely in these things there is a sign for you if ye but believe." (Surah 3:48–49)

As noted by Salman Rushdie, Muhammad was exposed to the teachings of the "heretical" Nestorian branch of the ancient Christian church, with its desert traditions concerning Mary and Jesus, in the years well before receiving the revelations concerning these things in the cave. It is of interest that, while much of this material is not in the traditional Gospels, some of it appears in the Gospel of Thomas, probably written down by Christians in Egypt halfway between the times of Jesus and Muhammad. This is an auspicious beginning to a messianic ministry that will be reviewed further in the next chapter, while we consider the role of Jesus' disciples in the Qur'an.

Meanwhile, this may be the place to consider more deeply what a renaissance in Muslim critical scholarship might mean in terms of an appreciative analysis of the Qur'an. It would merely be a "rebirth" of the type of scriptural investigation that occurred during an era of textual compilation in the century following Muhammad's death. This era also involved dynamic developments in source criticism, including the Hadith and other traditions that pointed to various background traditions, especially Jewish and Christian.

There was also a period of advanced scholarship in the fourth Islamic century (tenth century CE), before both Shia and Sunni schools began to cherish versions of what they both consider to be absolutely complete renditions of the revelation to Muhammad. It is not suggested here that there is anything whatsoever wrong with the text of the Qur'an as received. Indeed, the Muslims experience of textual re-evaluation could well be the same as the Jewish and Christian experience following the discovery of the Nag Hammadi Library (Egypt 1945) and the Dead Sea Scrolls (Palestine 1947). To the surprise of some, the confidence of scholars in the received texts has been immeasurably strengthened by comparison with these more ancient copies of the texts. With that reinforced confidence has come a deeper appreciation of what God has done in communicating both to and through the people of the book themselves, as well as to and through the oracular prophets.

Christians and Jews had pioneers in textual analysis in early centuries, like Origen in the third century, who proposed three ways of understanding the Bible: literal, ethical, and allegorical. At about the same time, Julius Sextus Africanus, living in Palestine, "proved" that the story of Susanna was a postbiblical work of Greek-speaking Jews and deserved to be among the books excluded from the Hebrew Canon (the official list of Holy Scriptures). Theodore of Mopsuestia, a Syrian contemporary of the great translator of the fourth century, Saint Jerome, illustrated that the author of the Book of Job was not Jewish, a fact never since disputed.

Of course, the ecclesiastical and rabbinical institutions are always nervous about such investigations. Baruch Spinoza, one of the leading founders of the modern critical school, was expelled from the Jewish community in Holland, and the Spanish Inquisition, with all its horrors, was designed to stamp out such questioning. To outsiders, it may appear that, until very recently, Islamic scholars wishing to pursue questions about the textual context of the Qur'an have faced something not unlike the Inquisition, with "fatwas" and charges of blasphemy.

This is rapidly changing and we are discovering that, because its texts have been so well preserved, perhaps Islam has little to fear from these investigations, as treasures begin to pour forth in the Qur'anic fields of science, women's studies, justice, and the acceptable standards of community life. Well-entrenched Muslim traditions that are not actually grounded in the Qur'an may be under attack, but more and more the Qur'an itself appears to be secure.

The next few generations of Muslims may witness a truly exciting flowering of their religion, but for this to happen there must be a confident openness to Qur'anic studies, no matter where they seem to lead. There will be false starts, dead ends, and disappointments, as well as thrills, inspirations, and progressive advances. Those who believe the Qur'an to be the Words of God have nothing to fear.

Just as a dream written down in the morning rarely makes literal sense but may be laden with insight for those who can interpret its meaning, so it was (in a more cosmic sense) with the revelations presented to Muhammad who was in a trancelike state (as the prophet himself describes it) when he was seized by God. As in a dream, these revelations from God may include images from many sources, such as the life experiences of Muhammad and his use of Arabic language, for example. The images and words may have been rearranged by God but can be identified, and may aid in interpreting the dream or trance. This could apply to images and material to which the thoughtful young Muhammad was exposed through the first forty years of his life (before the first revelation), and on through the series of revelations that came to him all through his mature years. If Muhammad's knowledge of Arabic was so obviously employed by Allah, what other preparations for receiving the revelations might Allah have provided to him?

Nestorian Christianity and other Christian traditions, especially those represented by his Abyssinian allies and certain members of his own family, were well known to Muhammad. The Jewish Diaspora, including orthodox and other Jewish traditions, was a major influence in his early search for truth and in his later years of working out communal relationships. Zoroastrian travelers brought even Hindu tales to his ears. One such Persian, named Salman, was a valued ally at the siege of Median and on other occasions. The Hanif monotheists who preceded Muhammad critiqued the idolatry of Arabian society and passed on ancient desert traditions about Adam and Abraham to him. The lore of the Sabeans, mentioned in the Bible but since forgotten, is now available only through the Qur'an, as filtered by Allah in the revelations concerning their beliefs.

The *textus receptus* for the Qur'an has come down in orderly fashion to the Muslim world. The original Qur'an is said to be authored by God (Surah 6:19), and written on a Tablet kept in heaven (Surahs 85:21–22). It was brought down, as tradition tells us, by the angel Gabriel, to the prophet's ear. Muhammad was chosen as God's messenger, having been prepared to receive the message and present it to the world. The sources behind the textual history of the Qur'an are exciting. They need not be seen as a challenge to orthodoxy, but rather as a means of shedding light upon it.

There is a pious tradition that the revelations were all promptly written down with the help of one scribe or another (usually Muhammad's secretary, Zaid). The serial additions were added to the collection and reviewed in detail by Muhammad and the angel Gabriel once a year, and twice in the year before he died.

There may be truth in the tradition to the extent that the revelations were certainly highly cherished and no doubt prayerfully reviewed, and that various compilations and collections were made by Muhammad and others. However, there is manifest evidence from trustworthy Islamic sources among the first generation of Muslims that when Muhammad died there was no collection of his revelations in any official form. Written portions had been collected during his lifetime by various persons in his community, certain portions had been memorized by individuals and groups, and it appears that some portions had been used liturgically in the worship of the community.

The first official collection, or codex, was made by the first Caliph, Abu Bakr, the successor to Muhammad and his first convert outside his own household. One tradition contends that the collection was made at the suggestion of Muhammad's nephew, Ali, who would eventually become the fourth Caliph and leader of the Shia schism. Secretary Zaid was employed in the work and the finished product was entrusted to Umar, the second

Caliph, and ultimately to Umar's daughter, Hafsa, who was its custodian until its universal acceptance.

There were attempts to gather all the revelations together, but several rival collections appeared in various places, each with particular claims to legitimacy, and the text in Hafsa's possession was not universally accepted until Uthman, the third Caliph, canonized this so-called "Medina Codex" and ordered that all other collections be burned.

The differences were perhaps not significant, but fragments still survive in quotations elsewhere. Hints as to their meaning or significance have been controversial. Some verses about stoning adulterers were left out of Hafsa's copy according to some early debates. There was the "Satanic verses" controversy . . . or were those simply some verses that were misunderstood and superseded by further revelations received by Muhammad himself through the process known as abrogation? Why do Muslims of North Africa use a variant of the official text, called the Warsh transmission? What is the official standing of Turkish and Farsi translations that are increasingly used in worship in Turkey and Iran, to the consternation of Arab purists? Such questions reverberate through the Muslim world these days. More questions may arise, but they are to be faced with confidence.

There is another pious tradition among less well-educated Muslims that every copy of the Qur'an in the world is identical. While there are no great differences, the fact that the original Arabic, like Hebrew, had no vowel marks, and the methods of transmission varied in early years of rapid expansion made it unlikely that all early copies would be identical. In fact, so many variations existed that in the fourth Islamic century (after 922 CE) that it was decided to codify the variations. Since then, as every Imam in the world knows, there have been seven official variant readings of the Qur'an, each of them with two recognized traditions of transmission, giving us fourteen versions of the Medina Codex alone, as authorized by Uthman. Not all of them are in general use today; some are used for scholarly purposes and others are used liturgically.

For example, a minor textual issue exists in the opening Surah, where Allah is described in Arabic as either the "Sovereign" of the Judgment Day or the "Possessor" of the Judgment Day. The consonants used by Muhammad's secretary are the same for both words in Arabic, but the vowel marks added later make a difference that is under dispute. A plausible solution to this conundrum is presented by Yusef Ali in his translation by using the English word "Master," but it still remains a problem in Arabic, at least for purists, including many Muslims in our time. This seemingly trivial puzzle is offered here merely as an example of dozens of textual questions now under discussion. An outsider hears all these things from Muslim colleagues, which suggests a larger area for possible fruitful investigation than is sometimes realized.

In early Muslim centuries there was an ever-evolving interpretation of the Qur'an by religious leaders, a centuries-old process called *ijtihad*. The decline of the process of *ijtihad* well before the modern era has led to the rigid and narrow interpretations of religious precepts that increasing numbers of Muslim thinkers see as a prison. Sadly, until very recently in the modern era, any such investigations of the Qur'an have usually been pursued by Christians and Jews purporting to be scholars of the Muslim Scriptures. In too many cases they were mere polemicists seeking to discredit Islam by exposing apparent inconsistencies and seeming flaws in its cherished text. Julius Wellhausen was an early exception to this judgment, but his goodwill toward Islam was not enough to overcome his limited knowledge of Arabic in the attempt to apply the principles of the Documentary Hypotheses to the Qur'an.

In addition to recognized variant readings there were also errors in copying in the Middle Ages, and modern printing errors, which produce clusters of versions in a process that will be described later when we compare this to the story of how Christians got two versions of their much loved Lord's Prayer. Then there is the problem of the many and varied translations. In the opinion of many, the true Qur'an is available only in Arabic for reasons intrinsic to its essence.

In the most recent era there are non-Muslims such as Professor Reuven Firestone of the Hebrew Union College who cherish the truth of Islam and bring exceptional and detailed knowledge of the Qur'an to the task. Professor Firestone's work respectfully complements the pioneering work of renowned Islamic scholars like the late respected Professor Edward Said of Columbia University in New York and Mehnaz Afridi of Los Angeles and the task continues on a collaborative ecumenical basis among scholars.

The most important work in this field and related fields is yet to be done by Islamic specialists in the ancient centers of learning, among whom many are exceptionally qualified. Initially, some of the modern work in this area by Muslims was done by knowledgeable individuals who were not specialists. Salman Rushdie in Britain and Ibn Warraq in America have brought biting negative critiques to the discussion, partly reflecting their frustration with what has seemed like intellectual dishonesty, or even cowardice, in contemporary Qur'anic studies.

The work has begun to advance in positive directions, in North America at least, by established intellectuals such as Dr. Khaled Abou el-Fadl, who is respected within the Muslim community as a professor of law at UCLA and an expert in Islamic jurisprudence. In the rising generation there are those like Reza Aslan, author of *No God But God*, with a degree in theology from Harvard and a doctorate from the University of California in Santa Barbara, who says reform within Islam is inevitable but is impeded by Western insensitivity and provocation. Such commentators are confident that their scholarship purifies Islam. They believe the vast silent majority of Muslims are with them in using the Qur'an itself as the basis of modern reforms.

Some of the most highly placed religious authorities in other parts of the world are said to be following these developments with positive interest, including possibly the Ayatollah Sistani, spiritual leader of the Iraqi Shia majority. This is hardly a "liberalizing" trend, since any errors are human errors and the quest for the purist rendition of the revelation is actually a conservative agenda in essence. Though reforms may challenge erroneous traditions that have evolved on a cultural basis over the centuries, the reactions of an entrenched establishment is never a match for the truth when embraced by the people, as is happening today around the Muslim world.

Finally, in an era of such dynamics, surprises will come. For many years the best text of both Hebrew and Christian Scriptures was the Codex Vaticanus, an old and well-preserved manuscript from the fourth century, which was used officially for Roman Catholic translations. Then in 1844, Konstantin von Tischendorf, a German biblical scholar, found an older manuscript, Codex Sinaiticus, in the rubbish heap of the Russian Orthodox Monastery of Saint Catherine at Mount Sinai. He presented it to the Czar, whose family lost it to the communists. They did not value it, of course, but sold it to the British Museum in 1933, when it became widely available to translators. A new era in Bible translation was begun on the basis of this more ancient authentic text. Its positive impact will be detailed in the next chapter, but even more exciting discoveries were to come.

In 1947 a fifteen-year-old Bedouin boy named Muhammad adh-Dhib threw some stones up into a Palestinian hillside cave to scare out a goat. He heard the sound of breaking clay pottery. Upon investigation, he made the single most surprising find in modern biblical pursuits, the discovery of the Dead Sea Scrolls. These ancient manuscripts, hidden in the year 70 of the Common Era, included complete scrolls of the Hebrew Scriptures in near perfect condition. The accompanying documents also shed light on Jewish sectarian practices and the context of early Christianity.

Wild rumors that the Dead Sea Scrolls proved that the Jews never crossed the Red Sea or that Jesus and John the Baptist were married were compounded by years in which Israeli authorities would not release full copies of these manuscripts. There was a nervous determination to control the out-come or at least the release of information. When it all did become public, the most amazing aspect of the discovery was the realization that Bibles used by Jews and Catholics, Orthodox and Protestant, have a textual integ-rity that was now beyond question. Nothing of significance had been changed by ignorant scholars, corrupt church officials, or Satan himself, as charged by reconstructionist cults and modern cynics from time to time.

In 1945 another Muslim party had made a discovery just as significant for Christians as the Dead Sea Scrolls, but eclipsed by that discovery until more of the documents have been published, which happened comparatively recently. An Egyptian farmer named Muhammad Ali and his brother had been digging for fertilizer in a potash deposit in the desert. They uncovered a jar, a foot tall and eight inches wide, crammed with small tractlike books. The Nag Hammadi Library, as it is called, contains writings of the Gnostic Christians. They were a sect who believed that the material world is bad and mortal flesh is evil, as explained in writings published in the name of those associated with Jesus, such as the Gospel of Mary and the Gospel of Phillip. Two of the Gnostic documents of interest of late, especially in New Age spiritual circles, are the Gospel of Thomas and the Gospel of Judas. There are also the Acts of Peter, the Revelation of Peter, the Revelation of James, the Gospel of Lazarus, and others, forty-five books in all, contained in thirteen volumes, each the size of a small paperback.

The existence of these documents has always been known in fragments and quotes. The ancient Church rejected them and then, for seemingly valid reason, banned them and ordered all copies burned. What would likely hap-pen when the authorities tried to destroy documents some group regards as precious? Quite naturally, someone hid a library of these writings! The story is reminiscent of the determination to destroy all rival copies of the Qur'an in early years.

After their discovery in 1945, it took twenty years for the world to fully appreciate that the Nag Hammadi Library contained authentic Coptic translations of Greek writings by the Gnostics, published at a time when Gnosticism was banned, after rivaling Orthodox Christianity and almost taking it over. In contrast to the Gnostics, Orthodox Christians believe this is not a bad world. In Genesis, as God completed each "day," or era, of creation He stood back and pronounced over each thing, "Behold, it is very good."

Again there was panic in certain conservative quarters in the Christian Church. The rumors were that the Nag Hamadi documents would dethrone the Pope with information about early church government, or even that

Jesus was married to Mary Magdalene. Hints of his love for her did actually lead to fictions such as *The Da Vinci Code*. However, close examination of the Nag Hammadi documents has merely enriched the study of Christian Scriptures, many of which were penned at the beginning of the controversy. Previously unintelligible arguments in their Scriptures suddenly made sense to Christian readers. We may yet discover the identities of the "false believers" disparaged in the Epistles of John and the Book of Revelation. Such discoveries have continued to justify the confidence of the church in its primary sources. There is never anything to fear from the truth.

Is there a codex of the Qur'an waiting to be discovered in an old library in Persia? Is there an early version in a cave somewhere in Lybia? Something like this is almost certain to happen, and rather than suppress it, Muslims would do well to welcome it, with its accompanying documents all shedding new light and promoting greater confidence in all that is true. As a matter of fact, it is virtually certain that just such a find has been made, but like earlier Jewish and Christian discoveries, the documents are being currently suppressed by nervous Muslim authorities.

A "paper grave" in Muslim tradition is similar to the Jewish custom of burying worn-out copies of the sacred scrolls. In some Middle Eastern Muslim circles there is a practice of removing damaged copies of the Qur'an from circulation by burying them in such a grave, a practice that respects the sanctity of the texts that are being "laid to rest" and guarantees that only complete and unblemished copies of the Qur'an will be read.

Just such a paper grave was found in 1972 by workers restoring the Great Mosque of Sana'a in Yemen. In an attic above the ceiling and beneath the roof they found a smelly, soggy pile of old documents of both parchment and paper. Mosques do not usually contain graves for either people or paper, so at first they did not realize what they had stumbled upon. The damaged texts and pages of Arabic text had been gnawed upon by rats and bored through by insects. The workers simply shoveled them into twenty large gunnysacks and stuffed them into one of the minarets. They stayed there until an inspection tour by Qadhi Isma'il al-Akwa, the president of the Yemeni Antiquities Authority, who realized that this had been a paper grave that could be of some importance. At al-Akwa's invitation, an international team, largely from Germany, began the arduous process of examining and restoring tens of thousands of fragments from more than a thousand ancient parchment copies of the Qur'an, plus a smaller number in book form.

Some of the parchments dated back to the seventh century CE, Islam's first century. They were pages from the oldest copies of the Qur'an known to be in existence anywhere. Indeed, some of them are what scholars call "palimpsests," that is, copies that had been used twice or more—parchments that had been erased or washed and reused. These are most exciting because in laboratory conditions, traces of the original text can usually be read, sometimes quite well. In this case, the evolution of the Qur'an, if any, will be possible to document since these copies represent a generation of material before the burning of variant texts by Uthman, the third Caliph.

By the turn of the twenty-first century, more than fifteen thousand sheets of the ancient Yemeni copies of the Qur'an have been carefully processed by flattening, cleaning, preserving, and restoration into complete volumes. Now they are stored in a vault in the House of Manuscripts in the capital. They await more detailed examination of such things as the palimpsest pages, but nothing is happening, as far as the rest of the world knows. The best summary of this find to date is possibly an article by Toby Lester in the January 1999 edition of *The Atlantic* magazine, available online.

Those who have read them are certain that these pages reveal small but remarkable differences from the Qur'an as we have it. For those who insist on believing that the standard text of the Qur'an contains the "inerrant" and perfect words of God, this could be a troubling development. There are other Muslim scholars who believe that study of these texts will place the Qur'an in its historical context, as called for in the foreword to this book. Combined with other factors, this could be the kind of spark that sets off an explosion of Islamic vitality in a positive direction.

Such a development of renewal was triggered by King Josiah when he found the scroll of Deuteronomy during a temple renovation, as reported in the Hebrew Scriptures at II Kings 22. The Protestant Reformation was initiated by such events related to scriptural accessibility and interpretation, unleashing a storm of social change in Europe. At the beginning of the twenty-first century, the Qur'an is the hottest ideological text in the world, and the possible consequences of these developments are immense.

There are few experiences more liberating and fulfilling than when blind faith is superseded by a faith that has eyes wide open, a faith that has no need to be fearful or defensive. Those who refuse to get onboard run the risk of drowning.

16

The Temple

Zacharias/Zakariya, John/Yahya

THE IDEA OF CHRISTIANITY as a "spiritual temple," rather than a physical church, has major appeal for many inside and outside the church. Few Jews and even fewer Muslims have any quarrel with Jesus, but many have serious problems with the institutional church, and sometimes for good reasons.

Within the Christian community, the debate between organized religion and spiritual life has occupied every generation to some extent, but the answer, in reality, always seems to be that these concepts are the opposite sides of one coin. It is difficult to sustain one without the other, and therein lie both the genius and the greatest challenge to Christianity in the church.

> Lay aside all malice, and all guile, and hypocrisies, and envies, and all evil speaking, as newborn babes, and desire the sincere milk of the word, that ye may grow thereby, if so be it that ye have tasted the graciousness of the Lord. By coming to Him, as unto a living stone, rejected by mortals, but chosen by God, and precious, ye also, as living stones, are built up as a spiritual temple, a holy priesthood, to offer up spiritual sacrifices, acceptable to God through Jesus Christ. (1 Peter 2:1–10)

The origins of Christianity in Judaism, and the origins of the church in the synagogue, are well known and appreciated, in spite of the horrific record of Christian church people toward their Jewish neighbors in history. One goal of this chapter is to see how Christianity and the church also may be able to relate to the aspirations and ideals so fondly expressed toward it in the Qur'an, ignoring for the moment that most Muslims have given up hoping for that which Muhammad looked for in the Christian community.

From the Christian tradition, the Qur'an recounts stories of Jesus and Mary, but it is in the disciples and others that we find the Qur'anic assessment of the church. Jesus' relationship to the disciples may be considered here while Mary's relationship with Zechariah has already been referenced. However, it is in the counterbalance between Zechariah and John the Baptist that the Qur'an recalls the nature of the church.

Zakariyah and Yahya as father and son, and especially as priest and prophet, define the church in the Qur'an in ways that may be helpful to the modern church in its quest to balance worship and social action.

> Kaf Ha. Ya. 'Ain. Sad. This is a recital of the Mercy of thy Lord to His Servant Zakariya. "Behold!" he cried to his Lord in secret, praying: "O my Lord! infirm indeed are my bones and the hair of my head doth glisten with grey: but never am I unblest, O my Lord, in my prayer to Thee!"
>
> "Now I fear what my relatives and colleagues will do after me: but my wife is barren: so give me an heir as from Thyself, one that will truly represent me and represent the posterity of Yaqub; and make him, O my Lord, one with whom Thou art well-pleased!"
>
> His prayer was answered: "O Zakariya! We give thee good news of a son: his name shall be Yahya: on none by that name have We conferred distinction before."
>
> He said: "O my Lord! how shall I have a son when my wife is barren and I have grown quite decrepit from old age?"
>
> He said: "So it will be: thy Lord saith 'That is easy for Me: I did indeed create thee before when thou hadst been nothing!'"
>
> Zakariya said, "O my Lord! give me a Sign." "Thy Sign," came the answer, "shall be that thou shalt speak to no man for three nights, although thou art not dumb."
>
> So Zakariya came out to his people from his chamber: he told them by signs to celebrate Allah's praises in the morning and in the evening. To his son came the command: "O Yahya! take hold of the Book with might," and We gave him wisdom even as a youth. And pity for all creatures as from Us and purity: he was devout and kind to his parents and he was not overbearing or rebellious. So Peace on him the day he was born the day that he dies and the day that he will be raised up to life again! (Surah 19:1–15)

> And Zakariyah and Yahya and 'Isa and Illiyas: are all in the ranks of the righteous. (Surah 6:85)

The story of the birth of John the Baptist is little different in the gospels than it is in the Qu'ran. With his emphasis on social justice, he would fit well among the prophets of Israel. With his emphasis on Judgment, it is easy to see why he fits so well into the Muslim prophetic tradition. Yet even "the most righteous man born of woman," as the Gospels call him, may have obeyed all the laws and still needed to be born again . . . born of the Spirit.

O ye who believe! be ye helpers of Allah: as said 'Isa Ibn Maryam to the Disciples, "Who will be my helpers to the work of Allah?" Said the Disciples: "We are Allah's helpers!" Then a portion of Bani Israel believed and a portion disbelieved: but We gave power to those who believed against their enemies and they became the ones that prevailed. (Surah 61:14)

Then in their wake We followed them up with others of Our Apostle: We sent after them 'Isa Ibn Maryam and bestowed on him the Gospel; and We ordained in the hearts of those who followed him Compassion and Mercy. But the monasticism which they invented for themselves We did not prescribe for them: We commanded only the seeking for the Good pleasure of Allah; but that they did not foster as they should have done. Yet We bestowed on those among them who believed their due reward, but many of them are rebellious transgressors.

O ye that believe! fear Allah and believe in His apostles and He will bestow on you a double portion of His Mercy: He will provide for you a light by which ye shall walk straight in your path and He will forgive you your past: For Allah is Oft-Forgiving. And Most Merciful, that the People of the Book may know that they have no power whatever over the Grace of Allah, and that His Grace is entirely in his hand to bestow it on whomsoever He wills. For Allah is the Lord of Grace abounding. (Surah 57:27–29)

When 'Isa found unbelief on their part he said: "Who will be my helpers to the work of Allah?" Said the Disciples: "We are Allah's helpers we believe in Allah and do thou bear witness that we are Muslims. Our Lord! we believe in what thou hast revealed and we follow the Apostle; then write us down among those who bear witness." (Surah 3:52–53)

These echoes of the gospel, as provided by Allah to Muhammad in the Qur'an, present a stricter gospel and a harsher gospel than the one presented in the Christian Scriptures. The same issue is debated among Christians, some of whom feel that permissive lifestyles, where "anything goes," are the undoing of the mission God has entrusted to the church. Others believe that union with God in Christ, far from licensing every sin, transforms every context and disciplines every action with a higher morality based on God's will, rather than the basic letter of the law.

But the Christian tradition to which the Qur'an bears witness is also more priestly (from Zechariah in the temple to the disciples and their sacraments) than expected from a source that might decry excessive ritual. There is no withdrawal from the rites and rituals of organized spiritual life in the church, as described by the Qur'an.

"And behold! I inspired the Disciples to have faith in Me and Mine Apostle: they said 'We have faith and do thou bear witness that we bow to Allah as

Muslims.'" And behold, the disciples said: "O 'Isa Ibn Maryam! can thy Lord send down to us a table set from heaven?" Said 'Isa: "Fear Allah if ye have faith." They said: "We only wish to eat thereof and satisfy our hearts and to know that thou hast indeed told us the truth; and that we ourselves may be witnesses to the miracle." Said 'Isa Ibn Maryam: "O Allah our Lord! send us from heaven a table set that there may be for us for the first and the last of us a solemn festival and a sign from Thee; and provide for our sustenance for Thou art the best Sustainer of our needs."

Allah said: "I will send it down unto you: but if any of you after that resis-teth faith, I will punish him with a penalty such as I have not inflicted on any-one among all the peoples." (Surah 5:111–115)

Those apostles We endowed with gifts some above others: to one of them Allah spoke; others He raised to degrees [of honor]; to Jesus the son of Mary We gave clear [Signs] and strengthened him with the Holy Spirit. If Allah had so willed succeeding generations would not have fought among each other after clear [Signs] had come to them but they [chose] to wrangle some believ-ing and others rejecting. If Allah had so willed they would not have fought each other; but Allah fulfilleth His plan. (Surah 2:253)

In the twentieth century, any reaction against secularism was muted in the face of "progress," but that reaction was clearly defined in some quarters. It broke out in the historic 1906 Azusa Street "revival" in Los Angeles, Cali-fornia, which marked the beginning of a century-long Pentecostal renewal of the spirit in the church, a spirit "not of this world."

In Eastern Europe, as elsewhere, wherever the Roman Catholic Church lost its privileged intimacy with power and influence it became strong enough to challenge the secular order. Where it remained entrenched, as in Central and South America, it has been challenged by Protestant, mainly Pentecostal, alternatives. The same thing happened to the disenfranchised Orthodox Church, outlasting Communists in the Soviet Union and the Ottoman Turks in Greece. We watch with equal amazement as the postcolo-nial church sets its own course in Africa and the underground church emerges intact and robust in China.

The exceptions to all this are the Protestant mainline churches in North America (Presbyterian, United, Methodist, Lutheran, and Episcopal) and the remaining state churches of Europe, (Lutheran, Reformed, and Angli-can). Their declared agenda has been to become relevant to the world and to address the issues of the time. They have remained viable, but in a dimin-ishing role, due to this emphasis on a secular agenda.

In Abraham's family, and with his example, Moses walked out on Pha-raoh, Jesus proclaimed a kingdom "not of this world," and Muhammad established a community that represents an obvious example of the rejection of secular values. All three branches of the family have struggled to find the balance of being "in this world but not of this world." The mainline churches of North America and the state churches of Europe have begun to realize again that the balance is not found in mere relevance to the world. Believers come together first to experience the "otherness" of God, something other than the issues of the time. When that experience of worship is genuine, the believers can then go back into the world to be relevant in the workplace and address the issues in the political forum.

Churches that were the most prominent one hundred years ago were temporarily seduced into either confronting or dialoguing with secularism as a first priority, but the church as recognized in the Qur'an went underground or into exile in the Pentecostal movement. Certainly, the National Council of Churches (U.S. mainstream Protestant) should lead the civil rights cause and question the American president every time he declares war, but not as its first priority. If the institutional churches are properly about their business of interfacing the people of the church with God, they should succeed in the social action agenda by merely pointing the people in the direction indicated in the gospel. Or God will raise up prophets in the way Al Gore became the "warner" on the environment.

Someone asked Jesus, "Master, which is the great commandment in the law?" Jesus said unto him, "Thou shalt love the Lord thy God with all thy heart, and with all thy soul and with all thy mind. This is the first and great commandment. And the second is like unto it, Thou shalt love thy neighbour as thyself. On these two commandments hang all the law and the prophets" (Matthew 22:36–40). The first is an otherworldly agenda; the second is a secular agenda that is only adequately accomplished after the first is fulfilled.

Jesus proclaimed that the second commandment, to love your neighbor, is "like unto" the first commandment, to love God. Far from denigrating social action, Jesus commends it that highly. The church only gets into difficulty when it reverses the order of these priorities.

The moderate majority in the church had reached a place where they were comfortable in electing a female priest with a positive approach to gay ordination and to gay marriage as the Presiding Bishop of the Episcopal Church of the United States in 2006: Bishop Katherine Jefferts Schori may well be right on these issues, or may not be, but she made the profound error of the mainstream in the last century as her answer to the first question put to her by *Time* magazine (July 17, 2006), "What will be your focus as head of the U.S. church?" Bishop Katherine replied, "Our focus needs to be on feeding people who go to bed hungry, on providing primary education to girls and boys, on healing people with AIDS, on addressing tuberculosis and malaria, on sustainable development. That ought to be the primary focus." Judging by the words of Jesus and the model of the priestly church recognized in the Qur'an, the Bishop was wrong. Her agenda is most laudable, but loving neighbors is second to worship. Her goals can only be accomplished by the people of God when the primary agenda is addressed, especially by the priestly leadership. In retooling for the twenty-first century, post-liberal denominations do not need to relinquish their cherished social justice agendas nor mimic the success of Evangelical friends with a more conservative gospel, but to simply put God first.

Spokespersons for the church have a duty to address world issues and national issues. Church regional units might well make relevant local statements, and congregations should be encouraged to have study and action groups, but a profound error is made when secular agendas dominate worship services in a reversal of priorities.

The contrast is stark in this regard when comparing the politically correct but somewhat anemic State Church of England with its robust Anglican counterparts in Africa and Asia. The first priority for the church is to connect people with God, and with eternal realities in an "alternate universe." The prophetic role in justice issues is of tremendous importance in Judaism, in Christianity and Islam, but taken alone, John the Baptist is the least in the Kingdom of God, as the Christian Scriptures attest.

Unless the loving, healing, and redemptive relationship with God is secured through an encounter with God in worship (a burning bush experience, whether spontaneous or planned), the social action of the Christian Church is at risk of becoming a temporary feel-good exercise with constantly diminishing resources and impact. This has been precisely the experience of mainline Protestant Churches in North America and the state churches of Europe, in spite of sincere and heroic efforts to be relevant.

Prominent in the Jewish community in this regard was the voice of the twentieth-century minor prophet Martin Buber, whose classic 1923 book, *I and Thou (Ich und Du)*, shows how this otherworldly approach works in personal relationships. Even earlier, in 1917, the Christian theologian Rudolph Otto wrote *The Idea of the Holy (Das Heilige): An Inquiry into the Non-rational Factor in the Idea of the Divine and its Relation to the Rational*, in which he described the human need for connecting to the *Mysterium Tremendum* in life. This classic was perhaps a hundred years before its time, as we note religious trends today where issue-centered churches are often empty and those with either Pentecostal spirit or high liturgy are increasingly robust.

The otherworldly emphasis of the Pentecostal movement in the church was paralleled by the rise of the Hasidic movement in Judaism and Wahabinism in Islam for exactly the same reasons. These were all unexpected developments in the twentieth century, which was thought to be a time of growing secularism. No one denies the influence of these movements in the world, but no one takes that agenda to be their priority. Mainline and established churches have taken note and the spiritual climate of the twenty-first century is changing rapidly.

Salman Rushdie frequently suggests that religion, as he sees it, might well be replaced by awareness of "transcendence," whether found in art, poetry, or music. Sadly, because of Islam's extreme manifestation of other issues, he misses seeing what is among the most powerful examples of what the world needs in its quest for religious authenticity. The Qur'an itself, as recited in haunting Arabic tones, is ethereal, mysterious, and imbued with qualities of both dread and awe akin to what the Bible calls "the fear of the Lord." Christians would want to say that Jesus is "transcendence personified," and when they realized that, the first impulse of the disciples was to worship—and only then to reach out to neighbors.

Some analysis of the Christian Scriptures is in order at this point. We have seen how textual analysis and criticism has worked in recognizing the sources of the Pentateuch. There is a similar exercise available to sincere scholars of the Christian Scriptures, both lay and professional, with equal value in appreciating the richness in the backgrounds of the first three gospels in particular. It is another detective story.

The texts of the gospels are sufficiently familiar in Western culture, and even in world culture for readers to make their own observations, based on the best-known stories. This exercise does not even require language skills, because, although the gospels were all written in Greek, this particular investigation can be pursued in English or any other translation.

We begin with the question of where the gospels came from and why the first three of them look so much alike and yet have such distinct differences. The relationship between Matthew, Mark, and Luke is a puzzle often referred to as "The Synoptic Problem." The Gospel of Jesus Christ According to Saint Matthew appears first in the New Testament, because it repeatedly points to the purported fulfillment of Old Testament prophecies concerning the Messiah. It opens with stories of the magi astrologers visiting Bethlehem following the birth of Jesus, a hint of the Persian or Oriental origins of this gospel. Like the Pentateuch, Matthew has four strands of material: a document that Matthew's gospel shares with Mark and Luke, another document shared with only Luke, a collection of sayings of Jesus unique to this gospel (probably the portion written by Matthew himself during his mission ministry in the farther east) and finally the unique opening section that presents Jesus genealogy (through Mary back as far as Abraham), the birth and magi stories, and the flight into Egypt.

The second gospel in the Christian Scriptures is the one by Mark. According to I Peter 5:13, Mark was like a son to Saint Peter, himself a disciple, then an apostle and the first Bishop of the church in Rome. Papias, Bishop of Syria, remembered Mark as Peter's interpreter in his missionary work, leading to the natural assumption that when Peter died the church turned to Mark to publish a collection of the stories of Jesus since no one wanted Peter's stories about Jesus to be forgotten. As interpreter, Mark probably knew the stories by heart and there is no reason to doubt that Mark was the author of this gospel. Both internal and external evidence suggests that the gospel of Mark appears to be basically one document. There are no nativity stories and only a few verses about the resurrection (possibly added later); it is mostly a collection of the stories of Jesus that the world knows in direct, unpolished language, like a transcription of Peter's gruff style.

Luke tells us at the outset that he is merely the compiler of the third gospel, the one that bears his name, having gathered material from many sources and having interviewed eyewitnesses to the events of Jesus' life. One of those sources must be Mark because virtually every word of Mark is reproduced verbatim. Luke has his own collection of parables not found in Mark—material from Jesus' ministry unique to Luke, though not written by him since, as we learn in his second volume, the Acts of the Apostles, Luke is a physician from Greece who became a Christian some years after the life of Jesus through the missions of Saint Paul. There is also a document in Luke that has material in common with Matthew, plus Luke too has a unique birth and boyhood section, with a genealogy through Joseph all the way back to Adam—no magi, but shepherds and other authentic Palestinian figures.

John's gospel is sufficiently different in style, purpose, and content to ignore in the synoptic question, but why do Christians have those three "look-alike" gospels, and what can be gained by comparing them? The answer gives a picture of the early church and the license for the church universal to present the essence of the gospel in the context of the lives of people in all the cultures of the world.

Mark gives the essence of the teachings of Jesus, implying that if we get that, the more esoteric doctrines of his birth and resurrection may be seen as presentations of messianic credentials. That is a subject for believers, once they have accepted his teaching. Matthew focuses on the Jewish Diaspora from east to west and develops the messianic claim within Hebrew "proof texts," quoting Jewish prophecies and tracing the lineage only within the family of Abraham. Luke presents a gospel to the non-Jewish world, not quoting Scriptures that would be unfamiliar, but eyewitnesses who could then still be verified. His genealogy relates Jesus to the whole human family, beginning with Adam. These distinct emphases remain despite the fact that two-thirds of all three gospels are virtually the same, and in the case of Matthew and Luke, eighty percent is practically identical.

We surmise that Mark's gospel was written between Peter's death in the year 64 CE and the year 70 CE, when Jerusalem was destroyed, because the text presumes the city is still standing. Matthew and Luke both integrated Mark's writing into their longer works. They both are two-thirds Mark, one-sixth something else they had in common, and one-sixth something unique to each. We believe that Luke and Matthew were written at about the same time, sometime after 70 CE because their gospels refer to the destruction of Jerusalem. It would have taken a few years for them to acquire copies of Mark if they were some distance away, and there is evidence that they were. Matthew and Luke must have been some distance from each other since neither of them had yet seen the work of the other—why else would Matthew leave out the story of the Good Samaritan and the Prodigal Son, masterpieces of world literature, and why would Luke omit the Ten Virgins, the Marriage Feast, the Laborers in the Vineyard, and the Parable of the Talents, if he had read them in Matthew?

We know from other sources that Luke was centered in the eastern Mediterranean and Matthew somewhere in the Orient, but there is more. They both had copies of Mark but neither possessed the work of the other, as illustrated above, so how do we explain that another sixth of Matthew's gospel and Luke's gospel are word-for-word identical, but not found in Mark? It is believed by source critics that this proves the existence of · another document circulating in the early church, and in the possession of both Matthew and Luke, but unknown to Mark at the time he wrote. A copy has yet to be found.

This document is called "Q" by the source critics (from the German *Quelle* meaning source) and because Matthew and Luke appear to have copied it meticulously, we assume that we have the whole of it. Q is a collection of information about Jesus, possibly originating as a supplement to Mark's collection of stories told by Jesus. Q includes such things as the temptations in the wilderness, Jesus' reply to questions posed by John the Baptist from prison, the conditions of discipleship, the mission of the seventy, some parables like Building on Rock or Sand, the Beatitudes (unexpected blessings announced by Jesus), and the Lord's Prayer. All these are significant additions and they appear to come from a source known to both Luke and Matthew.

Matthew (or the editor who finally put material by Matthew into the gospel that bears his name) and Luke both insert Mark's material to suit their agendas, but respectfully, in large sections, as befits something from the head office of the church. The Q material is scattered more creatively into the composite documents. The material from these multiple sources may be represented graphically when presented in multicolored diagram form. In side-by-side columns of gospel verses, Mark's material, Q, Matthew's unique material, and Luke's unique material are all assigned separate colors. The best known of these is possibly the 1939 version by Allan Barr of Edinburgh, which has been in wide circulation ever since. This is Exhibit A in any dispute about the validity of critical methods of scriptural analysis because even a child can clearly identify the strands of material and draw correct conclusions about such things as the order in which they appeared and the distinct agenda of each gospel.

An appreciation of the dynamics of the early church and the spread of the gospel is greatly enhanced by such study. This is similar to the enhanced appreciation of Hebrew history and God's dealing with people in the Pentateuch once the basic thesis of the documentary hypothesis was accepted. Something similar may be about to unfold in Qur'anic research.

The gospels agree that there were visitor witnesses to the birth of Jesus. On the basis of his research, Luke says they were shepherds. It is suggested that Matthew's unique representation of those visitors as "magi" to his Persian audience was the license for early missionaries in Canada, for example, to present the nativity story with indigenous imagery. This style of evangelism is demonstrated in the Canadian Christmas Carol in which God is given the name *Gitchi Manitou*, the Great Spirit of the first nations.

> 'Twas in the moon of wintertime, when all the birds had fled,
> That Mighty Gitchi Manitou sent angel choirs instead.
> Before their light the stars grew dim and wandering hunters heard the hymn
> Jesus Emmanuel; Jesus is born; in excelsis gloria.
>
> Within a lodge of broken bark the tender babe was found;
> A ragged robe of rabbit skin enwrapped his beauty round.
> The chiefs from far, before him knelt, with gifts of fox and beaver pelt.
> Jesus Emmanuel; Jesus is born; in excelsis gloria.

This phenomenon has its parallels in Chinese and African figures in nativity scenes on Christmas cards in those cultures.

Finally, in reference to the church and its relationship to the text of Christian Scripture, the discipline of "form criticism" (knowledge revealed from within the text) presents us with the delightful tale of the different versions of the Lord's Prayer. This may serve as a model for discoveries almost certain to be uncovered in the Muslim world. The story was pieced together by Christian scholars only after the finding of *Codex Sinaiticus* in Egypt by Konstantin von Tischendorf in 1844.

Prior to the invention of the printing press (for the purpose of speeding up Bible production), Bibles were mass-produced by monks in selected monasteries. Twenty or thirty brothers would sit in rows in a large room called a *scriptorium* copying by hand as a reader dictated. When perhaps twenty Bibles were completed they would be shipped to churches requesting them, or to other monasteries and church institutions, including libraries and theological colleges. Occasionally, a manuscript from one of the leading monasteries would be shipped to a new monastery, or one that was just going into the production of Bibles. If a copy with an error was shipped, and hundreds of copies were eventually made from it, that error would be repeated in all the copies distributed from that source. If the new producer was the only one in a certain country or region, the Bibles in that whole area would contain the error. As more copies were made, the church of that country might become insistent on its interpretation of the Bible because all its churches had that version. There are a number of well-documented examples of this reason for variant texts, but none so clear as what happened in the case of the Lord's Prayer.

We do not know where *Codex Bezae* originated, except that it was in the Western church because it is in Latin. Scientific dating of its pages and analysis of the style of script confirms the tradition that it is from the fifth or sixth century, so it is ancient. In the Middle Ages it resided in the library of the Monastery of Saint Irenaeus in Lyons, France. It came into the possession of Protestant Reformer Theodore Beza, who wished to promote translations into vernacular European languages. He presented it to Cambridge University in 1581, and Cambridge named it after him. *Codex Bezae* was used as the basis of translations into European languages used by many Protestants. An error in *Bezae* would be translated and incorporated into the text. Thanks to the new printing presses in Britain and on the continent, the error would soon have thousands of copies and possibly be repeated for hundreds of years, even into various Revised Versions.

Picture the scene as it must have happened: The monks have been writing all day except for washroom breaks, chapel services, and meals. Late in the afternoon, some of them have writer's cramp and Brother Adrian, the reader, has begun to get hoarse. They got into the New Testament that morning and were now up to the sixth chapter of Matthew. When he reached verse nine, Brother Adrian read, "After this manner therefore pray ye," which they wrote. He continued, "Our father who art in heaven," which they wrote. At this point he might have said, "Carry on, chaps, while I get a drink and rest my throat."

Twenty monks kept writing, transcribing the words of the prayer they knew by heart. Except that when they said this prayer in chapel seven times a day, they added a *doxology*, a liturgical ascription of glory, as follows: "For Thine is the kingdom, the power and the glory, forever and ever, Amen." It was like another doxology, "Glory be to the Father," which many Protestants, Orthodox, and Catholic Christians still chant after reading a Psalm.

Nineteen monks wrote the prayer, ending where Catholic and Orthodox Christians end the prayer to this day: "And lead us not into temptation, but deliver us from evil. Amen." Brother Michael, exhausted and trying to complete the task in his beautiful handwriting, carried right on as he had done four times already that day in chapel, "For Thine is the kingdom, the power and the glory, forever and ever, Amen"—absentmindedly forgetting that the doxology was not part of the prayer as given to the disciples by Jesus.

Guess whose copy got shipped to Lyons, placed in the library, cherished, and quoted on special occasions and copied two thousand times in their scriptorium? Guess which prized original, not even one of the two thousand copies, was acquired by one of the great reformers, presented to Cambridge, and used throughout Protestant lands as the basis for translations in Swiss, Dutch, and French Reformed Churches, and by British Presbyterian, Puritan, and Anglican translators? It was *Bezae*, of course, and that was the manuscript used most famously as the basis for the King James Authorized Version.

So for nearly four hundred years Protestants said a longer Lord's Prayer than Roman Catholics, and wondered why Catholics did not know the whole prayer. In popular Protestant culture, from America to Australia, this seemed like proof that the Catholics had a defective tradition. After *Codex Sinaiticus* confirmed the *Codex Vaticanus* version, there was nothing Protestants could do except humbly admit that they were wrong.

It took a hundred years for this to be acknowledged, and Catholics kindly included the ancient doxology from time to time, especially when there were Protestants present. In joint services of worship to this day, Catholics generally bow to Protestant intransigence, and Protestants continue with the longer version, even though in most other respects they are not as given to doxologies and liturgical flourishes as their Catholic friends.

17

Son of Man, Son of God, Son of Mary

Jesus/'Isa

THE QUESTION JESUS asked Peter still hovers over humanity today: "Who do you say that I am?" The question is featured in blockbuster movies and every major weekly news magazine devotes one issue per year to the world's fascination with this subject. This level of interest in Jesus would have been impossible to imagine in the twentieth century.

Jews have always said, "The Messiah is coming." Christians saw the prophecy fulfilled and said, "Here He is, the Christ." Muslims looked at Jewish prophecy and Christian fulfillment and announced, "Yes, Jesus was Al Masih, and He is coming again" on the strength of the testimony of the Qur'an.

The Messiah, the Christ, Al Masih, the Anointed One unites and divides Jews, Christians, and Muslims as no other. One of the surprises of the current theological scene is how the Muslim understanding of Jesus as the Messiah presents a remarkable opportunity for Jews and Christians to come to a new understanding. This is not a new agreement about the Messiah, but it is at least the possibility of a new understanding of each other. The rest of the world may appreciate any agreement among the members of Abraham's dysfunctional family these days.

Messianic theology illustrates the foundation, temple, and dome motif of the Jewish–Christian–Muslim relationship. The Jews did establish the messianic ideal and the foundation of this doctrine. Christians certainly believe they have experienced its reality in Jesus. Muslims look for final fulfillment of the doctrine in the second coming of Al Masih as he ushers in the all-important Day of Judgment.

If Jewish prophecies laid the foundation for the doctrine of the Messiah, and the Qur'an points the way to a future understanding, the so-called Gospel of Thomas has caught the imagination of many Christians in the opening years of this century. The best copy of Thomas has come from Nag Hammadi in Coptic translation, but good Greek fragments also exist from this second century collection of one hundred fourteen Zen-like sayings of Jesus. Though it has no official standing or recognition in the church, the Gospel of Thomas has so many parallels with the Christian Scriptures that it might be seen as a gospel with a different slant, rather than a different gospel. It also presents a Jesus whom Jews can appreciate, and it tells additional stories of Jesus found nowhere else, except in the Qur'an.

Marvin Meyer, author of *The Gospel of Thomas: The Hidden Sayings of Jesus*, suggests: "The kind of Jesus that is presented in the Gospel of Thomas is not the one who died for anybody's sins. This is not a Jesus who performs miracles, walks on water, changes water into wine, and so forth. This Jesus is a teacher of wisdom and one who invites others to join in the quest for wisdom with him."

The Gospel of Thomas does have a few "wonder stories," more like the Qur'an than the Christian Scriptures. For example, both Thomas and the Qur'an tell the story of the boy Jesus making clay pigeons that could fly, as an authentication of his lifelong messianic anointing. It does have a lot of material identical or similar to the traditional gospels, but the Gospel of Thomas also has sayings that make no apparent sense to Christians. Yet, it also appears to preserve some sayings of Jesus that have an attractive ring of authenticity and find an echo both in the tone of the Qur'an and in many rabbinical sayings.

> Jesus said, "If your leaders say to you, 'Look, the kingdom is in heaven,' then the birds of heaven will precede you. If they say to you, 'It is in the sea,' then the fish will precede you. Rather, the kingdom is inside you and outside you." (Thomas 8)

> He who is near me is near the fire; he who is far from me is far from the kingdom. (Thomas 82)

> His followers said to him, "When will the kingdom come?" Jesus replied, "It will not come by watching for it. It will not be said, 'Look, here it is,' or 'There it is.' Rather, the father's kingdom is spread out upon the earth, and people do not see it." (Thomas 113)

It is the loose style of this gospel as much as the content that many people find engaging. Ron Miller, author of *The Wisdom of the Carpenter*, man-

ages to link this with the Jesus presented in the Christian Scriptures. "Jesus'
wisdom teaching takes two classic forms: parables and aphorisms. Jesus'
parables were provocative and often surprising short stories that invite
reflection, and his aphorisms were brief, memorable, arresting sayings. They
are invitational forms of speech, inviting people to see in a particular way,
or to see something they might not otherwise see. Thus one of the most certain things we know about Jesus is that he was a storyteller and a speaker
of great 'one-liners.' In the gospels, the short sayings of Jesus are most often
collected into a series of sayings. This is perfectly natural in written documents. But this is not how Jesus would have spoken them. Jesus was an oral
teacher. As an oral teacher, Jesus would not have strung a bunch of unrelated sayings together in an extended series."

A collection such as Thomas—as well as that other collection of Jesus'
sayings called Q, which lies behind the Gospels of Matthew and Luke—
makes no pretence at narrative settings. The gospels, as presented in the
Christian Scriptures, brilliantly edit the sayings of Jesus into the narratives
of his life story, but the result is a picture of a rather disjointed Jesus, almost
thick in speech as he recites one pithy saying after another. Combine this
with an edited theological overlay by the church, and you have a Messiah
quite different from the itinerant rabbi whom people could not resist.

The editing of the traditional gospels may be brilliant, and the theology
may be correct, but it is the "Jesus Lite" of the Gospel of Thomas and of
the Qur'an that could appeal to both Muslims and Jews today, and perhaps
to disenchanted Christians as well. However, Christianity did not achieve
its position as the dominant religion in the world by compromising its
understanding of the salvation offered through the Messiah. In addition to
the simple stories, the church edition of the gospels includes references to
the anticipations of the Messiah in Egyptian imagery, Hebrew prophecies,
and Greek philosophy, as well as providing answers to the Gnostics.

No scholar of any repute believes that the Gospel of Thomas was written
by Saint Thomas, and no one is suggesting it should be regarded as Scripture. Its value is as a slightly later echo of another way in which Jesus' style
was remembered in a time still ancient to us, but at a time before any of our
existing scriptural manuscript copies were produced. In the same way, the
Gospel of Judas, recovered from the Egyptian desert after nearly seventeen
hundred years and "re-released" in 2006 by *National Geographic* magazine, is not actually by Judas Iscariot. It is valuable because it does give a
very early reflection on the possible motivations and feelings of the one who
represents many who betray Jesus, then and now. It does so in an ancient
context and with a mindset almost contemporary to the events.

A complete copy of the Gospel of Judas was found at Muhafazat al Minya in Egypt under circumstances yet to be documented about a decade after the discovery of the Dead Sea Scrolls. First reviewed by competent scholars in the 1970s, it is clearly a Coptic copy of a somewhat earlier document from a Gnostic sect called the Cainites, an offshoot of the heretical movement whose theology was rejected by the church after a century of public debate.

Christians call such books the *Pseudepigrapha*. Like the *Apographa* of unofficial Jewish books, they can be used, much as the Jewish Mishna and the whole Talmud, to illuminate the context of the writings that did come to be recognized as Holy Scripture. In writings about the life and sayings of Muhammad, Muslims also have a welter of other contextual documents that could enhance our understanding of the Qur'an and the marvelous methods of Allah in speaking to Muhammad in a context that the Prophet understood.

The Hebrew Scriptures pioneered the storytelling technique of parables, or fables with a parallel meaning, but Jesus raised that particular literary form to its highest level. He simplified the message through the use of everyday illustrations and deepened the sense of God's Kingdom, leaving listeners to make the connections for themselves. In the Christian Scriptures, Mark's gospel best reflects the miracles of Jesus, Luke specializes in the healings of Jesus, and John focuses on the poetic meaning of it all. Matthew emphasizes the teachings of Jesus, and Matthew is also the one who presents everything Jesus says or does as fulfilling the prophecies in Hebrew Scriptures.

A rare example of Jesus actually explaining a parable was the story of a farmer sowing seeds on hard clay, among weeds, in desert conditions, and in good earth—with differing results. The disciples did not get the connection with God's Word, but since they were to become the sowers to all people in every kind of situation, he did take a private moment to spell it out for them—probably with a sigh, because they often did not get the message.

One of his teaching techniques was the use of pithy sayings that went to the heart of the matter. This is illustrated in the story where he upbraided those same disciples for dismissing children. He pointed to the virtue of simple trust in God, saying, "Whoever is unable to enter the Kingdom like a child will never enter it." Jesus taught that the Kingdom of God is like a wedding banquet at which many honored guests failed to show up due to "important commitments" and other lame excuses. So, the father of the bride told the caterers, "We are going to have the best party here you ever saw. Invite everyone you can find at the food bank and the homeless shelter; go to the highways and hedges and compel them to come. We are going to celebrate." Jesus did not explain, but if there are those whose religious commitments are so heavy that they miss the meaning of it all, God will happily fill the Kingdom with people who may respond spontaneously, especially any who have been down on their luck in this world.

Neither the sayings of Jesus nor his stories reflect the common religious tone of "Thou shalt not do this" or "Thou shalt do that." Rather, the thrust of Jesus' teaching is more like, "Imagine this." When people heard him speak, they found him warm and approachable. Jesus also exuded authority, "not as the Scribes and the Pharisees" (people with education and position), but an authority that came from God with total integrity, unconditional love, and other signs of the Kingdom.

At the same time his warnings to city sophisticates and religious authorities link his ministry with that of the prophets in the Hebrew Scriptures as well as the Qur'an. Consider Matthew 23:15:

Woe to you, scribes and Pharisees! You hypocrites are like whitewashed tombs, which on the outside look beautiful, but inside are full of dead bones and filth.

There is the Parable of the Talents (use your talents or lose your talents), and the famous Good Samaritan story (you find out who your friends really are only in a crisis). Other well-known parables include the Lost Sheep, the Friend at Midnight, the Hidden Treasure, the Vineyard, the Silver Coin, the Mustard Seed, the Pearl of Great Price, the Wheat and the Weeds, the Wise and Foolish Virgins (also contained in the Qur'an), and about twenty more. All of them have one purpose—to connect people with God's spiritual Kingdom.

Possibly the most beloved parable of Jesus is his story of the Prodigal Son, (sometimes summarized as "Tough love is not enough love"), which is found only in Luke's gospel at Chapter 15.

And he said, A certain man had two sons: And the younger of them said to his father, Father, give me the portion of goods that falleth to me. And he divided unto them his living. And not many days after the younger son gathered all together, and took his journey into a far country, and there wasted his substance with riotous living. And when he had spent all, there arose a mighty famine in that land; and he began to be in want. And he went and joined himself to a citizen of that country; and he sent him into his fields to feed swine. And he would fain have filled his belly with the husks that the swine did eat: and no man gave unto him. And when he came to himself, he said, How many hired servants of my father's have bread enough and to spare, and I perish with hunger! I will arise and go to a ring on his hand, and shoes on his feet: And bring hither the fatted calf, and kill it; and let us eat, and be merry: For this my son was dead, and is alive again; he was lost, and is found. And they began to be merry.

With our study so frequently showing the estrangement of brothers, it is interesting to follow a second conclusion, almost another parable, again one for our times.

Now his elder son was in the field: and as he came and drew nigh to the house, he heard musick and dancing. And he called one of the servants, and asked what these things meant. And he said unto him, "Thy brother is come; and thy father hath killed the fatted calf, because he hath received him safe and sound." And he was angry, and would not go in: therefore came his father out, and intreated him. And he answering said to his father, "Lo, these many years do I serve thee, neither transgressed I at any time thy commandment: and yet thou never gavest me a kid, that I might make merry with my friends: But as soon as this thy son was come, which hath devoured thy living with harlots, thou hast killed for him the fatted calf." And he said unto him, "Son, thou art ever with me, and all that I have is thine. It was meet that we should make merry, and be glad: for this thy brother was dead, and is alive again; and was lost, and is found." (Surah 25–32)

If ever the story of Canaan, Noah's other son, were reworked to illustrate God's mercy, here it is, at least thematically. The Father in the story is God, of course, and all of us have played the role of the younger son in some manner, either in relation to our own parents or others, or in relation to God. Sometimes we also play the role of the elder brother. There is a corporate meaning to the story as applied to humanity in the twenty-first century. Hopefully, our self-destructive agendas do not have to be redeemed by God in another realm, as with Canaan. There is still time for the world and its people to cease squandering the resources of the earth and to desist from rejecting and abusing each other.

It is the role of religion to issue the warnings in these regards, but the first priority is to re-establish the relationship between parent and child. Canaan's relationship with his parents was strained, just like that between the Prodigal Son and his family. Moses at the burning bush became connected with God before confronting Pharaoh. Jesus, as the Messiah for Christians, came to make that connection universal. Muhammad was called by God to bring the transcendence of heaven to earth in the Qur'an.

This Jesus may be the same Jesus we meet in the church, even if he never churned out parables one after another or presented unrelated sayings in rapid fire, the way they appear in the collections made by the early church. Those who know him intimately by faith are not put off by his formal appearance in church or in the straightjacket of gospel narration, but there he is a Messiah different from the Messiah expected by most Jews.

Unlikely as it seems, Jews may find the Jesus of Islam more acceptable than the Jesus of Christianity. As presented in the Qur'an, Jesus is as different from the Messiah of Orthodox Christianity as he is in the Gospel of Thomas, where we see his style at least in a more authentic ambience.

Another surprise for those becoming familiar with the Qur'an is that the Jesus who is the Masih for Muslims is surprisingly similar to the Jesus of unorthodox Christian offshoots such as Unitarians, Jehovah's Witnesses, Christian Scientists, Catholic radicals, and liberal-fringe Protestants. Jesus in the Gospel of Thomas and Jesus as known by Muslims is even similar in some ways to the Jesus accepted with a measure of affection by those in the media and tolerated by academics. The difference is that Muslims embrace Jesus with an enthusiasm and a love that is not as evident among some in these groups.

According to the Qur'an, Jesus was born without mortal paternity, by an act of God. This is compared to the creation of Adam, suggesting that the miracle of the virgin birth introduces an event of cosmic significance. In the Qur'an, when gossips criticize Mary for giving birth without a husband, Jesus speaks from the cradle to defend her. This may be accepted as another literal miracle or as a figurative incident that can be understood in a similar manner to Christians who sing "no crying he makes" in their cherished Christmas Carol, "Away in a Manger." Like the boy Jesus making clay pigeons fly, these images are signs or symbolic authentications of his messianic destiny.

The ministry of Jesus, as reported in the Qur'an, is much as it appears in the Christian Scriptures but, as in the Gospel of Thomas, it is without tedium or dogma. The main difference is that Muslim tradition and the Qur'an deny that Jesus died on the cross. He is said to have escaped by God's grace, and someone else was killed. Muslim tradition outside the Qur'an holds that it was Judas who was crucified, even though the disciples and others believed it was Jesus, due to their distance from the scene and the melee confusion of the moment.

Ancient fringe traditions from India and southern Europe have also supported the view that Jesus escaped or survived, as witness popular novels and movies like *The Last Temptation of Christ*. This is diametrically opposed to the important Christian doctrine of substitutionary atonement and other atonement theologies based on Christ's death and resurrection. A final remarkable surprise for many Christians is the Muslim belief in the second coming of the Masih, Jesus, just before the final Judgment.

The details of Jesus' nativity, so similar in style to the Christian Scriptures, but with added detail, were covered completely in our chapter on the place of Mary in the Qur'an, except for the texts covering the divine initiative, that is, the Virgin birth. An interesting reference, distinguishing between "begetting" a son and "announcing" Jesus into existence is found in the Book of Mary, Surah 19:35:

> It is not befitting to the majesty of Allah that He should beget a son. Glory be to Him! When He determines a matter, He only says to it "Be" and it is.

To this, Christians may be tempted to say, "Begetting or Be-getting . . . you say tomayto and I say tomahto." Of course the debate has many levels, but the current empathetic discussion cannot help but lower the intensity. A more complete reference is found in the book of Mary's father, *Imran*:

> Behold! The angels said, "O Mary! Allah giveth thee glad tidings of a Word from Him: his name will be Masih 'Isa Ibn Maryam [Christ Jesus, son of Mary], held in honor in this world and in the hereafter, and in the company of those nearest to Allah. He shall speak to the people in childhood and in maturity and he shall be of the company of the righteous." (Surah 3:45–47)

> She said: "O my Lord! How shall I have a son when no man hath touched me?" He said: "Even so: Allah createth what He willeth; when He hath decreed a plan, He but saith to it 'Be' and it is!" This similitude of 'Isa before Allah is as that of Aadam: He created him from dust then said to him: "Be." (Surah 3:59)

Not all Christians have a literal belief in the Virgin birth, the meaning of which is simply that God initiated our salvation, and humanity is not required to somehow lift itself by its own bootstraps. The debate over the biological possibilities, or God's manner of action is superseded in this postmodern era into a discussion of the meaning of this be-getting, a discussion in which Muslims and Christians in particular may join together.

And about His adult ministry, in the Book of Golden Ornaments we read the following:

> When 'Isa Ibn Maryam is held up as an example, behold thy people raise a clamor thereat in ridicule! And they say, "Are Our gods best or He?" This they set forth to thee only by way of disputation: yea they are a contentious

people. But, He was no more than a servant: We granted Our favor to him and We made him an example to Bani Israel. (Surah 43:57–59)

And continuing in the Book of Iron:

We sent after them 'Isa Ibn Maryam and bestowed on him the Gospel; and We ordained in the hearts of those who followed him Compassion and Mercy. (Surah 57:27)

As noted previously in the similar words in another Surah, there may well be an echo of the Last Supper in this prayer of Jesus recorded in the Table Spread:

Said 'Isa Ibn Maryam: "O Allah our Lord! Send us from heaven a table set that there may be for us for the first and the last of us a solemn festival and a sign from Thee; and provide for our sustenance for Thou art the best Sustainer of our needs." (Surah 5:114)

Three short verses from the Book of Women touch on the rejection of the doctrine of crucifixion, hint about resurrection—which Christians might understand differently than Muslims—and refer to the Day of Judgment, which points to the role of Jesus as Messiah:

They said in boast "We killed 'Isa Ibn Maryam the Apostle of Allah"; but they killed him not, nor crucified him, but so it was made to appear to them, and those who differ therein are full of doubts with no certain knowledge but only conjecture to follow, for of a surety they killed him not.
    Nay, Allah raised him up unto Himself; and Allah is Exalted in Power and Wise.
    There is none of the People of the Book but must believe in him before his death; or on the Day of Judgement He will be a witness against them. (Surah 4:157–159)

The Qur'an, Islamic commentaries, and the many sayings of Muhammad outside the Qur'an have much more on the topic of the role of Jesus in bringing in the Day of Judgment than the Bible. Muslims may deny the crucifixion, but they have no doubt about the resurrection/ascension/return, according to their own understanding.

As a final note on Muslim messianic expectations, we should observe the tradition of the Hidden Imam, or the Imam *Mahdi*, so important in Shia circles, as explained well by Professor Richard Hooker in the World Civilizations website of Washington State University: "When Hasan al-Askari, the Eleventh Imam, died in 874 CE, a seven-year-old boy, Abu'l-Kasim Muhammad, declared himself to be the Twelfth Imam and went into hiding. He is to disclose himself shortly before the Final Judgment at the head of the forces of righteousness and do battle with the forces of evil in one final, apocalyptic battle. When evil has been defeated once and for all, this 'Imam Mahdi' will rule the world for several years under a perfect government and bring about a perfect spirituality among the peoples of the world."

After this Imam Mahdi reigns for several years, the Shia believe that Jesus Christ will return in judgment. The intensity of this expectation is said to explain many of the political developments in modern Iran and Iraq, as people prepare for Imam Mahdi's appearance with a frenzy not unlike the rapturous fanaticism of Christian adventist groups that arise from time to time. The end of the world may be near, according to all such people, and both suicide bombers and apocalyptic politicians are prepared to go out in a blaze of glory. The Christian equivalent is in the tragic saga of David Koresh and the Branch Davidian conflagration at Waco, Texas, in 1993.

In a close-up look at the Messiah in her book *American Muslims*, Asma Gull Hasan gives the details that might remind many of the Book of Revelation:

Jesus—Islam's Messiah at the End of the World

The Qur'an describes the beginning of the end of the world: famine, storms, floods, vandalism, and rampant immorality prompting the arrival of Dajjal, the name of the anti-Christ in the Qur'an. . . . Dajjal's reign of terror lasts only forty days, however, because God sends Jesus down from heaven on a white horse with a lance in his hand to save the world for righteous people—those who have lived their lives in service to God and with kindness to others. Jesus' throne will also be lowered to earth from heaven, and the faithful will rejoice upon seeing it. Jesus will lead an army of the righteous against Dajjal, who will be defeated by this army but will manage to escape. Nevertheless, Jesus finds Dajjal and kills him with God's lance . . . Jesus will bring a reign of righteousness over the earth for roughly eighty years. The apocalypse and Judgment Day are still to come though, with the death of Jesus. Jesus will return to Jerusalem at the end of the period of his reign, and pray at the Dome of the Rock, dying and returning to God. [There he will pray for those facing Judgment.]

Jewish theology, too, remains full of messianic expectations, as shown by the modern Lubavitcher movement, a sect founded over two hundred years ago in Lubavitch, meaning "town of brotherly love" in Russian, after the town that served as the movement's headquarters for over a century. In

Toronto, New York, and Israel, and with perhaps half a million devotees around the world, many of these Hasidic Jews believe that Rabbi Menachem Mendel Schneersohn (1902–1994), the seventh and final Lubavitcher Rebbe is the Messiah, or *Moshiah* in Yiddish. This phenomenon is not widely understood and is hardly even recognized outside Judaism, but exudes a vibrancy only known in messianic circles.

The *Canadian Jewish News* of January 17, 2002, summarizes their position thus: "Our long-awaited Messiah and Redeemer has arrived! Most Jews failed to recognize that he was the Messiah, but we, his disciples, did. Tragically, he died before completing the redemptive process. But he will soon be resurrected and will continue and complete his messianic tasks."

Jesus of Nazareth never attracted half a million Jews to the claim that he is the Messiah, but respectful interest in him as a son of Israel is a possibility. Judaism has absorbed many messianic movements, and certainly the majority of messianic Jews today are not Christian, but those who sometimes pose a special anxiety to the Jewish community because of their seeming alliance with Christian extremist movements that have threatened to overwhelm (if not exterminate) the Jewish community in the past.

Christians are almost completely dependant on earlier Jewish messianic visions in reference to prophecies concerning both the birth and the passion of Jesus. These are derived in part from Isaiah's vision of a Messiah born of a virgin and a suffering servant who dies for those he loves, as celebrated in Handel's beloved oratorio *Messiah*.

Given the absence of a king during several centuries of superpower occupation, it is clear that for most Jews in the time of Jesus, the messianic vision was expressed in the hope for a king and the restoration of Hebrew dignity and power as remembered under David and others. Jesus himself acknowledged to his followers that he had faced the temptation to rise to the pinnacles of political, religious, and military power, but he recognized the ephemeral and transitory nature of these powers.

From Jewish nobility such as Nicodemus and Joseph of Arimathaea to the humble fishers among his disciples, many Jews accepted his radical transformation of the messianic role into an incorporation of God's presence at the very heart of all earthly suffering through his acceptance of the ancient world's greatest symbol of ignominy, the cross. At his trial for treason against Rome, Jesus told Pilate, "My kingdom is not of this world." Many Jews looked, and still look, for a Messiah whose kingdom is of this world, but there has always been a spectrum of opinion and there is no one clearly defined Jewish position on this matter that is consistent throughout the ages.

However, it may be of note that while Christians have described Jesus mainly as the "Son of God," Jesus himself displayed a decided preference for "Son of Man," a term from the Hebrew Scriptures, as the appropriate messianic title. This appellation is closer to the usual Jewish understanding of a human Messiah, while, following the Qur'an, Muslims always prefer the title "Son of Mary" (*Ibn Maryam*) for Al Masih.

There is no anticipation that any amount of debate, even with the greatest goodwill, can significantly reconcile the images Son of Man, Son of God, and Son of Mary, but something else may be about to happen. Through the application of the Golden Rule of religion (interpret another's beliefs with the same positive attitude one wishes another to interpret one's own beliefs), Jews, Christians, and Muslims may now clarify and enhance their appreciations of the messianic vision with help from each other.

The entire Christian community is on the way to recognizing what the Roman Catholic Church has recently called "the covenant relationship" between God and the Jewish community, including a communal messianic element, which may be fulfilled at the end of time, or sooner. Pope John Paul II's visit to a synagogue in 1985 and later to the Western Wall in Jerusalem was not to observe, but to worship and pray. Christian programs aimed at Jewish conversion, based on the presumption of their exclusion from the Kingdom of God, are over, except in limited circles. American Southern Baptists are among the last significant denominations in the world to support programs for "the conversion of the Jews" and even they now face both internal debate and ecumenical pressure on this matter.

A problem for many Christians is a traditional misreading of chapter 8 of John's gospel and certain "I AM" passages elsewhere in John's gospel. For example, in John 14, when Jesus says, "I AM the way, the truth and the life; nobody comes to the Father except through me," he is here identifying himself as the voice Moses heard from the burning bush, the "I AM," the essence of the universe, rather than simply Jesus of Nazareth. Jesus spoke as the Cosmic Christ, the Eternal Essence that is in all of us when he said "I AM the Vine," "I AM the Gate," "I AM the Good Shepherd," "I AM the light of the world," and in all the other "I AM" passages. Jesus embodies the "I AM," as may we all.

Even before Moses heard God's essence described in this way, Abraham was regarded as righteous, or "saved" as Christians say, because he obeyed the one who is "I AM," though Abraham never heard that name any more than he ever heard the name of Jesus. Jesus deliberately uses the I AM phrase so often that there can be no doubt that he means "Nobody comes to the Father except through the life giving experience of I AM," which he embodied and invited everyone to share. This passage, which some Christians treat as the most excluding teaching in the Bible, is actually one of its most inclusive texts.

In verse 12, which some translations treat as the beginning of chapter 8 in the Gospel of John, Jesus says, "I AM the light of the world." The Jewish authorities, representing all religious authorities in their own exclusive outlook, make it clear that they too do not realize for whom Jesus is speaking, and in what voice. They assume him to be speaking as merely the upstart itinerate rabbi from Nazareth. To paraphrase the rest of the chapter, he tries to explain to them who he is and who they are. Again he uses the Hebrew phrase Son of Man, rather than the later Christian phrase Son of God, to describe his messianic role. In frustration, the authorities quote him back to the effect that, "You say whoever believes in you will never die. Abraham died, and are you greater than Abraham?" Jesus replied, "Abraham was delighted to see me. He did and he rejoiced." The authorities scoffed and said, "You are not even fifty years old and you claim to have seen Abraham?" Jesus replied, "Before Abraham was, I AM."

If the Jewish authorities did not get it, neither do many Christians, but the very awkwardness of the syntax in that last use of the phrase makes it abundantly clear what Jesus meant. He was not saying that only those who come to God in the name of Jesus of Nazareth can be saved or considered righteous, but rather all who come to God through the I AM experienced by Moses would be "saved." If Abraham knew the I AM instinctively, and Moses recognized the I AM, then so do all Jews who share the covenant and all people everywhere who experience the life of God.

This Messiah principle was integral to God from the beginning of creation. Allah/God said "Be" and it took the form of Jesus, but it is also found in a measure in all ages and all cultures. Christians see it perfectly in Jesus of Nazareth but Jesus himself says Abraham saw it, and if Abraham, then also the prophet Muhammad and Leonard Cohen and Yusuf Islam (a.k.a. Cat Stevens). This broader understanding of the messianic principle may be a basis for a "new ecumenism" in the multifaith arena. It is entirely based on the words of Jesus as they might also be understood by Jews and Muslims without violating their own precepts.

Abraham experienced the "I AM" and was accounted righteous because of his response. Moses heard the "I AM" and what transpired became the core code of Hebrew religion. Jesus articulated the "I AM" and embodied the messianic principal to the extent that his followers feel fully justified in calling him the Messiah. Finally, Muhammad bore witness to the "I AM" in reporting the revelation concerning the burning bush in the Qur'an, where he recites the words of Allah: "I AM the Lord" (Surah 20:10) and again "I AM Allah" (Surah 28:30).

The Christian Scriptures are clear with respect to God's eternal covenant with the Jewish people. Saint Paul writes to the Roman Church concerning the Jews:

> I ask then, Has God rejected his people? By no means! I myself am an Israelite, a descendant of Abraham, a member of the tribe of Benjamin. God has not rejected his people whom he foreknew. . . . As regards the gospel, they are enemies of God because of you, but as regards election, they are beloved, for the sake of their ancestors; for the gifts and calling of God are irrevocable. (Romans 11:1–2, 28–29)

Critics may say that these are verses selected out of context, but the evidence is that such a charge is more applicable to those verses of Christian Scripture used in the past to justify hatred toward Jews. Christians must recognize which of their Scriptures God is impressing upon them today, and how the Holy Spirit is guiding them in their understanding.

Some American fundamentalist leaders evince a stubborn resistance to extending their recognition of the Jesus of history to a recognition of the Cosmic Christ. For Christians, Jesus of Nazareth is the Christ in time and space, but the Cosmic Christ, present in the act of creation (John 1:1) and present with Abraham (John 8:56) is also present everywhere God is recognized. He is called Jesus by Christians, but he is also known in the hearts of many who cannot use that name, often for historical reasons related to their experience of Christians and the church.

In order for Jews to regard organizations such as Jews for Jesus with the indulgent tolerance or benign indifference that is appropriate, it is essential that Christian churches make their respect for the Jewish covenant relationship with God into part of the mental mindset of the whole church. The United Church of Canada document *Bearing Faithful Witness* has been recognized by Jews and Christians in many parts of the world as among the most helpful expressions of these principles (see Appendix I). The consequences of this could be enormous in the twenty-first century. Muslims already accept Qur'anic teachings with respect to the salvation of the People of the Book, but they might now let God judge as to who has been faithful to the teachings of Jesus and the prophets sent to Bani Israel/B'nai Israel, the Children of Israel. Muslims and Christians say each in their own way that Jesus was completely submissive to God, and this has helped both Christians and Muslims to build on the spiritual foundation first laid by the Jews. The Qur'an itself cries out for a Muslim reconsideration of God's love for Israel, in spite of the political conundrums in the modern world, which require a spiritual solution in order to come to a resolution.

The Muslim presentation of a non-divine Jesus as the Messiah could be of intense interest to some Jews and even certain Christians. Some Jews, including many of the secular variety, might be sincerely interested in this most famous Son of Israel/Son of Man, if interest did not involve conversion. Could it be that one of the greatest sources of division in Abraham's dysfunctional family, namely messianic theology, especially as related to Jesus of Nazareth, may now yield not unity, but at least growing respect? It is still an awkward area, but one in which it is unnecessary for anyone to be untrue to themselves in order to appreciate the beliefs of others.

Both the Gospel of Thomas and the Qur'an restore the humanity of Jesus in a manner at least compatible with Jewish, Muslim, and Christian theology, though neither Thomas nor the Qur'an diminishes the supernatural attributes of Jesus—attributes he said all people possess within themselves. As wonderful as this all may be, at this point not even Christians are in total agreement about the Messiah who is at the very center of their faith. The Christian community has had this discussion within itself in many eras, including the present. When anyone speaks of the Messiah, we should all develop greater sensitivity. Some good examples of misunderstandings among Christians may be found in the Christian mainstream represented by the United Church of Canada, a "confederation" of Methodists, Presbyterians, Congregationalists, Evangelical United Brethren, and including Community Churches, along with a number of Reformed, Lutheran, and Evangelical congregations and individual members of Orthodox, Catholic, Anglican, and Baptist heritage.

A United Church moderator (national church leader) who was once a famous missionary doctor in China was asked about the resurrection by students at a university. He said, "I don't believe in the resuscitation of a corpse." Some students suddenly felt justified in their own youthful cynicism, but the furor across the country was intense. He might have said, "I believe the resurrection means much more than merely the resuscitation of a corpse," which he said later is what he believed.

Since then, the United Church has had a moderator who shocked the nation in an interview with the *Ottawa Citizen* newspaper (November 2, 1997) asking, "Is Jesus divine?" He later enlivened a CBC radio talk show by asserting that Jesus Christ is not divine. Even his host, a practicing Christian of liberal disposition, was taken aback to hear this from the moderator of the United Church. The host tried to assist him to rephrase the pronouncement, to the effect that "divinity may not be the most helpful cate-

gory of thought to help modern people grasp the unique essence of Jesus."
The moderator would not go along. The shock approach briefly caught the
interest of some on the fringe of the religious community, but the damage
within the church was considerable. Some still assert that this "progressive
Christianity" position on "Christology" is identical to the Muslim view, and
that may be true, though this moderator also learned to temper his language
to more normative Christian expressions.

The United Church even had a former moderator say recently that Jesus
did not die for her sins. There may be some Christians who believe in a kind
of philosophical idea of God, not a God who shares the shame and feels the
pain of the world and its people, but while expanding the vision of God's
love for every person, she might have said something like "substitutionary
atonement does not begin to describe all that Jesus does."

These three moderators were exhilarating leaders of one of the youngest
denominations in the world, and their pronouncements enabled many to
perceive the presence of the Messiah in realms beyond the limits of orthodoxy. The doctor had represented the healing presence of Christ in the midst
of the revolution in China, even winning the friendship of a bandit chief by
mending his badly fractured leg with bicycle spokes, when the doctor was
kidnapped for that purpose and lacked medical supplies. The moderator
who was questioned in the media about the divinity of Jesus has brilliantly
articulated the position of Christ in the economy, on behalf of the poor in
our post-socialist/post-capitalist mixed economy. The third of these more
radical moderators interjected the compassion of Christ in a manner both
sensitive and firm, as the United Church played its leadership role in the
worldwide dialectic on human sexual orientation.

But Christians can be deeply hurt by careless or imprecise words in discussing Christ, which has been an article of faith since the time of the apostles. Three dozen other moderators in the life of this young church have
appeared more orthodox, or perhaps more careful of deep sensitivities in
this area, even while seeking to expand the Christian understanding of the
role of Messiah. It is only messianic Christology that makes the church specifically Christian. Other ideas about God, or even about the environment,
peace, fair trade, obeying the golden rule, and "being nice," are commend-
able but not necessarily Christian, or in any sense not *only* Christian.

Christians may also appreciate the non-divine Messiah of Muslims and
others, as well as the messianic component in the Jewish covenant relationship with God. However, at the same time, and without quarrelling about
it, Jews and Muslims might accept that for most Christians, Jesus is the
Messiah, and the Messiah is God's appearance on earth in the flesh. Other

views can be tolerated and appreciated, even within the church, but while poetry, artistic expression, and music may convey the concept best, this is the core teaching of the church and the most basic belief of Christian people. For Christians, no finer expression of God's love for the world has been expressed than God coming in the flesh (the doctrine of incarnation) and sharing of the pain of humanity on the cross. Christians believe that no cross can kill that love or kill the people who trust in it.

All earthly images or ideas of God are incomplete, insufficient, and inadequate, even the most cherished theological constructs. Christians cannot be expected to cease speaking of the Trinity and of Jesus as the Son of God, but these motifs only make sense after certain experiences that can scarcely be explained in any other way. Just as the covenant relationship between Jews and God is news to some Christians, and much of the Qur'an is a modern revelation to both Jews and Christians, some attempt to restate these Christian conundrums simply should be made in the context of this book for the benefit of Jewish and Muslim readers. The Trinity is a Christian expression to describe the experience of God as "Father, Son, and Spirit," but does not include Mary as one of the three personas of God, a misunderstanding still held by many Muslims.

The author of this book is one person with three personas. He is called "father" by a young woman who lives in Toronto, "son" by an older woman who lives in Halifax, and "husband" by a woman who lives with him near the Niagara Falls. He is not three persons, though in three very different contexts he has three *personas*. Would it be more helpful for Christians to say they have experienced three *personas* of God, rather than saying that God is three persons in one? There are limits to this construct also, as when the Son prays to the Father, does this mean that God talks to Himself? Why not, if God can be everywhere at once and experienced in different ways? While this simple illustration of the Trinity is helpful for some, it has obvious limits. Some Christians simply prefer to regard the doctrine of the Trinity as the symbol that God exists in community, within God's self and with us.

But Jews and Muslims are right to some extent when they protest the idea of Jesus as the Son of God, because for Christians, too, this construct also breaks down at some point. If Jesus is the Son of God, what kind of father sends his son to suffer in the most horrific form of torture yet devised? No, on the cross, Jesus is God in person, God in the flesh, according to Christian doctrine. It is as such that God gives Himself, to feel the pain and share the shame of the world. Jesus was not a lamb raised for the slaughter; he was and is the lamb who gives himself for others. Jesus said, "I lay down my life in order to take it up again. No one takes it from me, but I lay it down of my own accord" (John 10:17–18). The prophet Isaiah says presciently of the Messiah,

> Surely He hath borne our griefs, and carried our sorrows: yet we did esteem Him stricken, smitten of God, and afflicted. But he was wounded for our transgressions, he was bruised for our iniquities: the chastisement of our peace was upon Him; and with His lash marks we are healed. (Isaiah 53:4–5)

For Christians who have experienced God's identification with their sorrows and distresses, such claims of cosmic redemption can only be made of God Himself, as he is active in the messianic role on earth. He does not send his Son like an unfeeling father or a vengeful tyrant, but He comes Himself in a form that Christians refer to elsewhere as His Sonship, just as the author appears as a son whenever he visits Halifax.

So why is the cross so central to the faith of Christians? It is precisely because it is the most degrading torture ever devised. God used it to show how far he is willing to go to share our shame and feel our pain. Many other people have died horrible deaths but in this case, all the blood of Iraq and the starvation in Africa, all the enmity between Jew and Arab, all the spousal abuse and racism in America, every child abduction and rape in Toronto, and all the burdens of both personal sin and unwarranted suffering are taken upon Himself by God.

Nobody can ever say, "My situation is so bad that not even God knows what I am going through." God took human form in Jesus and is with humanity in the very worst circumstances. Without the crucifixion there is no resurrection, and God's promise that he will stand by people through rape, abuse, murder, terrorism, and every other kind of hell means nothing. God suffers with mortals to show that nothing can overcome his spirit of love and that nothing on earth can overcome them if they put their complete trust in Him. Then God calls these redeemed human beings to be that kind of presence for each other, in an ethic of self-giving love.

Of course this explanation itself is incomplete, as Christian critics will point out even before other members of the family can comment. Jews and Muslims may experience the fullness of God's grace in other ways, but these days they might more gracefully accept that Christian theology does contain paradox and seeming inconsistencies, even while Christians argue among themselves about how best to express what they have experienced.

If only Muslims were to follow the teachings of the Qur'an with respect to others who submit to God, including Christians who follow their messianic prophet Jesus and Jews who are related to them in blood and share in Abraham's covenant with God. If only Christians could acknowledge their own continual crucifixion of Jesus the Messiah whenever they reject their Muslim and Jewish family members, or any others. If only Jews could trust again the communities involved in the *Shoah* (holocaust), and the pogroms, in confidence that others who love their most famous Son would now act differently.

But how can these disparate family members love and trust each other when the holocaust of the recent twentieth century threatens and continues on so many fronts in the twenty-first? Elie Wiesel, in his book, *Night*, the classic testimonial of a holocaust survivor, tells of a concentration camp hanging of a child whose neck did not break and who slowly strangled. A fellow prisoner cried out in anguish, "For God's sake, where is God?" Wiesel, himself a child at the time, answered, "Where is he? This is where— hanging from this gallows."

French novelist and Nobel laureate, François Mauriac, upon meeting Wiesel as not much more than a child after the war, and hearing that story, later wrote in a foreword to *Night*, "What did I say to him? Did I speak to him of that other Jew, this crucified brother who perhaps resembled him and whose cross conquered the world? Did I explain that what had been a stumbling block for *his* faith had become a cornerstone for *mine*? And that the connection between the cross and human suffering remains, in my view, the key to the unfathomable mystery in which the faith of his childhood was lost? . . . That is what I should have said to the Jewish child. But all I could do was embrace him and weep." It is little wonder that Muslims find it almost impossible to imagine that such things actually happened, but *Night* should be in school curricula for children in Pakistan and Indonesia, as it is now in much of North America and Europe. We all still need some time to hold each other and weep.

While it may seem to some observers that the Jewish experience of the holocaust is retold excessively in the media, this should be understood not as an inference that no other people have suffered as much but as an articulation of the horrors of all such events. Jews were once restricted by law to certain professions, writing (and media) among them. In the twentieth century, this literary heritage resulted in a unique documentation of horror that is a service to the whole world. Let this holocaust stand for all time as among the worst of such atrocities and certainly the best documented so that it may never happen again. In places where it happened (and happens)—Armenia, Cambodia, Rwanda, Darfur—one of the reasons for it is the failure to educate the people about the nature of genocide, mass psychoses, and war hysteria that permit such atrocities.

The role of the Messiah has been a logjam for millennia. The resolution will not come with bigger bombs in the hands of one clan or another. The resolution can only come on the spiritual plane, though this may have many practical ramifications. "Praying for the peace of Jerusalem" today means a resurrection in human hearts of a messianic vision. For the Messiah to stand among us in his first coming, yet to happen among Jews, in his ancient appearance to Christians, and in his final coming in Judgment for Muslims, we must accept each other and embrace each other, not for the sake of agreement, but for the sake of the Messiah, the Christ, Al Masih, coming, having come, and coming again.

In his novel *Light in August*, William Faulkner compares a person's ability to remember to a photograph in the imagination. All the events and people ever experienced by a person are gathered, as in a valley. It is possible to see them all at once, in one scene. If God has the ability to "remember" in a forward direction also (premember?) perhaps eternity is that valley we have experienced, the valley we stand in now, and the valley we will stand in yet.

In the most positive Christian perspective, the Messiah is in this valley and those who have not seen him and yet been faithful, as well as those who have seen him and been faithful, and those who live in faithful expectation, will all see him in his glory. He will introduce us to each other and take us before the throne of the One who was and is and is to come, the "I AM" we have all known.

Quantum Theology, as described by Diarmuid O'Murchu in the book by that title, is the theological counterpart of Quantum Physics. Both question the nature of physical reality and insist that time as we know it is merely a figment of human experience in a "seemingly physical" world. The Hebrew, Christian, and Muslim Scriptures all agree on that point, but only recently has science concurred.

Whether the Messiah is yet to come, has already come, or is coming again must ultimately appear irrelevant from God's position above and beyond the realm of time and space. Again, from a positive Christian perspective, what is required is for each of us to hold the Messiah in our hearts, Jew, Christian, and Muslim. We will notice a difference, and so will others, if we put our trust in God who comes in Messiah, Christ, Masih, who is everywhere in the world, and waiting to be recognized more personally and less dogmatically in Abraham's family.

18

The Dome

Muhammad

SALMAN RUSHDIE threw down the gauntlet to Islamic fundamentalism in the *Satanic Verses*, published in 1988, before others in the Muslim community or outside it realized the extent of the problem. In 1990, after violent protests and a death edict, or *fatwa*, issued by Iran's Ayatollah Khomeini, he offered an apology for the "distress caused" and acknowledged a respect for Islam, including a personal relationship with the community.

Though he has now no ongoing participation in the Muslim religion, he comments incisively and helpfully about the role of religion in every society. Indeed, in a comic aside to Bill Moyer in an interview on PBS (*On Faith & Reason*, June 23, 2006), Rushdie admits, "Athiests are obsessed with God, as you may have noticed." In the same interview, Rushdie also agreed with the thesis of this book that "religious fanaticism is a response to disillusionment with secularism." Our purpose here is to point to the solution as neither a return to secularism nor an acceptance of religious extremism, but an acknowledgment that religion is here to stay and needs to be promulgated with wisdom and moderation.

As a nonreligious person, Rushdie is an even more articulate theologian than the atheist Sigmund Freud, mentioned earlier in reference to his investigation of the roots of monotheism. It is the lack of frank and open discussion in Islam and the absence of scholarly discourse on religion and subjects concerning the text of the Qur'an that contribute to widespread misunderstanding, and even provokes ridicule in some quarters.

Rushdie is right in his unrelenting quest to shed light into dark corners of Islam. Though still reviled in the Shi'ite community in particular, Salman Rushdie may be one of progressive Islam's best allies in the twenty-first century, recognized and accepted or not. Along the way, in addition to writing further masterworks of English literature, Rushdie has become a world leader in the quest for freedom of speech.

The fact remains that almost any modern critique or analysis that raises questions about the Qur'an is still subject to dismissal or anger in much of the Muslim community, whereas in the Jewish and Christian experience, such disciplines have proven to verify the sacred texts among scholars and increase the confidence of believers. Such openness has the advantage of giving believers the confidence of "eyes wide open" faith, as opposed to "blind faith."

There may be a few circumstances in which blind faith can be accepted, but when it is employed unnecessarily it produces a negative result, undermining confidence in the sacred texts by believers and nonbelievers alike. The world needs more from the dome of Abraham's family shrine if the undoubted treasures of the Qur'an are to be appreciated. This is equally true for the future within the Muslim community itself.

In the eyes of the world, unanswered questions about the Qur'an remind friends of Islam of the worldwide reaction of Muslim masses to published cartoons of Muhammad wearing a turban bomb in 2006. No thinking person agrees with egregious insults, and Muslim leaders were right to urge peaceful protest to insist on respect for the holy Prophet, but it did not advance the cause of Islam for bloodthirsty crowds to rampage under slogans to the effect of "Muhammad is the Prophet of Peace and we will kill anyone who says otherwise." Muslims are even likely to take umbrage at depictions of the likes of Lot in the Hebrew and Christian Scriptures, given the view that the prophets were holy persons sent by God to warn people and to provide role models for humanity. Muslims may be right about such things, but it is civil discourse that is required. Meanwhile, we might remind ourselves that it has not been many decades since laws against blasphemy and other restrictions on free speech inhibited public discourse in the West.

In 1930, the Motion Picture Producers and Distributors of America adopted a "Production Code" that included the rule that "References to Deity, God, Lord, Jesus, and Christ shall not be trivial." That made it so risky to invest in any movie focusing on the life of Jesus that until the 1960s Jesus had only a few nonspeaking roles, such as his appearances in Academy Award–winning films such as *The Robe* and *Ben Hur*.

People got over the half-time entertainment "wardrobe malfunction" of pop star Janet Jackson at the 2005 football Super Bowl, whereby she contrived to expose an inch more of her breast than the cleavage normally permitted, but the issue of censorship is alive and well in America. Comedian

Michael Richards (Kramer on *Seinfeld*) may have been legally exercising freedom of speech in a 2006 Thanksgiving week performance, when he called some hecklers "Niggers," but it is highly dubious that his career will ever recover.

In the West, with restrictions on anti-Semitism, prohibitions against child pornography, and hate laws still functioning with widespread public support, the jury is still out on certain fine points of free speech and the limits of civil discourse. Islam simply has a different set of parameters in which spiritual matters are also to be respected.

According to Islam, it is prohibited to reproduce images of the Prophet, far less to depict him as an aggressive terrorist in cartoons that vilify and mock him, so the reaction is not entirely surprising. If someone were to describe the Battle of the Boyne as a piece of fiction, the Protestant paramilitaries in Northern Ireland would possibly put out a contract (read: *fatwa*), even to this day. Jewish attempts to ban Mel Gibson's movie *The Passion of the Christ*, and the successful campaign to have it excluded from consideration for an Academy Award also shows that Muslims are not alone in these reactions.

Over the course of history it is easy to illustrate such hypersensitivities in the Jewish and Christian communities, sometimes with good reason. In the present world situation, both Christians and Jews are equally culpable in actions contradictory to their faith. As Islam takes its place in the mainstream of the West, and as Western values are exhibited in the Muslim world, everybody might thoughtfully reassess their positions on these matters.

The dispute over cartoon depictions of Muhammad was entirely within Abraham's family, but seen objectively, say from Mars, it might look like a rather healthy discussion, were it not for the loss of life and the destruction of property. Somewhere between an extreme, and now old-fashioned, Western secular view that "nothing is sacred" and a more typically Oriental view, that "everything is sacred," comes the balanced Muslim position that "some things are sacred." That is actually the traditional position of the whole Abrahamic family. If everything is treated as sacred, as it may ultimately be, no one can move lest they step on an ant. If nothing is sacred, there are no models to show the ultimate value of anything. None of this is to suggest that Muslims lack humor, as indicated by their widespread delight in the 2007 sitcom *Little Mosque on the Prairie*. Starring Zaib Shaikh and created by Zarqa Nawaz, this Canadian production has been picked up for syndication throughout the English-speaking world in 2008, and is frequently quoted and dubbed on Arabic channels in the Middle East.

The reaction to the publication of the Danish cartoons might be seen as an eruption of reawakening to awareness of sanctity in the shared psyche of the human community. If this incident is regarded as a breach of human norms in the realm of holiness, it may be also the best example to date of the inappropriate transfer of outdated twentieth-century Western secular ideals into the more spiritual twenty-first century.

That secular ethos and the idea that freedom means "anything goes" possibly reached its zenith in the *Piss Christ* artwork, and has been receding ever since. *Piss Christ* is a controversial American work of art by Andres Serrano. It depicts a crucifix submerged in a glass of the artist's urine. Because of its reddish tint, some have suggested that the glass may also contain the artist's blood. The piece was a winner in the Southeastern Center for Contemporary Arts' Awards in the Visual Arts competition. It was sponsored in part by the United States National Endowment for the Arts, which offers support and funding for projects that exhibit artistic excellence. *Piss Christ* caused a mild scandal when it was exhibited in 1989, with detractors accusing Serrano of blasphemy and his supporters presenting this as a major issue of artistic freedom. On the floor of the United States Senate, Senators Al D'Amato and Jesse Helms expressed outrage that the piece was supported by the National Endowment for the Arts, as it is a federal taxpayer–financed institute.

Was this artwork offensive, ridiculously laughable, sad, or helpful? Possibly it was all of these things, depending on the life experience of the viewer. If there is any virtue in testing the limits of freedom, it can only be ascertained by actually testing them. *Piss Christ* possibly has meaning to some seeking to understand the cross, or to challenge its impact in Western and world cultures, but the Christian churches simply ignored it, as did even their most devoted members, except for a few insecure fundamentalists.

On the other hand, in the matter of criticism and analysis of Scripture, the mature response of Christians and Jews in the last century brought undeniable benefits, a position that the Muslim community could now emulate with profit. If the West can reassess its position on free speech, as it is doing across the spectrum of gender and race issues, and if the rest of Abraham's family can rediscover reverence for sacred texts from Islam, as has been suggested in this investigation, Muslims should now be able to develop their confidence that respect for their own Scriptures will be enhanced rather than diminished by the kind of scrutiny called for by Rushdie and others. This is the cutting edge of one of the most exciting intellectual discussions of our time, with ramifications as much on the street as in the classroom or the media. Salman Rushdie pleads for Muslims to "study the revelation of their religion as an event inside history," and this may simply be describing the way God speaks, even when Allah is speaking through the voice of Muhammad.

It is unlikely that Salman Rushdie's growing status as almost a cult figure in the world of literature will ever be extended to the Muslim community. His gift of his papers to Emory University in 2006 and his acceptance of an academic position there, at least through 2012, seem to have completed his "coming out" to function again without restrictions in the mainstream community. Even among Muslims, there may yet come a grudging acknowledgment that his questioning of the way sacred Scripture is studied is a significant contribution to the renaissance of Islamic scholarship in the twenty-first century. Nowhere is that more easily illustrated than with the example of the infamous, and possibly nonexistent, Satanic verses, an area of investigation that has now received the full benefit of critical analysis in many quarters.

Salman Rushdie has written things that many Muslims regard as egregiously insulting to the memory of the Prophet and his wives, as well as other "sacred cows," to borrow an image from another tradition, equally subject to lampooning. But the so-called Satanic verses to which the title of Rushdie's most famous book refers were possibly nonexistent, at least as treated in the most offensive renditions of the story. The episode is a clear example of the thesis that believing communities have nothing to fear in the full airing of questions surrounding their Scriptures.

Modern scholarship is increasingly confident that the verses in question were planted very early in the movement by opponents of Islam and preserved in their commentaries by Islamic scholars in the first Muslim century, when it was still acceptable and safe to discuss such things. This example of ancient Muslim scholarship is worth examining in some detail as a basis for the argument that such discussions are appropriate today. The fact that modern Islamic scholars concur in the analysis of the Satanic verses may provide a paradigm for a broad range of investigations into questions about the Qur'an that otherwise are still taboo in the modern era. The verses in question are found in all versions of the Qur'an:

"Have ye seen Lat and Uzza and another the third [goddess] Manat?"

"What! for you the male sex and for Him the female? Behold such would be indeed a division most unfair! These are nothing but names which ye have devised, ye and your fathers for which Allah has sent down no authority [whatever]. They follow nothing but conjecture and what their own souls desire! Even though there has already come to them Guidance from their Lord!" (Surah 53:19–23)

The controversial addition was said to be the words allegedly whispered into Muhammad's ear by Satan, or by some sinful spirit of compromise, masquerading as the voice of Allah through Gabriel, dictated not in the cave but on the spot in the Ka'bah, and spuriously added in reference to these three goddesses at the conclusion of ayah 19 or 20:

"These are the high-flying ones, whose intercession is to be hoped for!"

Before reviewing the story, let us be clear why Muslims find these words so offensive, when they are attributed to the Prophet. It is as if Muhammad, who established a whole new religion based on the strictest monotheism, here acknowledges that three older female deities or goddesses not only coexist with Allah but are to be prayed to in hopes of their favor. The inference is that Muhammad was willing to sacrifice the greatest principle of Islam in order to present a watered-down version acceptable to idolaters who were making his life miserable.

This is enough to distress the faithful, especially when taken in the context of the story which follows, far less with the possible interpretation of ayahs 21 and 22, which can then be twisted to suggest that Allah is cavorting on high with females while his followers below are uniting with males.

The whole thing is so bizarre that the likelihood of its fabrication has been only exceeded down through the centuries by the eagerness of Christian and Jewish opponents of Islam to keep this false tradition alive and to embellish the story out of context. The best we can do now is to reconstruct the events in the most probable manner, based on whatever reliable information is known.

The main opposition to Muhammad was found among the leading families of Mecca, the Quraysh Tribe, an establishment that had the greatest vested interest in the old ways. They were in control of the commercial idolatry associated with the Ka'bah shrine and its thousands of pilgrims. From petty harassment such as piling excrement at his door, to a more significant economic boycott of Muhammad's own tribe, which failed after about three years, the opposition continued. Some of Muhammad's followers emigrated to Ethiopia to find peace and establish a community based on Islamic principles. Quraysh attempts at corrupting Muhammad and his followers by including them in the economic benefits of the old system also failed, as did outright bribes.

On an occasion when Muhammad boldly presented a recitation of some of his revelations in the Ka'bah, at about the time that tactics of harassment, boycotts, coopting and bribes were all failing, some of the Quraysh, desperately needing a resolution, spread the word that they heard Muhammad recite something inclusive of the old goddesses, and how it would not hurt to pray to them too. We surmise they may have said such a thing after he left the Ka'bah, and they got the ball rolling toward a reconciliation.

They offered to join the Muslim religion on the basis of this compromise. If Muhammad did indeed say something about those three goddesses, which is highly doubtful, he possibly could have compared them to "high-flying cranes," which is another possible interpretation of the Arabic words (without vowel marks) in the half-verse in question.

> Have ye seen Lat, Uzza, and the third goddess, Manat? They are but high-flying cranes!

This could have been a disparagement of the three goddesses, not an invocation of their intercessions. Depending on how you interpret such a possible incident, it was perhaps good enough for the Quraysh. Somehow a rumor may have spread quickly regarding a possible reconciliation. Muslims in Ethiopia were quick to support rumors of reconciliation and a few of the homesick may have returned.

The inference taken from the more negative version of the incident is that Muhammad had become weary of beating his head against the wall and was ready for compromise, not on minor details but on the very essence of Islam. Those who chose to believe the story, even in its more acceptable version, also believe that in the following verses, accepted today by all as part of the Qur'an, Allah comforted Muhammad when he realized the damage done.

> And their purpose was to tempt thee away from that which We had revealed unto thee, to substitute in our name something quite different; [in that case], behold! they would certainly have made thee [their] friend! And had We not given thee strength, thou wouldst nearly have inclined to them a little. In that case We should have made thee taste an equal portion [of punishment]) in this life, and an equal portion in death: and moreover thou wouldst have found none to help thee against Us! (Surah 17:73–75)

This might be read to indicate that Muhammad had not succumbed to such temptation, nor even considered it. Allah appears to be congratulating Muhammad, even while acknowledging that someone had made such an attempt to corrupt him. No one disputes the text or the validity of these verses.

Those who think there was something to the Satanic verses episode also believe that Allah let Muhammad off the hook by pointing out that all the prophets have been corrupted by Satan at some point, as pointed out in

Surah 22. If there is any verse in the Qur'an, as conveyed by Muhammad, that could be reasonably suspected by Muslims of having Satanic origins, it would surely be this one that still stands in all texts and translations of Surah 22. Yet these ayahs remain universally accepted as being from Allah, so it is not as if Muslims cannot possibly consider such matters.

> Never did We send a messenger or a prophet before thee, but, when he framed a desire, Satan threw some [vanity] into his desire: but Allah will cancel anything [vain] that Satan throws in, and Allah will confirm [and establish] His Signs: for Allah is full of Knowledge and Wisdom: That He may make the suggestions thrown in by Satan, but a trial for those in whose hearts is a disease and who are hardened of heart: verily the wrong-doers are in a schism far [from the Truth]. (Surah 22:52–53)

While not identified as Satanic, as presented here in the treasured Yusuf Ali Version, with his elucidations in brackets, these verses clearly state that all the prophets have been corrupted by Satan at some time or other, and that Allah redeems those corruptions by substituting His own teaching later. This is the "warts and all" view of the prophets that Jews and Christians accept, but which is normally rejected by Muslims, even though explicitly spelled out in the Qur'an in these verses.

The very idea that Muhammad was prepared to throw away his life's work, the monotheism that was the basis of his new community, and the precious revelations of Allah in a compromise designed to gain peace with the Quraysh is offensive to those who love his memory. But even the existence of the Satanic verses is now rejected by the majority of Jewish, Christian, and Muslim scholars of repute on the basis of critical analysis of the text of the Qur'an, as we shall now attempt to illustrate.

Take, for example, the whole idea of accepting the above version of events is rendered highly improbable by the time lapse determined by the dating of the three Surahs in question. The offending "Satanic" verses were to have been spoken in Mecca before the *Hajra* exodus of the whole Muslim community to Medina, two years later. Allah's comfort in Surah 17 came six years after the Satanic verses. That would be "cold Comfort" in a crisis. Moreover, Allah's acknowledgment that the incident is to be understood in the context of all prophets making mistakes came another two or three years after that, in Surah 22, according to the universally accepted dating of the Surahs.

The damage occasioned by this uncertain position would have been too great over nine years for the movement to have remained cohesive. In the opinion of analysts of religious trends and group dynamics, the pure zeal that sustained Islam would have been so compromised by this that the Islamic movement would have disappeared into the ebb and flow of petty revivals of spiritual energy throughout history. This did not happen.

The coining of the phrase "Satanic verses" to describe this controversy is attributed to Sir William Muir, an anti-Muslim polemicist writing only a hundred years ago. The first reports of the incident go back to the first full and official biography of Muhammad, written by Ibn Ishaq about a hundred and thirty-five years after the death of the Prophet. His complete work, the *Sirat Rasul Allah*, is no longer available in its entirety, but is quoted extensively by two other ancient authorities. Al-Waqidi and al-Tabari both wrote in Baghdad in the next two succeeding generations. They were careful scholars representing the two major Islamic traditions, quoting Ishaq at length, and including the purported Satanic verse incident. None of the three endorse the story, but they boldly examine all aspects of the prophet's life and career from every conceivable angle. Would that they were alive today.

The rejection of the Satanic verses on the basis of timelines is perhaps the simplest basis, but there are many other convincing textual arguments. Using Western critical techniques, in this instance at least, plus analytical techniques of their own, Muslim scholars have turned this issue inside-out, so important is the integrity of the monotheistic tradition. However, because so many other questions in Muslim circles seem to be settled on the basis on blind faith or raw emotion, many outside observers have suspected the veracity of such in-house conclusions that the Satanic verses are false.

Recently, a few respected Muslim scholars, notably scholar-activist Isma'il al-Faruqi and academician Fazlur Rahman, have even suggested that if Ibn Ishaq included this story it is worth considering at some level, since Ishaq is trusted on virtually every other matter. Their position is courageous but unnecessary if we accept that Ishaq and the others were simply and appropriately reporting a controversial debate as part of their historical surveys.

Modern Western scholars, both Jewish and Christian, have largely come to the conclusion that the opinion of the great majority of Muslim scholars is actually correct, and that the Satanic verses incident was fabricated in the early Islamic years by opponents of Muhammad. If the flame of this spurious lie was fanned by Christians a hundred years ago, the arguments that put it to rest were published in 1970 by another Christian, John Burton, in the *Journal of Semitic Studies* (15, 2, pp. 246–65), using the most exhaustive critical analysis of the Arabic text. Burton was the career specialist in the Arabic language at the University of Saint Andrew in Scotland, where he had collegial access to the critical techniques of the Faculty of Theology.

The very title of his article is "Those Are the High-flying Cranes," suggests that the whole notion is a high-flying farce.

Rushdie must have known that most scholars regard this as a bogus issue, but if such rigor were to be expended on all such questions, and there are many of them, the whole world would benefit from a true renaissance of Islamic scholarship, values, and mores, all focused on the Qur'an. If Islam is to correctly counter the charges that it is prone to terrorism, anti-Semitism, misogyny, and homophobia, for example, it can do so on the basis of a confident understanding of the Qur'an, including a complete airing of all such questions. The world is waiting to receive such blessings from the dome of Abraham's family shrine.

Christians may soon learn the identity of the heretics in the Epistles of John and the Book of Revelation. As in finally discovering of whom Noah spoke in cursing, "Canaan," some of these discoveries may now come from Muslim sources, like the biblical references to the "sabeans" who the Qur'an identifies as living in Yemen. Both Jews and Christians have benefited immensely from the discovery of the Dead Sea Scrolls and the Nag Hammadi Library by Muslims. Jews and Christians have gifts for the Muslim community in techniques of research, if nothing else, and in appreciating and using such new information. Increasingly, the joint Jewish–Christian–Muslim programs in religious studies at major universities are facilitating the new scholarship.

But to continue with Muhammad himself, a vast body of literature about him has come down directly from contemporaries, his "companions and others who knew him well." This fact distinguishes his story from, say, Moses, the Buddha, or Jesus, where the material was collected later from communal sources and heavily edited. The Muslim literature has never gone out of sight, like the Qur'an itself, which has a textual history with an integrity unlike any other of the classic holy books of the great world religions.

In the "Dark Ages" of Europe, which was Islam's period of enlightenment, Islam not only salvaged Europe's classics of antiquity, but Muslims also maintained their own materials as a sacred trust. That period being followed by Europe's Renaissance, with its collections of European and Islamic classics, means that the world has always had authentic texts of the Qur'an and records about Muhammad that are both vast and reliable. The most notable of these are the Hadith (his own sayings, as distinct from those given to him by Allah) and the *Sunna* (the accounts of his actions and lifestyle), written by his companions and eyewitnesses to the events of his life. The basic integrity of this material would seem ready for verification from independent sources, such as the Yemeni parchments, now becoming available.

For that reason, the scope of the subject is greater than can be managed with justice in this context, except for a few comments to dispel some prejudices about Muhammed, and a brief summary of his ministry. Indeed, the Qur'an contains quotations from the Hebrew and Christian Scriptures, which all Muslims believe to be direct references to the Prophet Muhammad, appearing prophetically in those earlier Scriptures. This may be the final and, for Jews and Christians, among the most startling pieces of new information from this study.

Muhammad was a sensitive young man, aghast at the corruption, immorality, and idolatry of Arabia in his time and initially eager to discover what other religions could offer to remedy the situation. He was frequently exposed to both Jews and Christians in his work, accompanying caravans on the trading routes through the Middle East. During this time, several of his relatives were converted to Christianity, never to join his new religion despite relationships that remained mutually supportive. He also entered into relationships with a considerable number of Jews as well as other desert Semitic people called *Hanifs,* who were monotheists and preserved much of the same Middle Eastern lore from ancient times, in versions complementary to Jewish and Christian stories.

Muhammad cherished these relationships throughout his life, in spite of occasional tensions and even strife with Christians and especially with Jewish tribal entities in the Arabian Peninsula. Late in life, he is quoted in the Hadith as saying, "He who wrongs a Jew or a Christian will have me as his accuser on the Day of Judgment." He also said to his followers, "Do not consider me better than Moses" and "I am closest of all people to Jesus, the Son of Mary."

Critics have traditionally suggested that the Jews had a great opportunity for conversion of the Arabs, but that they were typically disinterested in proselytism, and that Christians somehow ignored one of the greatest opportunities for evangelism in the history of the world. Be that as it may, Muhammad was interested, but capable of making his own judgments, and neither the synagogue nor the church was able to deliver what he felt Arabia needed—the unity of the warring tribes under a strict moral code. As referenced in the Qur'an, the strictness of that code has been well recognized, but there is a grace in the Qur'an that many have professed to find missing in Islam, as practiced in various historical circumstances.

A word search on the computer text of the Qur'an, for example, reveals that, while many people regard punishment as the dominant theme of the Qur'an, the balance is actually tipped toward mercy. There are 137 references to "punish" compared to 149 references to "merciful," and 387 references to "punishment" compared to 452 references to "mercy." The fact is that Islam has an emphasis on consequences, but some long-standing prejudices have prevented many non-Muslim readers from noting the balance that the Qur'an attributes to God's graciousness or "grace" (439 references). These prejudices are partly due to ignorance about Muhammad himself and his gentle nature.

During his busy life as a commercial traveler, Muhammad's private moments at home were spent on retreat in his favorite cave. These quiet times were taken over by God, and some of them became episodes when he received inspired revelations that he never expected. The revelations were accompanied by a compulsion, seen as a command, to "recite this" to others on God's behalf. The Qur'an is the record of these recitations. He recounted his cave experiences with his wife Khadia, the love of his life, and she insisted they visit his cousin, Waraqa bin Nawfal, a Christian, who was equally moved and assured them that this was the very truth of the Hebrew Torah and the Christian Gospel, but in an Arabian context. This cousin is also the person who pointed out a certain prophecy in the Hebrew Scriptures, that an Arab prophet was to bring God's word to Arabia.

Before very long a growing group recognized that this illiterate but sincere young camel drover was not speaking or composing on his own. No one expected to see him as their religious leader, but no one who heard his beautiful poems, psalms, or revelations, could doubt that they were from God.

The movement spread through the city of Mecca and inspired a new moral tone of living. The idolatry, drunkenness, prostitution, and gambling of that city were not harmless pastimes, but destructive habits that ruined lives and prevented Arabian culture from developing. There were vested interests in all these areas of questionable activity, and their influence led city officials to seek to ban the new religion.

Muhammad was hounded in Mecca for ten years, but also admired more and more by a growing minority in the city and by others throughout Arabia. A delegation from the city of Yathrib arrived from several hundred miles north. Pilgrims to Mecca's ancient shrine had sung Muhammad's praises, and Yathrib needed someone to lead its factions into harmony. They made him an offer he could not refuse and, after he extracted a promise that the whole city would worship One God, Allah, Muhammad's followers migrated to Yathrib to exercise their new lifestyle free from harassment. Muhammad followed soon, after eluding a police dragnet attempting to arrest him.

The year of this "exodus" from Mecca was 622 CE, and it is the beginning of the transformation of the world, in Muslin opinion. It became the first year in the Muslim calendar, and Yathrib changed its name to Medinatun-Nabi, the City of the Prophet, eventually shortened to simply Medina, the City. The revelation literature of the Qur'an was growing, and being collected and published piecemeal by his followers. His friends and family would not get the final edition out until after his death, which came sooner than expected.

If Muhammad had astounded his friends as a Prophet, his transformation into civic leader was no less amazing. He skillfully drew five city tribes, three of them predominantly Jewish, into a cooperative confederacy that was so successful that Medina soon rivaled the much larger Mecca in trade and tourism. Muhammad lived simply, in contrast to most rulers, dwelling in an ordinary clay house, milking his own goats, mending his own clothes, and remaining accessible, day and night. We see a deliberate attempt to emulate that style of leadership in Libyan President Muammar Qaddafi, for all his erratic ways, but rarely elsewhere among Muslim potentates.

Muhammad's reputation for blending justice and mercy led people throughout the Arabian Peninsula to wish that he would do for the whole area what he was doing for Medina. The divisions and constant warfare were devastating to the people, except for the few who always thrive on war and the troubles of others, a group still centered at Mecca and still determined to destroy the new religion and its moralistic leader.

Several pitched battles were fought, as they sought to capture or kill him. On one famous occasion his intuitive military strategy paid off politically, when a small Medina force bested a huge army from Mecca, as the clamor for him to unite and lead a new nation grew. The following year, in a reversal of fortune, Muhammad was severely wounded, but the Meccans foolishly let the moment pass, and he recovered.

The next year, Muhammad made a discreet pilgrimage to the Ka'bah, the ancient shrine at Mecca, and determined that things must change there at the ancient heart of Arabian culture. The following year, Muhammad marched on Mecca with tens of thousands of troops from all over the peninsula, just eight years after leaving as a fugitive. Mecca had seen the storm clouds gathering and laid in supplies, hired mercenaries, and armed itself to the teeth for the final showdown. They intended to lure him into a battle he could not possibly win in their stronghold. They were determined to make an end of Muhammad and his movement.

Then, one of the most amazing developments in world military history took place. Muhammad approached the city with a huge army that raised dust in the distance, and Mecca braced for the bloodshed. Just out of range of the archers, but well within sight and earshot, Muhammad gave loud orders for his troops to lay down their arms and to march forward. Everyone obeyed, and they entered the city unarmed, to the dumbfounded amazement of the defenders. The population embraced them with relief, and together they circled the Ka'bah seven times, tearing down the idols and praising God.

Why is the story of this peace march not better known? It is the story of Joshua at the Battle of Jericho and Mahatma Gandhi's salt march all rolled into one. There has been a vested interest in old prejudices among Jews and Christians in particular, but times are changing. A converse prejudice clouds the perception of many in reference to Islam's reportedly "warlike" nature, a fire stoked by a radical minority who are well placed to exploit Western ignorance.

Following the destruction of the World Trade Center on September 11, 2001, and, in reference to other terrorist actions, various Muslim spokespersons have appeared in the media to protest that "Islam is a religion of peace," while many observers were inclined to mutter, "But, is it really?" Realistically, the same question could be asked about Jews, quiescent in Europe for centuries but recently provoked in tit-for-tat violence in Palestine to ensure that pogroms and holocausts "never happen again." As for Christians, possibly the only events to supersede the Crusades in brutality and stupidity were the World Wars of the twentieth century, in which Christians killed both Christians and others in record numbers.

Christians almost eliminated the Jews from the face of the earth, the Axis Powers using ovens and gas chambers, and the Allies resisting Jewish immigration. In the twentieth century, Christians became the only community ever to actually use nuclear weapons of mass destruction on civilian populations. At least, that is how much of the world sees it. Islam is not alone in its warlike reputation, and there are peaceful aspects of the Muslim story that need to be told. This is a project for Jews, Christians, and Muslims together.

As for Muhammad, he is perhaps more to be compared with David than with Gandhi, with at least that one special exception. Willing to fight to win when cornered, and prepared to use the "pre-emptive strike" when necessary, he deserves to be remembered for possibly the most successful peace march in world history, the event that brought him the victory made further warfare unnecessary for his followers or for their enemies in Arabia.

But this book is primarily about the Scriptures, and how biblical characters relate to the Qur'an and to the events of our time. Is there anything to suggest that Muhammad, who barely figures in the Qur'an personally, has any place in this study of biblical figures who also appear in the Qur'an?

I will raise them up a Prophet from among their brethren, like I did unto thee, and I will put my words in his mouth, and he shall speak unto them all that I shall command him. (Deuteronomy 18:18)

Muslims believe, as did Muhammad himself, that this Hebrew Scripture referred to Muhammad in a prophecy from the lips of Moses. Israel's most holy prophet and lawgiver spoke specifically about the surrounding Arab nations at the end of his ministry. Moses had just finished announcing God's promise that He would raise up another leader to replace him as Prophet in Israel, taken as a reference to Joshua. Then, almost parenthetically, as it appears in the text of Hebrew Scripture, Moses makes an almost identical prophecy regarding a Prophet for the Arab peoples, as quoted above.

No such prophet of the stature of Moses arose for centuries in Arabia but, when he came forth, Muhammad was recognized by Jews, Christians, and other Arabians as the one foretold by Moses. This central dogma in the Muslim religion is also based on several references in the Qur'an, but especially where Allah speaks of those to whom he extends mercy:

"Those who follow the apostle, the unlettered prophet whom they find mentioned in their own [Scriptures], in the Law and the Gospel; for he commands them what is just and forbids them what is evil: he allows them as lawful what is good [and pure] and prohibits them from what is bad [and impure]; He releases them from their heavy burdens and from the yokes that are upon them. So it is those who believe in him honor him help him and follow the light which is sent down with him it is they who will prosper." (Surah 7:157)

There can be no doubt that in the Qur'an, the unlettered prophet is a reference to Muhammad, and of further interest is the comment that he is mentioned in what the Qur'an calls *Tawrat* and *Injil*, the Old and New Testaments, the Law and the Gospel. Muslims everywhere regard Deuteronomy 18:18 in the Hebrew Scriptures as a clear example of this, along with a few other less emphatic texts of Hebrew Scriptures.

Perhaps equally impressive is what Muslims see as the reference to Muhammad in the Christian Scriptures. Muslims believe that in the Gospels, Jesus validates the prophecy concerning Muhammad by Moses, and specifically affirms and strengthens it. The Qur'an itself supports this understanding of the role of Jesus in acknowledging Muhammad, as recorded in the Surah known as Battle Array.

And remember that 'Isa Ibn Maryam [Jesus, Son of Mary] said: "O Bani Israel! I am the apostle of Allah sent to you confirming the Law which came before me, and I give you glad tidings of an Apostle to come after me whose name shall be Ahmad." (Surah LXI:6)

For Muslims, the first part of this ayah is a "proof text" of the role and ministry of Jesus in fulfilling the prophecy of Moses, which is found in the Qur'an. It is then coupled with what Muslims take as a sure prophesy about Muhammad from the lips of Jesus, which is recorded in several specific Christian Scriptures, as they read them.

It appears to Muslims that Jesus prophesies the coming of Muhammad through the identical words in Greek, Arabic, and English when Jesus promised the coming of an "Advocate," as read by Christians. The Greek word is *Paraclete,* which translates into English as *Advocate,* which in Arabic is spelled *Ahmad*—the closest to the original Aramaic spoken by Jesus.

Muhammad's first name was Ahmad, the name used in his childhood and among his intimates. The references to this prophecy in Christian Scripture, as recalled in the Qur'an, are in John's gospel 14:16, 14:26, 15:26, and 16:7, where Jesus uses the word four times in promising to send a Paraclete, that is, an advocate or an Ahmad. The promise is repeated in I John 2:1 and has received more notice in the Muslim world than Christians have ever realized. The Muslim reading that God would send Ahmad is certainly plausible, though it is news indeed to Christians who have presumed that these prophesies refer to the coming of the Holy Spirit.

This Muslim interpretation is no more esoteric than many Christian or even Jewish traditional translations or understandings of specific verses that support their various theological positions. How do Roman Catholics come to the conclusion that every later Bishop of Rome is the successor of Peter in the matter mentioned in Matthew 16:18, where Jesus says of Peter, "Upon this rock I will build my church"? The inference is no more, nor any less reasonable than the Muslim reading of the references to the coming of Ahmad. That this comes not from the Hadith or from any later tradition, but from the Qur'an itself as Muhammad received it, is of profound significance to Muslims. It seals the argument that Islam should be seen as in the succession of Israel and the Church, following Moses, Jesus, and Muhammad.

Muhammad's principal identity to Muslims is not as the Advocate, but as "The" Prophet, in fact the final prophet in the line of prophets identified in the Hebrew and Christian Scriptures. He does not bring new revelations but, rather, a spiritual summary that completes and corrects the record of previous revelations and presents them, at last, to Arabs, and, through them, to the world not reached by Jews and Christians.

For Muslims who hold Jesus and Moses in such reverent regard, it is a painful mystery that Christians and Jews accord Muhammad such little honor as any kind of prophet. Christian assemblies have recently issued statements recognizing the covenant relationship Muslims have with God, in words similar to the loving expressions directed toward Jews, but the recognition or acknowledgment of Muhammad as a prophet has not happened, though small steps in that direction have been taken in a few places. Hans Kung, one of the most beloved and respected Roman Catholic theologians of the twentieth century, has made some helpful observations in this regard in a compendium of writings on "the new ecumenism" called *Christianity and the World Religions*, published in 1986. Kung suggests that the Christian Scriptures appear open to the expectation of prophets after Jesus, provided that their message is in basic agreement with his. Kung's reading of the Qur'an highlights some aspects of the teaching of Jesus that the church has neglected since the early Hellenistic period. He proposes that Christians look again at Muhammad's prophetic role in reminding the church of certain of its own doctrines.

Just as Christians are now acknowledging that Jews have a covenant relationship with God, Muslims need to be open to a similar acknowledgment of their debt to the Jews, a debt Muhammad frequently acknowledged. Moreover, each in their own way, Jews and Muslims employ "messianic theology" in the debate about the Son of Man/Son of God/Son of Mary question. That question is of the essence of Christianity but it is also among the issues of primary interest to Jews and Muslims as well.

If Jews and Christians are not yet prepared formally to recognize Muhammad as the final prophet of a certain kind, they might now at least accept the Qur'an, not as a Scripture of their own, but as a Scripture of the family of Abraham, with Muhammad as the mouthpiece of God in this regard. Implicit in this is the realization that, along with mutual appreciation of the Foundation and of the Spiritual Temple, comes recognition of the Dome of Islam as the harbinger or symbol of Judgment and Paradise for all those to whom God extends grace and mercy, regardless of the simplistic expressions of this reality in certain populist Muslim circles.

Some of these steps can be taken at Jewish Congresses, Church Assemblies, and Islamic Conventions. The purpose of this book has been merely to present again the stories of familiar characters in the Bible who also appear in the Qur'an, as a way to become more familiar with the things these three traditions have in common. It also presents, in the style of the Qur'an, a "warning" to all those who refuse to listen or to heed the messages from God. It is the story of Noah's other son, retold before disaster engulfs us all.

Hopefully, this study may serve as part of the groundswell of goodwill that is the positive side of certain aspects of the world in the twenty-first century—the spiritual century. The scourges of racism, anti-Semitism, and Islamophobia remain active, and the dangers implicit in a "clash of civilizations" are very real in our time, but in the understanding of their Scriptures, the members of Abraham's dysfunctional family have a basis for blessing others, perhaps beginning with each other.

Christians and Jews can learn again from Muslims about the poetic authority and the aural beauty of Scripture as presented in the Bible. We may also be living in a time when Muslims can learn from Christians and Jews how to have confidence in the Qur'an as the source of what their people seek today.

How much more about Mary, Jesus, and the Hebrew prophets will the world learn when critical methods become established in Islamic studies? Without denigrating the present study methods of the Qur'an, or the emphasis on memorization, recitation, and devotion, how much richer and fulfilling could the Muslim community become through a renaissance of Islamic life based on a more confident connection with the sources of the Qur'an and the true life setting of its production, dissemination, and propagation?

The face of modern Islam is changing. No official statistics are yet available, but Heshmatollah Riazi, a former professor of philosophy and theology in Iran, believes, for example, that up to five million Iranians have switched to Sufism from orthodox Shia practice in recent years. (Sufism is a mystical form of Islam which, while not "reformist," has little patience with traditional restrictions.) These surprising statistics from **www.freerepublic .com/focus/f-news/1615880/posts** compare to just one hundred thousand Sufis in Iran before the Islamic revolution in 1979. Few in the West can keep up with such rapid changes, but some attempts at understanding are required before misunderstandings result in everybody drowning.

EPILOGUE

THE CHURCH BELLS ring out to summon the faithful to Sunday Sabbath worship. The shofar ram's horn sounds in the synagogue at the beginning of Saturday *Shabbat* celebrations. It is the muezzin chanting the *adhan* call from the minaret of the local Mosque on Fridays for Juma prayers that is new in urban parts of Europe and North America. This is a significant and permanent change in Western community life. We should get used to it and welcome it.

Muhammad knew of both Christian Sabbath and Jewish Shabbat, but he was instructed in the Qur'an to adopt neither as the Muslim "United Day of Prayer," but rather to set aside time on Friday for this purpose. Because prayer is required five times each day, the Friday service was not to rival the Christian or Jewish practices, which were both honored and breached in excess at the time. Friday is important, but not necessarily the whole day.

The Western weekend used to be just Sunday, the Christian day of worship. When the weekend expanded, it did not grow to include Monday, but rather Saturday, the Jewish Sabbath. This happened partly because of the Jewish presence in business and industry. Lately, the weekend has grown to begin at noon on Friday for many businesses and institutions. Again, it might have grown to allow time to get back from the cottage, or to let people return to work at noon on Monday. However, for various reasons, now including a significant Muslim factor, expanding the weekend to include Friday makes sense in Toronto and Montreal, New York and Chicago, London, Paris, Madrid, and Berlin, where millions of Muslim workers, doctors, and politicians are seeking Friday afternoon off to attend prayers at the Mosque. Everyone's cooperation could become a valuable symbol.

The voice of the muezzin is heard and the three-day weekend is coming, or at least a two-and-a-half-day weekend. It serves as a symbol of the weekly worship pattern in Abraham's family on Friday, Saturday, and Sunday. If, as widely reported, worship attendance *every* week is now limited to *only* some twenty percent of the population, that is a million or more people in each of the aforementioned urban centers. This would be regarded as an astounding phenomenon, if it were attendance at sporting, cultural, or political activities. Religion is here to stay in the twenty-first century.

A professional colleague was lamenting the decline of the Sunday School in Protestant congregations of the old mainstream, many of which had a thousand students or more within our memory, and indeed, even in our own experience as senior clergy in our denomination. In response to several sessions of his whining about the current generation of children being illiterate about the scriptural stories and their meaning, I asked the principal of a local school and the teacher of a grade five class of ten- and eleven-year-olds if we could interview the class for research purposes. There was no objection, once the politically correct balance of our questions was ascertained.

In a class of twenty-four children, there wasn't one who could not recount the story of the nativity of Jesus, and most could articulate the difference between that understanding of Christmas and the Santa Claus version. This was not a Catholic or Conservative Christian school, but a public school in the Canadian province of Ontario. While we did progress to the stories of Noah and Moses, which were also well known, it was of interest to us that Jewish and Muslim children were as able to accurately recount the scriptural nativity stories as the Christian children. They had learned these stories from their parents and various other sources, as did many Christian children, but some of the latter learned from Sunday School. The largest number had gained their basic scriptural literacy from Vacation Bible Schools sponsored by neighborhood Evangelical churches. My colleague suggested a bias in the sample due to our small-town test case, so we repeated the test in a large city class nearby, with practically identical results. New methods of teaching may yet be required in the twenty-first century, such as home study kits provided by churches for the cultural religion constituency, but the interest is there.

The presence of several thousand churches, synagogues, and mosques throughout the world's major cities is another feature of postmodern life that comes as a surprise to many of those who do not participate. Be that as it may, it is the sound of Muslims gathering for worship that is the new part of the weekend. Neighborhood parking problems and traffic patterns are not nearly as important as the rest of the population gaining some sense of the meaning and feel of those words from the Qur'an emanating from the neighborhood minaret.

Of course, just as some Jews attend synagogue only on "High Holy Days," and there are many Christmas and Easter Christians who possibly believe that there are either poinsettias or lilies in church every Sunday, there are so-called "Eid Muslims" who only attend on Eid al-Fitr at the end of the Ramadan season or Eid al-Udha, marking Abraham's obedience to God in possibly giving up even the dream of having a family.

As for the Scriptures, in various revisions, the Tanakh may now continue as the most widely accepted English version of the Hebrew Bible. But modern Jews have completely mastered the revival of their ancient language, so the Hebrew Bible in the Hebrew language is now the norm among Jews throughout the world. Such a development would have been unimaginable a hundred years ago.

Christians will continue to read the latest translations of their Scriptures in English and other languages, and the Bible will continue to be the world's best-selling book, as it has been every single year since the invention of the printing press (though secular best-selling lists may continue to ignore that fact, fostering the mistaken illusion that we live in a post-religious era). However, classic texts like the King James Version in English, Old Slavonic in Russian, the Aramaic-based Syriac text in India, and countless other treasured versions around the world may well continue to be increasingly appreciated in an age craving depth and authenticity.

However, the Arabic Qur'an has never been lost and never revived, nor has any translation gained the status of a "standard" version in any other languages except for Turkish and Farsi. Non-Arabic Muslims will continue to learn the Arabic language version in which the Qur'an first appeared, direct from the voice of Allah, speaking in Muhammad's heart, through the voice of the angel Gabriel.

The various translations of the Qur'an will be helpful for study and discussion, but it is clear that the sonorous tones of the original are part of the impact of the Qur'an. The sound does incorporate the message in the medium in a fusion that is more significant than in either the Jewish or Christian Scriptures. Christians and Jews may actually appreciate the true depth of their own traditions even more after growing in understanding of these aspects of the Qur'an, and perhaps acknowledging some limited parallels in their own experience of God's Word.

But the Bible, even if somewhat jumbled, remains a precious communal document, with layer upon layer of authenticity and validation. The Dead Sea Scrolls and other findings have virtually proven that there have been no substantial corruptions or changes down through the ages since the original oral traditions and autographed manuscripts were first edited and adopted.

Muslims may insist that God did give his Word directly through Moses and Jesus, as the Qur'an attests. But the community of believers had a role in preserving that revelation in a way that made it live in each generation through the long process of telling, reciting, writing and editing, selecting books for inclusion, and producing copies by hand. The printing press was invented to speed up the process, and its first product, in the Western world at least, was the Guttenberg Bible. That led to even wider dissemination and the demand for more meaningful translations, versions, and editions. Rabbinical scholars and Sunday School teachers all have roles to play with this "work in progress," but it is, finally, in the heart and mind of each believer that God speaks through the Holy Spirit. The Bible is the "cave" where the Word of God is heard and the command is given, "go and tell this story."

Muslims call the original and "uncorrupted" Hebrew and Christian Scriptures by the Arabic names *Taurat* (Torah), meaning Law, and *Injil*, meaning message (as in angel) or gospel. They wish that their Jewish and Christian neighbors, in Muhammad's time and in modern times, had never lost the Taurat and the Injil, and that they lived by the Taurat and Injil precepts. There is news for them, as more and more Muslims get to know their Western neighbors better in the cities of Europe and the suburbs of America.

As Jews and Christians more willingly recognize that God did, indeed, speak directly to Muhammad in the cave, Muslims may be pleased to recognize that the Taurat and Injil have not been lost. The Word of God is received directly every day in the cave of Hebrew and Christian Scripture, through the hearts and minds of believers. Many devout people are anxious to live up to those precepts these days, especially their relationships with the alienated members of the family, those descendants of Abraham through Ishmael, who have remained faithful to what has been revealed to them.

A literal understanding of the Scriptures, Jewish, Christian, and Muslim, suggests that the earth is the center of the universe and the sun revolves around the earth. This terracentric (technically called "Ptolemaic") view of the universe works quite well everyday, as we speak of "sunrise" and "sunset." Land surveyors all over the world actually conduct themselves everyday as if the earth were flat, and nobody has a deed that acknowledges the curvature of the earth. The literal view of Scripture can also work well enough to if believers get the true spiritual message: loving their neighbors and worshiping God.

Fundamentalist problems arise only when the believers' energy is directed to insisting that the earth is central and flat—speaking metaphorically, of course. A more enlightened view, in the opinion of some believers, is that the Bible speaks poetically about such matters as sunrise and sunset, and that the earth actually rotates around the sun at the center. Proponents of this heliocentric (or "Copernican") view of the universe expend much time and effort correcting those who have a more existential perspective, but

again, the crux of the matter is the spiritual approach to love of neighbor
and worship of God. Problems arise when these more enlightened believers
devote their energies to politically correct speech and social justice in support of current causes, without equal passion for the spiritual basis of their
commitments to God.

Of course, both are wrong in their view of the universe, which is actually
omnicentric. The earth is not the center of the universe and neither is the
sun. The conservative terracentric view and the liberal heliocentric view
both work well day to day, but the omnicentric universe is the only adequate
scientific model that is completely accurate as a spiritual model for life in
the twenty-first century.

Properly understood, the Scriptures of Judaism, Christianity, and Islam
all point to God as the center, and God is everywhere. Jews, Christians, and
Muslims, both conservative and liberal in all three traditions, need to move
to this new space in the twenty-first century. It need not cause great disrup-
tions in their everyday spiritual life, if they got the basic message, but in
their relations with each other, the omnicentric model of faith in God is not
only the true model, it is also the most helpful. This is a model that is
already the basis of understanding the universe employed by our fellow
earth dwellers of Hindu and Buddhist orientation—possibly the subject of
my next book!

Meanwhile, the West has much to learn about Islam. The awarding of
the 2006 Nobel Peace Prize to a Muslim banker from Pakistan came as a
surprise to many. Muhammad Yunus received the award in recognition of
his leadership in establishing "micro-credit" loans to replace discredited aid
programs in lifting people from poverty around the world. Again we see an
obliteration of a pointless Western prejudice about Islam, among those who
believed Muslim strictures against "usury" to be a barrier to their participation in an advanced economy. Now it becomes clear that what is forbidden
is extortion by "loan sharks" or even banks, whereas simple interest is
regarded as that which can enable even the poor to prosper.

The value of demolishing these prejudices, and the influence of these traditions upon each other, was dramatically illustrated by a decree from the
Vatican in late 2006. The announcement from the Holy Father that
"limbo," as a theological construct, cannot be sustained was a direct consequence of the competition among these three major faiths for the soul of
Africa, where even Judaism has a stake in Ethiopia, South Africa, and elsewhere. Limbo, as the place or state where infants go when they die before
baptism, was one of the least satisfactory constructs of medieval theology in
any event, but as Muslim influence begins to expand into even Sub-Saharan

Africa, the Islamic doctrine that the souls of stillborn babies go straight to heaven represented a graciousness that Christians found irresistible.

Perhaps the most helpful aid to understanding in the whole Western–Muslim interface has come from the pen of Haroon Sadiqui, the recently retired editor of Canada's largest newspaper, the *Toronto Star*, with a daily readership of about one million. Sadiqui's little paperback book *Being Muslim*, garnering awards through 2007, betrays an appropriate touch of testiness from the Western world's most respected senior journalist of Muslim background—testiness toward people of liberal disposition who, in his opinion, might have been expected to "get it" before this.

Almost like a prophet of old, this doyen of the Canadian literary establishment chides the public for its failure to recognize the roots of Islamic militancy by comparing it all to the anguish and the sense of futility in the face of similar extremism on the part of the Black Panthers in America a generation ago. On that "Black Day in July," when Chicago was burning, and in the subsequent riots in the Watts suburbs of Los Angeles, the main victims of black frustration and violence were blacks themselves. Their rage needed expression and the opportunities to lash out at "whitey" were limited at best.

Does this remind anyone of the sectarian violence in Iraq? The fact that nearly three thousand people of many nationalities died in New York on September 11, 2001, will always be an unspeakable tragedy, but nearly three hundred thousand Muslims worldwide have died in related violence, largely self-inflicted, in Palestine, Chechnya, Indonesia, Malaysia, Saudi Arabia, Jordan, Lebanon, Bosnia, and Turkey, not to mention Iraq and Afghanistan.

It may at last be time for North Americans and Europeans to become constructive partners in the dialogue with our Muslim family members. At the same time, on the matter of the Rushdie fatwa, although not formally lifting it, the Government of Iran has declared that he is not to be killed. While crackpots can do anything, as we know from shots taken at popes, presidents, and pop stars, Salman Rushdie's re-emergence as a public figure is a tribute to his courage. His safety and his secure place in the community must also be recognized at the litmus test of maturity and moderation in the Western Muslim community. In spite of grievances we can all now recognize, and despite his role as a lightning rod for disaffection in the Muslim community, we must be confident, as he is, that Salman Rushdie is safe, and that his free movement and his contribution to the discussion is proof positive that we are moving into a new era. Which will be the first major Muslim institution to invite him to the dialogue?

APPENDIX I

Bearing Faithful Witness: United Church–Jewish Relations Today

Preamble

THE UNITED CHURCH OF CANADA is called to be faithful to Jesus Christ in worship, prayer, word, and action in the midst of our neighbors and in the world. Accordingly, the 36th General Council, meeting in Camrose, Alberta, in 1997, authorized for the whole church a study of the document "Bearing Faithful Witness: United Church–Jewish Relations Today."

People of the United Church responded thoughtfully and prayerfully to the study document and to the proposed policy statement. This statement encompasses that response, and seeks to be a faithful expression of our understanding of United Church–Jewish relations.

The 38th General Council, meeting in Wolfville, Nova Scotia, in 2003, overwhelmingly and enthusiastically approved this policy statement on the United Church of Canada–Jewish Relations today.

We believe this statement reflects our faith in Christ and is consistent with our historic witness as part of the Body of Christ. We believe that the God whom we know in Jesus Christ is the One who called Sarah and Abraham, gave the Torah to Moses, and put passion for justice into the hearts of the prophets. We believe, above all, in the faithfulness of God.

Holy Scripture teaches that the eternal Word became flesh in the person of Jesus, a Jew. The One who is "our judge and our hope" lives as a Jew, dies as a Jew and is raised as a Jew. In making these affirmations we seek to bear faithful witness to the Jewishness of Jesus.

We believe that the Holy Spirit calls us to bear faithful witness concerning God's reconciling mission in Jesus Christ. In Jesus Christ, God has opened the door in a new way to those previously outside the covenant. Our understanding of the faithfulness of God would be at risk if we were to say that God had abandoned the covenant with the Jewish people. As Paul says in Romans 9:11, the covenant is irrevocable because God is faithful.

We believe that our faith issues in action. Jesus commands us to love our neighbours, but all too often Christians have treated Jews, our sisters and brothers, as enemies. We believe that our faith calls us to repent when the church has been unfaithful in its witness by not loving Jews as neighbors.

Statement

Therefore, as an act of repentance and in faithfulness to the commandment that we should not bear false witness against our neighbors, the United Church of Canada

A. ACKNOWLEDGES:
    a history of anti-Judaism and anti-Semitism within Christianity as a
        whole, including the United Church of Canada;
    a history of interpretation of New Testament texts which has often
        failed to appreciate the context within Judaism from which
        these texts emerged, resulting in deeply-rooted anti-Jewish
        misinterpretation;
    a history of insensitivity with respect to the importance of the Shoah
        (Holocaust) for Jews;
    anti-Semitism and anti-Judaism as affronts to the gospel of Jesus Christ.

B. REJECTS:
    all teaching of a theology of contempt toward Jews and Judaism;
    the belief that God has abolished the covenant with the Jewish people;
    supersessionism, the belief that Christians have replaced Jews in the love
        and purpose of God;
    proselytism that targets Jews for conversion to Christianity.

C. AFFIRMS:
    the significance of Judaism as at once a religion, a people, and a cove-
        nant community;
    that Judaism, both historically and currently, cannot be understood
        from knowledge of the Old Testament alone;
    that the gifts and calling of God to the Jewish people are irrevocable;
    the uniqueness for Christianity of the relationship with Judaism;

that both Judaism and Christianity, as living faiths, have developed significantly from a common root;

that the love of God is expressed in the giving of both Torah and Gospel;

that the State of Israel has the right to exist in peace and security;

our common calling with Jews and others to align ourselves with God's world-mending work;

the opportunity for growth in Christian self-understanding that exists through closer dialogue with, openness to, and respect for Judaism.

D. ENCOURAGES MEMBERS, CONGREGATIONS, PRESBYTERIES, CONFERENCES, AND THE GENERAL COUNCIL:

to seek opportunities to meet with Jews and to learn about modern Judaism;

to continue to study the issues raised by the study document, "Bearing Faithful Witness," along with other issues of significance within the Jewish–Christian relationship;

to be vigilant in resisting anti-Semitism and anti-Judaism in church and society;

to create ongoing worship opportunities within the church for highlighting the importance of the Jewish–Christian relationship, such as at the time of Shoah Remembrance in April, or the high Jewish Holy Days in September/October, or Kristallnacht in November or Brotherhood/Sisterhood Week in February.

APPENDIX II

That We May Know Each Other: United Church–Muslim Relations Today

Preamble

THE UNITED CHURCH study document and this resulting statement were written for the Canadian context. Many of our global partners find themselves in situations of much greater complexity than what is represented in our study document. The Interchurch Interfaith Committee hopes, nevertheless, that engagement with this statement can contribute in some small way toward the larger exploration of Muslim–Christian relations.

Statement on United Church–Muslim Relationships

As an act of witness to our desire to find new ways of understanding and working with Muslim neighbors for the sake of the well-being of our world, the United Church of Canada:

AFFIRMS that Christianity and Islam are in essence religions of peace, mercy, justice, and compassion.

ACKNOWLEDGES hostility and misunderstanding between Christians and Muslims and between Christianity and Islam.

AFFIRMS a vision of Muslim and Christian relations no longer bound by past histories, and free from ignorance, indifference, and ill will.

AFFIRMS that the United Church of Canada is committed to a journey toward reconciliation, understanding, and cooperation with our Muslim neighbors.

AFFIRMS that we share with Muslims a belief in one God and a common heritage through Abraham.

AFFIRMS that God is creatively at work in the religious life of Muslims and Christians.

ACKNOWLEDGES another common bond in that Jesus, as understood in Islam, is accorded special honor as a prophet in the Qur'an and by Muslims.

ACKNOWLEDGES the prophetic witness of Muhammad, and that the mercy, compassion, and justice of God are expressed in the Qur'an, which is regarded by Muslims as the Word of God.

AFFIRMS that God, whose love we have experienced in Jesus Christ as boundless and resourceful, works creatively and redemptively in us and in others.

AFFIRMS that the United Church of Canada is committed to a vision that leads us to work with Muslims and others for peace and justice for all humanity.

INVITES all people of the United Church of Canada to participate in conversation and study that upholds and respects the integrity and faithful witness of our traditions.

ENCOURAGES all people of the United Church of Canada to seek out opportunities to work together with Muslims to seek justice and resist evil for the sake of the world we all inhabit.

AFTERWORD

The Bridge Between Judaism and Islam

By Reuven Firestone
Director of ISEMJI (Institute for the Study and
Enrichment of Muslim–Jewish Interrelations)

WHAT IS IT THAT bridges the world's religions? It is God, of course, whether known as El or Allah, God, Dios, or any other name. But we cannot know God directly. The immeasurable hugeness and the infinitesimal smallness of the Lover is beyond human knowledge, beyond knowing in human terms. So God reveals, and the record of that revelation is Scripture. Although conceived in the divine will, it can be articulated for humanity only in human speech and then inscribed into the texts that we know. It is Scripture that records that bridge between Judaism and Islam.

Scripture first recorded that bridge, but it then became the bridge itself. It speaks to us in God's name about the ethics of monotheism. Through narrative, poem, parable, and legal precept, the Scriptures of Judaism and Islam link the spirits of these religions through the One who revealed them both. The Scriptures span the gaps of culture, language, and time with the images of biblical personages.

Whether Avraham or Ibrahim, the first monotheist rejects the idols of his people to follow or seek out the One Great God. Abraham obeyed God with a whole heart. He submitted to the divine will. As Moshe or Musa, the lawgiver brought his people to the mountain to receive the revelation and learn the ways of God. He led his people from the egotism and pig-headedness that is epitomized by Pharaoh and into a holy land that could remain sanctified only as long as its inhabitants, whether Israelite, Christian, Jewish, or Muslim, acted righteously.

It is the nature of Scripture to tell stories about the heroes of ancient days, and to refer to the narratives with which its audience is already familiar. Scripture refers to itself and to the Scriptures that came before, and even to tales whose origins and ancient meanings are only hinted at in the Scriptures themselves. By referencing ancient pasts, Scripture draws attention to the meaning of the present.

It is the nature of Scripture, despite its own claims to be fully comprehensible, to remain obscure enough to elicit a deep striving on behalf of its audience to understand. It is unrealistic to expect Scripture to be truly understood if it is the sublime will of God conveyed in the limiting language of humanity. Scripture thus demands humility according to both Judaism and Islam—humility, diligence, striving, and patience, all for greater understanding and improved deeds.

Scripture is the bridge between two related religions, Islam and Judaism. But these two religions and the civilizations that they spawned are different from one another. Related, yes, and similar in many respects. But they represent distinct human articulations of the divine will. The divine emanations, like an eternal broadcast from the heavenly radio tower, are absorbed differently by each and every receiver. Should we expect anything different? How can we know that we, and only we, are right?

Scripture bridges Judaism and Islam. But it does not reduce them to tedious sameness. Their individual integrity and unique expressions of the divine will are maintained when Jews and Muslims come together to explore their own and each others' Scriptures and the messages, both hidden and revealed inherent within them. One religion will never reign over all humanity. If it were truly the divine will, it would have happened many generations before.

ACKNOWLEDGMENTS

I SAVED THIS FOR LAST because readers may now understand that I have so much for which to be grateful. An author will often acknowledge the assistance of others and graciously insist that any errors are the author's own responsibility, not theirs. That has to be my opening statement, particularly to my Jewish and Muslim colleagues who contributed so much but cannot be held responsible for final opinions and judgment calls on some of the more controversial aspects of this material. I will thank Christian friends, colleagues, and family members also, but I am close enough to most of them that they may also share the blame for my treatment of the difficult subjects that we wrestled through together.

I owe much to the congregations with whom I have worked over the several years in writing this book. Lansing United Church in Toronto provided the multicultural setting for my ministry in that city. Devoted seniors, who had me come to their homes to discuss the sermon series, asked me to consider publishing the Year of the Bible series and the Under the Shadow of War sermons as a book. They were shortly supported by a group of Canadian-born and new Canadian young professionals with the same request. Lansing proofreaders of the first complete draft were Orville Green and Karen Arbour.

I received technical assistance from Charles Cheng and research assistance from Olga Zhelvakova, two Lansing students at the Emmanuel Theological College in Toronto. Dr. David Alan Bruce, my colleague at the Donway Covenant United Church, assisted me with the Foundation–Temple–Dome motif to describe the Jewish–Christian–Muslim family connection.

Most recently, Saint John's Stevensville and First United Churches provided an environment for writing and a location in the Niagara area on "the south coast of Canada." These churches across the bridge from Buffalo offered valuable connections with American Jewish, Christian, and Muslim communities, as well as proximity to the North American offices of my publisher in New York and Harrisburg, Pennsylvania, from my home in the city of Niagara Falls.

I am grateful for encouragement from Rebekah Chevalier, Senior Editor of the United Church Publishing House, and wise counsel from Dr. Bruce Gregerson, General Council Minister for Programs for Mission and Ministry of the United Church of Canada. They also arranged permissions for copyrighted material from the church.

Members of my Niagara area congregations in Stevensville and Sherkston formed a study group to discuss the material, and, in some cases, to do extra proofreading. Chief among them were my colleague in ministry, Dr. Deborah Grimes, and members John and Sandra Dunn, Jane Elson, Marion and Robert Grimes, Marilyn James, Katherine and Robert Morningstar, Howard and Phyllis Page, Cathy Pikel, John Plyley, Donna and George Reeves, Aileen and the late Donald Schneider, bookseller Ada Sherk, and Janet Boyce, a professional grammarian from a neighboring congregation.

In the Jewish community, reference has been made to the contribution of Rita Vinnikov who gave me a student's perspective. Dr. Grigori Itkis, retired Professor of Philosophy from the University of Moscow, gave me an academic perspective on the wider Jewish experience. Milton Winberg, developer and humanist, contributed a community perspective as well as an affirmation of our common quest. Reverend Walter Mittler reflected the position of the small but significant Jewish presence within my own denomination. Rabbi Harry Rosenfeld of the Temple Beth Zion congregation in Buffalo balanced things out from the perspective of the solid Jewish religious establishment. Rabbi Irwin Tanenbaum of Temple Beth Am in Williamsville, New York, cautioned me on certain "political" aspects, and Rabbi Jacqueline Mates-Muchin, the associate rabbi at Temple Sinai in Oakland, California, contributed a feminist perspective, all from the Reform tradition. Rabbi Eliyahu Courante of Congregation B'nai Israel in Saint Catharines, Ontario, vetted a number of issues from an Orthodox Jewish perspective.

Some of these nearby colleagues also arranged helpful meetings for me with Rabbi Reuven Firestone, who was then Professor of Medieval Judaism and Islam at the Hebrew Union College in Los Angeles. His lectures on Parallel Narratives in the Hebrew Bible and the Qur'an have informed my own work. I am his disciple on many of the most difficult points of the interface between the three religions. I am grateful for his original contribution to the appendix section of this book, specifically addressing Jewish–Muslim relations, as current Director of ISEMJI, the new Institute for the Study and Enhancement of Muslim–Jewish Interrelations in Los Angeles. I also feel honored in his personal encouragment in this project and in the interest shown by Rabbi Harold Kushner, who gave his personal permission to use an illustration from his book, *How Good Do We Have to Be?*

I express my thanks to Tracy Bohan and Luke Ingram at the Wylie Agency for facilitating the contribution of Salman Rushdie in the Foreword. What he had to say there was originally penned for an opinion piece in the *Washington Post* of August 10, 2005, and the *London Times* of August 11, 2005, and made possible in this format by his personal permission and through the good graces of his agents.

My brother-in-law, Kazim Boodoo, son of a prominent Muslim Imam in Trinidad, got me thinking first in these directions several years ago. In a sense, the book began with him, even before September 11, as an idea emerging from one of those discussions a person has with someone on a patio killing time while dinner is materializing.

The Muslim community in Canada has been especially gracious in expanding my understanding. Javed Akbar and Mehboob Kamadia spent endless hours with me early in this project, as did Dr. Kazem Mesbarh Moosavi, Director of the Imam Ali Islamic Centre in Toronto, a fellow student at McGill University when we were both in training for the ministry some decades ago. In the Niagara region, Dr. Murtaza Najmudin, the Imam at Brock University in Saint Catherines, Ms. Samah Marei of Muslim Educational Outreach at the Niagara Islamic Centre, and the Saint Catherines Islamic Centre have been especially helpful in relating Islamic traditions to the Western context.

Outside my congregations, another circle of Christian critics lent their interest and support. I lived for a time in an enclave of nearly a hundred United Church clergy, spouses, and former church workers. There, the Albright Book Club spent a month previewing, reviewing, discussing, dissecting, and, again, proofreading. To them I mentioned my recollection that a certain famous University Press employs at least twenty-five proofreaders per book, but has yet to publish a book without error. My friends and colleagues determined to surpass that standard if possible, though we are under no illusions. The several authors in this little community have also been encouraging, but I must acknowledge the club members who did both proof work and reviewing, especially Carol and John Bunner, Gloria Christian, Les Edmonds, Ian and Kathy Kirby-Smith, Robert and Wilma Lindsey, Bette Mittler, Audrey Scott, and Eva and Milt Schwartzentruber.

The founder and leading spirit of that club was my wife, Jenny, who has researched and edited, done proofreading, and entered into discussion at almost every level of this study. Authors usually acknowledge and thank their families, but only other authors know the extent of that debt. We are frequently hard to live with while birthing a book, and authors seem to require a special level of "care and feeding" anyway. I have been blessed in all those ways, plus the invaluable direct contribution Jenny makes to my books as research assistant and copyeditor. My children, Arthur and Indira, and Indira's husband, Judson, have also done proofreading. Arthur researched the Ten Commandments segment, and years ago in high school Indira did a research paper on Nefertiti, which we always thought should be published. It is now, in large part.

My grandchildren, Indira Sarah, Arthur Ishwar, David Vishnu, Ariel Anjani Emily, Jennifer Vashti Anne, and James Judson Allan, will all be required to read this book, so perhaps I may be permitted to acknowledge them for doing so and living out its precepts in a world that may be very different than we now know.

After all these corrections and suggestions, the final touches were undertaken by my friends Dr. and Mrs. Roger and Beth Grant, the final readers, who still found many bits and pieces that needed improvement. My very dear friends, Bob and Anne Keys, simply say they cannot find anything wrong with the text, and every author needs a few friends like Bob and Anne.

In a similar vein, my final acknowledgment of gratitude is to you, the reader, and especially any of you who decide to acquire or pass on a copy for a Jewish, Muslim, or Christian friend, not of your own tradition, in hopes of furthering the goals we share.

BIBLIOGRAPHY

Ahmed, Qamar. *Stories of the Prophets from the Qur'an*. Mumbai: Bilal Books, 1970.

Aslan, Reza. *No God But God*. New York: Random House, 2005

Armstrong, Karen. *Islam: A Short History*. New York: Modern Library, 2000.

Broadhurst, Tom (ed.). *Year Book and Directory*. Toronto: The United Church of Canada, 2005.

Brown, Brian Arthur. *Your Neighbor As Yourself: Race, Religion and Region—North America Into the Twenty-First Century*. Notre Dame, IN: CrossRoads Books, 1997

Bucaille, Maurice. *The Bible, The Qur'an and Science*. Paris: Islamic Books, 1999.

Cleary, Thomas. *The Essential Koran*. New York: HarperCollins, 1993.

Craig, Kenneth (ed.). *Common Prayer: A Muslim–Christian Spiritual Anthology*. Oxford: Oneworld, 1999.

Feiler, Bruce. *Abraham: A Journey to the Heart of Three Faiths*. New York: William Morrow, 2002.

Grose, George B., and Benjamin J. Hubbard (eds.). *The Abraham Connection*. Notre Dame, IN: CrossRoads Books, 1994.

Halsell, Grace. *Journey to Jerusalem*. New York: Macmillan, 1981.

Hussain, Iftekhar Bano. *The Astonishing Truths of the Holy Qur'an*. London: Ta-Ha, 1996.

Kathir, Ibn. *Signs Before the Day of Judgement*. London: Dar Al Taqwa, 1991.

Kushner, Harold. *How Good Do We Have to Be?* New York: Little, Brown & Company, 1996.

Lester, Toby. "What Is the Koran?" The Atlantic online at www.theatlantic.com/doc/199901/koran.

Meyer, Marvin, and Harold Bloom. *The Gospel of Thomas*. New York: HarperCollins, 1992.

Murphy, Nancy. *Beyond Liberalism and Fundamentalism: How Modern and Postmodern Philosophy Set the Theological Agenda*. Harrisburg, PA: Trinity Press, 1996.

Mooney, Clint, et. al (eds.). *Bearing Faithful Witness: United Church–Jewish Relations Today*. Toronto: 2004.

O'Murchu, Diarmuid. *Quantum Theology: Spiritual Implications of the New Physics*. New York: Crossroad Publishing, 2002.

Osman, Ahmed. *Stranger in the Valley of the Kings*. New York: Harper & Row, 1987.

Qutb, Sayyid. *In the Shade of the Qur'an*. 9 Vol. Cairo: Dar al-Shuruq, 1952.

———. *Milestones*. Beirut: Dar al-Shuruq, 1964.

Sadiqui, Haroon. *Being Muslim*. Toronto: House of Anansi Press, 2006.

Schwartz, Stephen. *The Two Faces of Islam*. New York: Doubleday, 2002.

Smith, Huston. *Islam*. New York: HarperCollins, 2001.

Unland, Rinkah, et. al (eds.). *That We May Know Each Other: United Church–Muslim Relations Today*. Toronto: The United Church of Canada, 2005.

Vandenberg, Phillip. *Nefertiti*. Philadelphia: Lippincott, 1978.

Vidyarthi, Maulana Abdul Haq. *Muhammad in World Scriptures*. Vol. 1. Lahore: Ahmadiyya Anjuman Isha'at Islam, 1999.

Syed, Ashfaque, and Muhammad Ynus. *Terrorism and Islam*. Toronto: Islamic Learning Media, 2001.

Warraq, Ibn. *The Origins of the Qur'an*. Buffalo, NY: Prometheus Books, 1998.

———. *The Quest for the Historical Muhammad*. Buffalo, NY: Prometheus Books, 2000.

Wiesel, Elie. *Night*. New York: Hill and Wang, 2006.

Yahya, Harun. *Jesus Will Return: A Muslim View*. London: Ta-Ha, 2001.